Constitutional Ethos

Constitutional Ethos

Liberal Equality for the Common Good

ALEXANDER TSESIS

OXFORD
UNIVERSITY PRESS

OXFORD
UNIVERSITY PRESS

Oxford University Press is a department of the University of Oxford. It furthers
the University's objective of excellence in research, scholarship, and education
by publishing worldwide. Oxford is a registered trade mark of Oxford University
Press in the UK and certain other countries.

Published in the United States of America by Oxford University Press
198 Madison Avenue, New York, NY 10016, United States of America.

Cataloging-In-Publication Data is on file at the Library of Congress
ISBN 978-0-19-935984-4

1 3 5 7 9 8 6 4 2

Printed by Edwards Brothers Malloy, United States of America

CONTENTS

ACKNOWLEDGMENTS

Every book is a journey consisting of physical and intellectual excursions. On the physical side, the author must travel to brick-and-mortar libraries or virtual repositories of information. On the intellectual side, many hours must be spent alone, pondering collected research, evaluating existing arguments, working out stylistic puzzles, developing reasoning, and so forth. Fortunately, the journey is not entirely undertaken alone. Each author benefits from the wise counsel of mentors, friends, relatives, and even chance acquaintances.

In the investigation, writing, and editing of this book, I have been blessed by the abundant support of great constitutional law scholars. Their substantive guidance has been as important as their organizational advice. Where this work fails to achieve the standards they set, the fault is entirely mine.

I began receiving advice on the project when it was only a kernel of an idea during a remarkably productive dinner with Lawrence Solum and Randy Barnett. Once I put pen to paper—or more accurately fingers to keyboard—Mark Graber, Mark Tushnet, Jack Balkin, Louis Michael Seidman, Laura Underkuffler, and James Fleming gave me helpful advice on the proposal that sustained me throughout the project. Andrew Koppelman, Jeff Powell, and Insa Blanke provided me with feedback on early versions of the introduction.

I had the honor of presenting the book at the Cornell Law School, the Duke Law School, and the University of Iowa College of Law. The hospitality I received was exceptional and the penetrating insights were even better. While I am grateful to all those who engaged with me at those events, I most benefitted from the feedback of Joseph Blocher, James Boyle, Curtis Bradley, Michael Dorf, Odette Lienau, Darrell Miller, Jens Ohlin, Todd Pettys, Aziz Rana, Neil Siegel, Gregg Strauss, Bradley Wendell, and Ernest Young. They provided profoundly important reactions, analyses, and suggestions.

One thing that never ceases to amaze me about academia is how many scholars are incredibly generous with their time. Many extremely busy people have so graciously given me the gift of their time, their feedback, their competence, and their expertise. Amy Barrett, Caroline Mala Corbin, and Timothy Zick read, commented, and guided me toward improving various versions of chapters. Several other scholars were so considerate as to read the entire manuscript. They provided me with bird's-eye views on how to improve the project as a whole. Alan Chen, Katie Eyer, Randy Kozel, and Sharmila Sohoni commented on the complete monograph at various stages of its development. I owe a special debt to William Araiza who read an early draft of the book and helped me restructure several chapters to create a more compelling and cohesive argument.

I first explored this book's conception of constitutional theory, albeit in different formats, in *Maxim Constitutionalism: Liberal Equality for the Common Good*, 91 TEX. L. REV. 1609 and *Principled Governance: The American Creed and Congressional Authority*, 41 CONN. L. REV. 679 (2009).

My family is the greatest anchor of my life. Alexandra Roginsky Tsesis, my wife, is effervescently inspirational. She and our children, Ruthie and Ari, have for years been kind enough to listen, inquire, and engage in this book's construction and argument.

Introduction

Over the last two-and-a-half centuries, the founding commitment of the US Declaration of Independence to preserve the inalienable rights to life, liberty, and the pursuit of happiness has influenced the development of law and culture. The Preamble to the Constitution set a framework for carrying out the national mission to "establish justice, insure domestic tranquility, provide for the common defense, promote the general welfare, and secure the blessings of liberty." Constitutional law provides aspirational goals, sovereign mandates, and structural mechanisms for ordinary people to hold government accountable for fair treatment and the betterment of the national community.

This book develops a theory of constitutional law structured on the public duty to protect individual rights for the general welfare. The maxim of constitutional governance synthesizes the protection of individual and public rights. The ideal is neither solely theoretical nor customary but tied to a firm foundation that the people then build upon by lobbying elected officials and petitioning appointed judges. Representative government has an interlinked obligation to the individual and to the general welfare. This paradigm for responsible governance sets the baseline against which citizens can hold policy makers accountable to the structural and normative commitments of the Constitution. A pluralistic system must respect human dignity and govern for the betterment of the body politic. This ideal is objective in the sense that it is independent of any extant judicial opinions or contemporary social mores that justify injustices, such as slavery, Indian Removal, or the exclusion of non-whites from citizenship. The premise is not only one that embraces human uniqueness but also the need for government offices to function in the interests of citizens. The Declaration and Constitution codify the fundamental social ethos of human equality and set the basic structure of governance.

Books interpreting the Constitution of the United States often separate these two factors: Libertarians believe that the individual should be left free to pursue a vision of the good life without government interference, while communitarians tend to find mutual obligation that must be fulfilled to further some collective well-being. Too often lines are drawn between these theories without recognizing a synthetic perspective for enforcing institutional mechanisms that are conducive to equality and freedom.

The state is a means of optimizing the well-being of individuals. Human productivity can best flourish in a society of equals, where talents can be brought to bear in the betterment of self and other members of the community. In the United States, the Declaration and Constitution are the highest textual sources of normative law, granting limited powers for the augmentation of well-being. The Supreme Court of the United States recently recognized that the Declaration and Preamble are interlinked guarantees of the people's representative sovereignty over representative governance.[1] The realm of human initiative is expanded by cooperation in an open political society. As essential to a representative democracy as are deliberation, sharing, and collective will, the constitutional principle of liberal equality for the common good cannot be legally gainsaid, even by supermajorities.

The aspirational limits of representative democracy cannot, however, be realized by strictly adhering to the text of those two formative documents. They provide the initial framework of governance; clear, albeit limited, list of rights; and a federal structure. Yet neither the Constitution nor Declaration of Independence make any mention of some of the most important issues of our day: healthcare, economic welfare, gay marriage, abortion, drone strikes, education, child-rearing, right to die, and so on are not even hinted at. Even the power to print paper money is nowhere directly referred to in the text, nor are free speech and the exercise of religion explicitly guaranteed against states' infringements. Understanding the documents must therefore begin with the written clauses but take seriously both deductive and inductive reasoning filtered through the ethos of dignity and community interests.

My argument is that constitutional interpretation should aim to secure the people's right to enjoy their autonomy. The constitutional community shares correlative rights by virtue of their humanity. The Declaration and Preamble are statements of the people's public charges to their governments. These documents propound the standards and rules that federal, state, and local governments— within their separate spheres of authority—are duty-bound to fulfill in the enforcement of policies that are likely to conduce to the public good. To stay true to the central premise of the Constitution, public policy must be developed that allows individuals to pursue their goals while placing limits as well as creating programs crafted for the entire community to share in the boons of liberty. Each person is free to set his or her trajectory for life but also obligated to respect the interests of others. The Constitution creates limited governmental powers for running public programs that benefit individuals while placing necessary safety limits for the good of society. Civic cooperation through representative institutions facilitates the enjoyment of mutual human rights by creating legally enforceable standards of behavior—in the form or statutes, regulations, executive orders, and judicial interpretation—for the flourishing of individuals in a community of equals.

The Constitution does not create rights but protects those universal ideals of representative democracy first set out in the Declaration of Independence. It further grants authority to political institutions for the enforcement of policies and concrete laws for the betterment of society or some relevant segment of it. Many scholars with legal realist and process theory leanings believe that the authority of government is a social construct created by popular majorities, while I believe no law, even those enacted by popular majorities, to be authoritative unless it is in accord with a central maxim of constitutionalism, which is the protection of individual rights for the common good. I use the terms "constitutional maxim" or simply "maxim" throughout this book to refer to the overarching goal of government, which sets limits on power and holds the obligation to act for the public benefit. In some cases, constitutional maxim is interchangeable with constitutional principle, but I prefer the former to refer to the legal ethos that is not only aspirational but mandatory on all government institutions. The term refers to a synthetic principle and mandate for governance that is derived from the Declaration of Independence and the US Constitution.

I will seek to demonstrate that the Declaration of Independence and the Preamble to the Constitution are substantive statements that should bear significant weight on constitutional decision making. Unfortunately nearly all constitutional scholars—with the exception of a handful of prominent constitutional experts like Jack Balkin, Mark Tushnet, and Sanford Levinson—exclude them from discussion of interpretation, deeming them too nebulously general to be of any value for understanding specific clauses of the Constitution. To the contrary, both assert the central purpose of constitutional law: establishing stable, egalitarian norms for the creation of government institutions; placing obligations on their functions; and contributing to deliberative popular dialogue about representational self-government.

The Declaration and Preamble jointly establish the framework for deliberative discourse, containing normative principles that cannot be violated by other laws. Together they describe the purpose of government, the sovereign role of the people, ideals of the United States, and political representation. They render certain motives for laws—prejudices, hatred, bigotry, viewpoint suppression, and the like—illegitimate.

In a society of free and equal citizens, different priorities are inevitable. Therefore, the Preamble to the Constitution directed those holding the reins of power to seek the people's general welfare, a statement that required the Union to safeguard liberties and to create institutions to maintain safety and happiness.

The Declaration and Constitution provide legal stability in a pluralistic nation, where each person has a different conception of the pursuit of happiness. They set the general terms for a collective ethos, one that should empower individuals and guide politicians setting policies for the collective good.

This joint concept of individual rights and public welfare constitutes a unified mandate of government to maintain, refine, and advance a system by and for the people seeking their personal goods and exercising their collective judgments through elective franchise and deliberation on the means for achieving social goods. Succeeding generations have defined and redefined the meaning of those documents through social movements, statutes, and judicial opinions.

The terms of the Declaration and Preamble restrain decision makers and render them answerable to the people as a whole rather than a constituency that happens to be powerful enough to pass popular laws that violate the rights of certain classes of the population. Together they require public actors to effectuate civic values in accordance with the principles of nondiscrimination, mutuality, and the public good. The Declaration and Preamble proclaim a unified maxim of public civility that the people can identify and use to analyze, debate, and criticize all incompatible uses of authority. Thus any contemporary issues—including the most contentious on minimum wage, public assistance, public health plans, abortion, campaign financing, business regulations, and so on—should be treated through the prism of constitutional maxim found in those documents.

A. Constitution and Theory

The US Constitution, like constitutions throughout the world, establishes a system of governance with structural, procedural, and substantive norms. Its terms are broad enough to facilitate legal development without having to regularly ratify a new version to meet the changing demands of modernity. In combination with the Declaration of Independence's statement of norms, the Constitution provides the structural provisions along with additional proclamations on the rights retained by the people. The dual normative and institutional structure that they create sets the mandatory framework for a stable government that is not as easily modified as by statutes. Understanding their underlying purpose empowers citizens to determine the legitimacy of specific policies and laws, empowers legislatures to pass laws to safeguard rights and to advance the general welfare, blocks the presidency from becoming an autocracy, and provides judicially reviewable provisions and standards to prevent government overreaching. Reformers' efforts are bolstered by a clear understanding of the shortcomings of existing institutions.

The United States Constitution and Declaration are ancient documents; indeed, the national constitution is the oldest in the world. Their clauses were composed at a time when the art of constitution making and popular sovereignty were little understood. Inevitably, they are chock-full of ambiguities. What precisely does "due process" mean? And what is the "pursuit of happiness"? How specifically shall the federal government provide for the people's "safety and happiness"? What are the "privileges and immunities" of national citizenship? What acts constitute "high crimes and misdemeanors," and what about "good behaviour"? At what stage of negotiating a treaty with foreign envoys must a president seek the advice and consent of the Senate? By what metric should "general [w]elfare" be measured and which branch(es) of government should measure it? How literal should translation of the Constitution be? What rights are unenumerated? How should the people exercise their sovereignty? What forms of commerce may Congress regulate? What matters can Congress keep secret without publishing its deliberations in official journals of debates? Which of the president's functions are reviewable? Who should have the final say in the interpretation of the Constitution? Did the Declaration retain interpretive value after ratification of the Constitution? These and a host of other questions do not lend themselves to easy, textual, much less irrefutable answers. The Constitution's open-ended clauses and the Declaration's aspirational-sounding statements about human rights make them ripe for deliberations and analyses. In the end, we are left with supreme legal authorities that remain stable but set out methods for amendment; contain protections for political, civil, and procedural rights; provide the basic structure of governance; and set written mandates but cannot resolve all disputes without reference to norms.

Constitutional theory should contain a framework for holding officials accountable to ordinary people, each with his or her unique family, friends, social circles, likes, and anxieties. A normatively grounded and pluralistic approach to theory should not merely be a compilation of empirical, epistemological, and normative insights but rooted in the human will to act as an autonomous, social being. Yet the unconstrained exercise of power, without the restraint of national norms, carries the danger of unconscionable abuse by self-aggrandizing ruling elites or charismatic autocrats. That is, in turn, likely to lead to favoritism for select groups rather than evenhandedness and to suppression of outsiders' abilities to partake in a greater social community. A comprehensive constitutional theory must explain the reasons why some public actions are just and others unjust, going beyond positivistic explanations and assessing the fairness of outcomes; hence, theory should be more than a study of whether the government has followed existing rules or judges have relied on existing modes of interpretation. A deeper question is whether public officials have met their duty of trust to the people or, to the contrary, engaged in discriminatory conduct, suppressed democratic speech, or malapportioned the electoral system. In philosophical terms, in this book I propose a theory of constitutional law that integrates deontology and consequentialism.

Enforceable mechanisms—in the form of constitutional norms, statutes, judicial proceedings, executive orders, and administrative actions—are essential for guaranteeing individual rights for the whole body politic. Procedural constraints on conduct, most cogently explained by John Hart Ely,[2] are by themselves no guarantee against state overreaching by majoritarian oppression of less powerful groups. No doubt self-interest will win over many who hold the reins of authority, but a standard of legitimacy makes them accountable to the public through various channels of redress such as courts, elections, petitions, and public protests. The obligation (or put another way, the constitutional pledge) of public servants is to protect rights and to administer to the public good. Deontologists, who argue only for a rights protecting regime, miss the second part of the dual responsibility of governance. Rights cannot be absolute where the context of their exercise involves irresolvable conflict between rights holders. Take for instance free expression. United States citizens regard this to be a core entitlement. Alongside it are reasonable statutory or common law restrictions on defamation, disclosure of business secrets, trademark infringement, incitement to imminent violence, and false advertisement. These limits are predicated on social norms recognizing the simultaneous existence of conflicting claims that must be balanced against the interest of the speech rights holders. As a judge or legislator balances the relevant concerns, no absolute right to speech dictates the outcome. Some social concerns must come into play in balancing the claims of speakers and those who wish to prevent them from harms to reputation, intellectual property, and tranquility. Judgments, both in the formation of law and in the adjudication of cases, often raise public policy concerns that require resolutions about socio-constitutional issues about the nature of representative democracy and the equal freedom of the collective people, whom the Preamble to the Constitution recognizes as the real sovereigns, who make up its identity.

The US Constitution is a repository of ancient and modern values needed to resolve normative and pragmatic concerns of private and public concerns. It encompasses core provisions against autocracy, amendments guaranteeing rights, and its interpretation by courts reflects cultural sensibilities about contemporary debates. Constraints against tyranny, which run the gambit from tricameralism to the guaranteed privileges or immunities of citizenship, are not merely structure; rather they provide a format of government to retain representative sovereignty in the people's hands. All three branches of government are responsible to the public and obligated to pursue policies for its betterment. This, at least, is true in theory. In reality, partisanship and favoritism enter constitutional determinations and too often infuse irrelevant consideration into decisions that should benefit people equally, but often result in inapposite treatment based on race and other suspect classifications.

B. Written Constitution and Norms

Stability of a pluralistic society requires a principle of justice to help maintain its multifaceted character and the flexibility to recognize each person's unobtrusive right to pursue personal preferences. Judgment must take into account constitutional text, historical background, and specific context from which a dispute arises. It is too limiting to look only at original perspectives of the Constitution or to focus solely on contemporary values. What is needed is a stable foundation, one that does not change with shifting politics, that permanently demonstrates respect for human dignity while recognizing the value of history and ethical advancements. This foundation must be clear enough to interpret constitutional ambiguities, such as the meaning of "due process" and "equal protection," but general enough to enable each generation to grow as a people in light of changed social circumstances. Systemic stability is not only a function of text. Any textualist approach would be too narrowly focused, too fixated on syntactic meaning to deal with the enumerable issues that arise in an evolving democracy.

Legal stability requires structure for the administration of law and limits on the use of state powers. In order to remain relevant to anyone engaged in public debate, a blueprint of government should avoid factionalism; constitutions create systems of checks, and, overall, prevent the unbridled abuse of power. Even provisions setting out functions of the three branches of government are incomplete and must be further elaborated while staying within the parameters of text. Like the United States, other democracies with written constitutions have found the need to establish adaptable policies. While statutes can be changed to reflect political preferences that emerge with each election, a written Constitution sets expectations that transcend the existing debates between political parties and among their leaders. Complex amendment procedures make amending constitutions more difficult than changing or altogether repealing ordinary laws. I should add, on the other hand, that the amendment device is only one way in which the meaning of the US Constitution has evolved from a period of slavery to one recognizing the abomination of that institution and involuntary servitude, its incidents, as well as many other equal protection and fundamental rights concerns.

Provisions of the written Constitution only set a skeletal structure for efficient administration and for the protection of people's will to enjoy their rights on an equal basis without arbitrary restrictions. Constitutional provisions like the Unenumerated Rights Clause of the Ninth Amendment establish that an underlying ethos permeates the written text. While it stabilizes legal institutions,

the Constitution's wording is ambiguous enough to lend incompatible conclusions. For instance, the Supreme Court of the United States has both interpreted
the Equal Protection Clause of the Fourteenth Amendment as a justification
for racial segregation and as a statement prohibiting its practice. I will argue
that underlying ethos of equality, liberty, and public good rendered the Court's
acceptance of exclusionary practice in its decision in *Plessy v. Ferguson* the morally wrong interpretation of that Clause: Not simply wrong because it was an
illogical way of reading the text, nor wrong only now but legitimate when it was
decided. The holding in *Plessy* made no more sense then than it does today given
the nation's fundamental commitments to justice that finally led to desegregation after *Brown v. Board of Education*. Those commitments include the rejection
of racist state practices purporting to treat people of different races equally, while
being grounded in racist assumptions. That sensibility derives in part from the
post-Civil War Constitution's commitment, on national and state levels, to abide
by the ideals of liberal equality. In theory, although certainly not in practice, the
ideal had been a part of the Declaration of Independence and Constitution from
the time of independence.

C. Theoretical Validity

Any theory of constitutional law must provide the norms of legal culture and the structured authority for following through on them. Since the
Constitution is the highest law that no other laws can violate, no other branch
of government can legitimately overturn it. Theories of constitutional legal
doctrine, as the philosopher Robert Alexy points out, should include analytical, empirical, and normative dimensions.[3] Their breadth requires analytical
considerations of procedural and substantive questions. That is not to say that
the Constitution is pertinent for answering all legal questions. In the United
States, judges typically resolve matters of child custody, questions about the
alienation of property, and issues concerning contract formation without
resorting to higher legal principles. But where those same questions contain
elements of fairness that transcend the statutory or common law provisions
that govern their adjudication, questions of normative constitutional law arise.
For instance, in child custody cases the key question is about the best interest
of the child. Resolution requires assessment of specific claims, but if the question is complicated by discrimination based on suspect classifications (such
as race or nationality), then resolution of the claims transcends the facts of
the case and raises constitutional questions. To take another example, if two
people claim title to real estate or disagree about whether they have entered
into a legally binding agreement, the case is context-specific and resolution

is predicated on ordinary laws made by courts or legislatures. But if a party raises racial or ethnic inequality claims, the question includes constitutional components of private rights and social morals. In the latter case, resolution should draw from the higher principle in dignity and social goods asserted in the Declaration and the Preamble.

I am only dealing here with constitutional inquiry where normative values are essential for definition. Along with a design of how federal government should function, the US Constitution is a statement of national ethos. Hence resolution of sex, racial, or ethnic state discrimination claims raise national, not simply local, normative questions. Disputes about core values cannot be resolved solely by reference to an extant law or social practice. Knowing that a law or custom exists does not resolve whether it is fair on its face or in its application.

Constitutional theory must provide normative answers, or at least tell us what normative questions to ask. The normative approach, which I commend to the reader, differs from the judicial supremacy of the United States, where only court opinions, especially those of the Supreme Court, are definitive interpretations of the Constitution. Nor is my approach like the British system where Parliament has the final say of the Constitution's meaning, even when that means gainsaying judicial opinion. Instead, I argue that rational evaluation of constitutional meaning is a project for both government actors and the people. The texts of the Constitution and Declaration of Independence place limits on that approach, but their open-ended language leaves room for an evolving public ethos in keeping with the central premise of US representative democracy.

The relevance and meaning of the general principles are always controversial because on their interpretation rest policy choices about subjects of such moment as school prayer, legal tender, commercial intercourse, and taxation. Without some core ideal these topics would become even more politicized than they already are. Given the significance of these topics to individuals and society as a whole, conflicts about their resolution are rarely free of rancor, but at least with a central constitutional norm nonsensical and harmful solutions can be ruled out. Debate can be better focused on core values rather than on personal and group interests.

The inevitable differences of public opinion make it necessary to have some means of achieving finality, providing definitive rules and standards. The Supreme Court has granted itself the power to resolve constitutional debates, and the other two branches have recognized that authority.[4] The Court's claim to interpretive finality, a power never explicitly granted by the Constitution, has largely gone unchallenged by the American public. But that has not stopped a few academics—most notably Mark Tushnet, Larry Kramer, and Jeremy Waldron—from taking on this premise. Through the years, the Court has often shown itself to be just as influenced by the trends of its day as any other branch of government. The results of judicial supremacy have been mixed. While the Supreme Court's opinions have proven to be relatively stable because of the doctrine of *stare decisis*, its periodic changes of mind about such matters as economic rights, campaign financing, racial relations, and national origin discrimination make the judicial opinions incomplete for the establishment of a stable theory of the Constitution. The legislative branch of government is even less likely to render objective opinions on interpretation than the judiciary because senators and representatives are typically overtly political in supporting policies that are likely to help them win reelections, something the judiciary need not worry about since federal judges have lifetime appointments. So prone are elected officials to voting on the basis of the changing tides of personal or public opinion that the US Constitution sets a bicameral system of separate functions to check lawmakers and their constituents from manipulating majority voting in order to harm minorities. So, too, an empirical study of presidential actions is a specious way of defining portions of the Constitution. This is especially the case with the executive branch, whom the framers believed to be most prone to corruption, autocracy, and militarism.[5]

D. Constitutional Rights and Social Equality

In this book, I seek to demonstrate that in the face of institutional, textual, and historical changes, a stable principle of accountability is needed for maintaining constitutional norms. Constitutional theory must accurately describe constitutional aspirations, criticize failures, clarify goals, and provide a trajectory for social improvements. Accordingly, I posit that a simple principle is at the root of the constitutional legitimacy; one that is not solely born of the "logical craving for unity," as philosopher Nicolai Hartmann put it in the context of overall ethical theory,[6] but included in the constitutive documents of the US legal system. Its basis is not natural law but holistic constitutional adoption. The principle I propose has textual roots in the Declaration of Independence, especially as it was incorporated into the Constitution by the Reconstruction Amendments, and the Preamble to the Constitution. It exists at a level of abstraction sufficiently broad enough to bind government to one consistent standard against which all official actions can be gauged. To be fully relevant, it must mandate the proper scope of sovereign authority, setting the limits of power and ordering the priorities of public actions. All three branches of government must abide by its formula for representative governance. Stated briefly, I claim that the foundational maxim of authority to be:

The underlying purpose of government is to secure equal rights for the common good.

I will explain its scope and meaning in the pages that follow.

This is a simple statement of the people's overall expectation to be treated justly by government. Its value is both as a theoretical construct against which specific actions can be tested and as a mandate for practical actions. Structural portions of the Constitution—those granting powers, assigning spheres of responsibility, and establishing methods for deciding conflicts—all serve this normative goal. As we proceed to parse this principle, we should be mindful of Alexy's insightful counsel that too high a level of abstraction not become so malleable as to render its formula meaningless.[7] I hope to demonstrate that my pithy statement of overall constitutional purpose provides both a theoretical and practical construct for fair governance, demonstrating concerns for individual rights while placing appropriate limitations on them in cases of overriding public interest. The state's sovereign authority derives from the will of the people, whose vital interests public officials are charged with safeguarding. My formulation takes into account the intrinsic value of each individual but also the need for formal assessments of how law impacts relevant communities. In the pages that follow, I derive this maxim from the structure and substance of the Declaration and Constitution, the logical consequences of their provisions, how those inform government in its exercise of duties, and the effect of consistent and fair norms on ordinary citizens.

The theory will inevitably encounter resistance from competing theories of constitutional structure and rights, most prominently those of the originalist and living constitutionalist schools of thought. In response it is not necessary to wholly disown others' contributions to the field. One can do better by examining their arguments and conclusions to understand where their ideas offer valuable understandings on our legal system. But it is at least as important to identify their shortcomings in an effort to present a more comprehensive and accurate explanation. Better results can be achieved by learning from the intellectual trajectory of others rather than simply discounting their efforts out of hand. This does not require getting lost in their ideas but rather learning from them while identifying a better explanation for the central ideal of representative constitutionalism.

The text of the US Constitution provides the starting point for any analysis of the normative purposes of the Constitution. Interpretation should liberally take into account the rights of all people, irrespective of their particular backgrounds or characteristics. In a society of equals, individuals impact others' lives. Rights can be limited when they cause others harms or are overridden by overwhelming public concerns, such as the need to prevent communicable diseases like tuberculosis.

Constitutional adjudication is concerned with norms, facts, and analyses, not simply a mechanical application of past precedents and accepted modes of rhetorical interpretation. Principles should and do play a role in judicial analysis. Unfortunately, in many cases normative claims are no more than a restatement of political preferences. The formulation of public policy, unlike private decisions, should be made impartially. The application of generic norms to the facts, as former President of the Supreme Court of Israel Aharon Barak points out, derives from "an expression of the national ethos, the cultural heritage, the social tradition, and the entire historical experience of that nation."[8] The extent to which any or all of these factors weigh in a particular case will vary based on context and facts. Analytical fit is predicated on a variety of factors, including rights involved, existing or potential public risks, historical facts, realistic or extraordinary choices, public input, governmental powers, and procedural avenues.

While the problems lawyers, judges, and politicians deal with are never purely theoretical but always practical, a clear statement of national ethos is needed to demarcate the lines between justice and injustice. My perspective on abstract norms is quite different from those of process theorists, who argue that constitutional legitimacy requires only organizational values like judicial consistency but not immutable norms like racial fairness.[9] Proceduralists believe inclusive deliberation will ultimately lead to stable democracy.

Procedural fairness is no doubt essential to the exercise of impartial governance, but it does not get at the most basic principle of constitutional purpose. More is needed than democratic theory to push the system in the direction of pluralistic equality. Democracy itself must be defined in a way that prevents majority rule from becoming a vehicle for arbitrary policies and encroachment on people's pursuits of happiness. Fairness, human dignity, and autonomy are not simply procedural but normative values that the Constitution protects against arbitrary state conduct. Even prominent procedural advocates tend to indirectly concede that there is at least one substantive value that precedes administrative assessments. For instance while Ely argued that judges should eschew substantive values, Frank Michelman and Laurence Tribe have pointed out that Ely commits to a "substantive vision of human rights" and a "thoroughly substantive proposition that everyone is to have an equal chance to count politically for one and no more than one."[10] Ely's project then is not solely proceduralist, but concedes that judicial inquiry must be conscious of safeguarding equal-access democracy and its essential features.[11]

Likewise, Jürgen Habermas, another proceduralist, ties legitimate public deliberation—defined as a communicative process in which everyone can "take part, freely and equally, in a cooperative search for truth, where nothing coerces anyone except the force of the better argument"[12]—to the successful operation of a democratic state. In working out a quasi-transcendental process of deliberation, Habermas himself commits to an intrinsically valuable legal norm: deliberative impartiality.[13] Procedural approaches, like his and Ely's, presuppose some stable norm of communicative action—sometimes neutral about the treatment of participants, as in ordinary political discourse, and at other times giving more weight to expert opinions, as in regulatory agency considerations. Therein lie unavoidable substantive criteria: In some cases everyone's voice is equal and at others preference must be given to the specialists, as in the drafting of environmental regulation or in the construction of public works. Norms are needed to avoid abuse and social ends come into play in weighing collective goods (e.g., maintaining clear water and air standards or structurally sound highways). Moreover, the unavoidable historical fact is that some groups, usually minorities, have too often been excluded from democratic deliberations. The recognition of stable principles that transcend the positive laws upon which voluntary legal associations agree is necessary to guard against overreaching and outright purposeful animus.

Judicial assessment of the constitutionality of statutes should not simply be a process of making sure that some methodological rules have been followed. We evaluate precedents on the basis of outcomes as well as administrative procedures. Supreme Court judgments, like *Dred Scott v. Sandford*[14] or *Ableman v. Booth*[15] are not merely wrong because they misapplied law but because they reinforced slavery and contributed to national divisiveness that eventually led to the Civil War. Both opinions sought to resolve sectional conflicts between the South and North, but by conceiving of property to only be the birthright of whites and of slaves as chattel subject to seizure, the Court caused irreparable harms to society as a whole, not just to blacks whom the majority opinions claimed were not and could never become citizens. Those two decisions were among the reasons the North and South became embroiled in civil war. The harm was not confined to a few, but all experienced the consequences of invidious ideology as eventually brother fought brother.

Safeguarding dignity and advancing democratic institutions are substantive social aims. Their combined nature in a polity requires reflection on private interests and public results. A dispute about whether a statement hurts a plaintiff's reputation or enjoys First Amendment protection, whether the welfare benefits of an out-of-state migrant can be limited, or whether state law can prohibit catering businesses from discriminating against homosexual couples are value-rich questions that require reflections on the facts of each case and the resolution's impact on society. Where constitutional rights are involved, the outcome of legal disputes has significance to the community as a whole because many of its members are affected by the resolution of the doctrinal questions.

For anyone whose life is affected by constitutional doctrine, the interpretation of the text is not merely a matter for rhetorical consistency with the founding generation. Whether the Constitution is interpreted as a document of majoritarian power or an instrument for the protection of minority rights and liberties is not solely an abstract philosophical question in the search for logical resolution. For persons seeking public assistance or filing a lawsuit for cyber stalking, the accurate interpretation of constitutional norms has direct impact on their lives. Answers do not come solely from the "original position" but from a regular reevaluation of foundational norms through the lenses of contemporary social practices and rules.[16] Economic realities; advancement in knowledge; the lessons born of wars and hardships; and the recognition of policy shortcomings through judicial opinion, political deliberation, and social group advocacy should also augment wisdom that had been unavailable to the founders. Abstract concepts of justice are, therefore, fruitful starting points for reflecting on political justice, but by themselves insufficient for contemporary policy making, requiring steady and persistent supplementation by historical observations and repeated reassessment of how the original constitutional contract advanced or harmed the central purpose of nationhood. Technically, the initial social contract can only be directly changed through amendments to the Constitution, the ratification of an entirely new Constitution, or revolution; but over the centuries ordinary citizens have relied on the legislative and judicial processes to make relevant to their own lives the general constitutional statements on such things as due process and equal protection. Constitutional interpretation is not solely a matter of describing American culture and its ideological origins, but should deliberatively advance the fair society of equals.

If neither past practices nor original meanings can provide an undisputed way forward away from past injustices, we must look for direction outside the plethora of judicial opinions as well as institutional and personal styles unavoidable in regulatory administration. They can tell us something about accepted and controversial practices of a particular day and age, but this inductive method will be too variegated to derive a stable idea of a comprehensive government. A foundational standard is essential for maintaining pluralistic constitutionalism against special interests, especially those with enough resources to manipulate the electoral process. With a unified legal obligation in place, the limits of pluralistic practices can be tested through a reviewable standard. The overall purpose that is essential for legal reasoning is not solely a matter of empirical reflection but a reliable ideal against which state actions can be tested. Such a principle facilitates the evaluation of past and present practices and projects national commitments into the future. What is needed is a legal obligation against which all constitutional practices, holdings, and mandates can be tested. The common core must apply to all constitutional subjects, no matter how disparate. The anti-autocratic principle that also requires all branches of government to respect the individual while working for the general welfare achieves just that.

If, as I claim, the Declaration of Independence and Preamble to the Constitution set out a norm of liberal equality for the common good, we can judge bygone exploitations like slavery and find them unjust even for the time period when the institution was legal and accepted by a large percentage of the American public. What's more, it provides a basis for arguing that clauses that protected that institution were constitutionally illegitimate. Once a general principle of governance is established, the justice of specific practices, both past and present, can be assessed through reasonable deliberation about empirical facts and positive laws.

Irrespective of systemic shortcomings—due in no small part to favoritism, widespread prejudices, failure to comprehend long-term ramifications, and weakness of collective will to act according to the highest social norms—the Constitution's and Declaration of Independence's principles remain indispensable for administering a just society. The public objective of securing liberty for the common good has allowed the United States to evolve into a more egalitarian country despite historic injustices, such as the Indian Removal, Japanese Internment, and Red Scare. Interpretation and reconceptualization of the Constitution's general language has enabled Americans to advance an understanding of its substantive content,[17] especially in the years following the Second World War when human rights became more prominently endorsed throughout the world. Each generation must reinterpret the text in an introspective manner to determine whether its legal institutions live up to the standards of the Constitution's and Declaration's humanistic values. Jack Balkin has expressed the need for an evolving understanding of constitutional ideals: "When the Constitution uses vague standards or abstract principles, we must apply them to our own circumstance in our own time."[18] A mutually accepted constitutional cause enables partisans of differing views on issues as diverse as abortion, assisted suicide, and war powers to debate vigorously but to work within the system rather than trying to overthrow it through revolution or some other violent alternative. Even losers of political disagreements are more likely to accept results that they rationally recognize to be in accord with the administrative and substantive functions of constitutional democracy.

E. Other Theories

Constitutional theory is the method of unpacking the text, understanding its relation to society, determining the role of the three branches of government, and developing a consistent and predictable interpretation. There are a variety of theories for interpretation, which I detail in Chapter 8. Here I wish to provide only a preliminary survey to help situate this book in the broader dialogue about

constitutional meaning. Philip Bobbitt elegantly described six accepted grammatical modalities of US jurisprudence:

> the historical (relying on the intentions of the framers and ratifiers of
> the Constitution); textual (looking to the meaning of the words of the
> Constitution alone, as they would be interpreted by the average con-
> temporary "man on the street"); structural (inferring rules from the
> relationships that the Constitution mandates among the structures it
> sets up); doctrinal (applying rules generated by precedent); ethical
> (deriving rules from those moral commitments of the American ethos
> that are reflected in the Constitution); and prudential (seeking to bal-
> ance the costs and benefits of a particular rule).[19]

Bobbitt's approach resists any grand constitutional meanings.

Missing from Bobbitt's list, as Tushnet pointed out, is the possibility that
ideological purpose might also be a modality of constitutional argument.[20]
Elsewhere, Tushnet stated that "the substantive criteria for identifying the people's vital interests" are grounded in the Declaration of Independence and the
Preamble to the Constitution.[21] His statement has profound implications for
understanding judicial doctrine. Tushnet's account is positivistic, derived from
extant legal pronouncements and the people's will, whereas I believe that the
Declaration codified a political morality that remains binding on each generation of government. The Constitution, later, detailed limits on power, offices
for carrying out the national mandate, and structures for exercising representative democracy. All constitutional interpretation must be grounded in the social
compacts of sovereign independence and constitutional ratification.

Sanford Levinson similarly posits, "To the extent that recourse to transcen-
dental and ostensibly eternal natural law is different from reference to more
contingent social norms of an 'ethos,' then reference to natural law might serve
as a seventh modality."[22] I would take this seventh modality a step further than
Levinson, understanding it to be both idyllic and proscriptive: It creates the
aspirations and duties that government must strive to achieve. The maxim that
government must protect inalienable rights through policies designed to benefit the community of equals is not solely something to which government can
aspire; rather, it creates an obligation on all public officials to impartially seek the
people's safety and happiness. The Declaration and the Constitution codified
a political ethos predicated on the people's decision to enter a political compact for creating representative government with the power to pass rules for the
maintenance of life, liberty, and the pursuit of happiness.

Bobbitt's lexicographical description of constitutional interpretation is broader
in its descriptive scope than Ely's suggestion that the Constitution is principally
concerned with "political process" and "representative-reinforce[ment],"

not "particular substantive values." Ely contended that the Constitution's primary concern with representative democracy implies that judicial review must reinforce participation-oriented policies. He asserted that the Constitution was principally concerned with judicial protection of participation in democratic governance. Judicial review, on his reading, "unlike its rival value-protecting approach, is not inconsistent with, but on the contrary (and quite by design) entirely supportive of, . . . representative democracy." The judiciary's role in preserving democratic institutions can hardly be doubted; however, contrary to my point of view, Ely believed that talk of rights, in the Declaration of Independence, was no more than legal posturing to convince rather than set any public principles.[23]

While Ely convincingly argued that the judiciary must guard against political failures to secure equal participation for all segments of the population, he was mistaken to discount the ethical values inherent in portions of the Declaration and Constitution that provide for equal participation, equal treatment, and fundamental rights. Focusing just on the Constitution for now, it no doubt sets many of the structures intrinsic to federalism and representative governance—such as the timing of presidential elections, the sequencing of presidential vetoes and legislative overrides, and the diversity required for federal assertion of subject matter jurisdiction. However, there are other clauses that create explicit substantive norms on which the nation's sovereign legitimacy is predicated: the Free Speech, Establishment, Due Process, and Equal Protection Clauses. Some portions of the Constitution that are concerned with process, such as the Habeas and Ex Post Facto Clauses, also place a value on rights like liberty and justice. As H. Jefferson Powell pointed out, many of the process elements of the Constitution, such as protection of property rights against misappropriation, are substantive in purpose. Judges cannot, Powell demonstrated, "identify legitimate occasions for judicial intervention without" making "substantive political and moral choices."[24]

The critique of any accepted method of interpretation is itself a meta-analysis of existing norms and hierarchies, which might take the form of extralegal arguments—be they philosophical, sociological, or political. Many questions about the meaning of constitutional text will require some normative reference; that reference point is the foundational principle of representative government to protect individuals and to provide policies for the common good. The First Amendment, for instance, provides little about the meaning of "free speech"; indeed, by its word it is only an injunction against congressional interference. Safeguarding political and autonomous speech requires integrity to a deeper value, one predicated on a structure of government created by the people to serve their needs, without abridging innate human entitlements, and setting reasonable commensurable goals with a pluralistic state.

Reflection on whether any line of analysis is valid to a given situation is a parsing of constitutional meaning that provides mandatory guidance to all three branches of government. One of the most influential statements for a "moral reading" of the Constitution appears in Ronald Dworkin's writings. Dworkin asserted that all levels of society—be they lawmakers, judges, or citizens—should interpret abstract clauses of the Constitution to derive "moral principles about political decency and justice." The central political ideal embodied in the Constitution, Dworkin argued, is the concept of justice in a "society of citizens both equal and free," where judges are constrained by the principle of "equal concern and respect." The judiciary plays an important role in American constitutional practice in which "judges [historically] have final interpretive authority."[25] Dworkin's profound insights into the overlapping constitutional concerns about equality and liberty need not, however, lead to his adopted supremacy of judicial opinion on justice. While judges play an important role in advancing the best reading of the Constitution, the people have never lost their sovereignty to define its meanings through their elected representatives. Indeed, courts, like all of the branches of government, must keep an eye to the sovereign will of the people as it was guaranteed by the Declaration of Independence and the Constitution.

A variety of scholars, like Daniel Farber and Suzanna Sherry, call out Dworkin and other expositors of foundational theories for presuming that there are "clear-cut answers" for "difficult moral dilemmas." Farber and Sherry's criticism is not, however, limited to progressive thinkers like Dworkin. They also take Robert Bork, Antonin Scalia, and Richard Epstein to task.[26] The three latter theorists adopt various strands of originalism, currently one of the most popular approaches to constitutional interpretation.

The driving sparks of originalism are the desire for interpretive consistency, legal stability, and judicial credibility. Its proponents seek to restrain judges in order to prevent them from politicking from the bench.[27] Bork, who represents the early direction of the movement, adopted a position that "original intent is the only legitimate basis for constitutional decisionmaking."[28] Criticism of original intent theorists was pointed and effectively reframed the debate. Justice William Brennan, arguably the most influential living constitutionalist, asserted that originalism was naught but "arrogance cloaked as humility."[29] He adopted a nontextualist method, in which scholars and judges were to flesh out the many ways constitutional tradition evolved through judicial opinions and practices of other public institutions. As may be expected in such a contentious field of study, living constitutionalism also has its detractors, who denounce its often inattention to constitutional text as a threat to a well-ordered society, putting at risk the very institutions of an accountable democracy.

The theory I will elaborate in this book is one that does not discount texts but rather regards them as gaining legitimacy insofar as they apply a basic principle that is grounded in human nature but likewise consistent with the needs of a complex, pluralistic society. Text is important because it provides consistency and predictability for the entire system of constitutional law; however, without a moral basis the text is so ambiguous that the Supreme Court in the past relied on the Equal Protection Clause to justify racial segregation,[30] the Declaration of Independence to justify slavery,[31] and the Due Process Clause to strike minimum hour and maximum wage laws.[32]

This book elaborates a foundational theory of United States representative democracy. I have discussed its application in a variety of articles.[33] In this work I deal with the practical applications of the theory primarily in the final chapter. My principal focus is on constitutional governance, unlike most studies of constitutional theory, which tend to focus on adjudication. I seek to identify a maxim grounded in constitutional text that can remain constant through generations. A statement of national purpose must be general in order to enable government to advance policies to safeguard individual rights and exercise authority to accommodate conflicting tastes and interests. The people must benefit from its stability of general laws and yet be empowered as voters and social actors to deliberate, lobby, and pass laws reacting to changing conditions in commerce, agriculture, industrialization, exploration, defense, international relations, reform, sentiments, and any other aspect of social evolution. A constitutional ethos should provide an overarching mandate for government, while being abstract enough to enable each succeeding generation to build on the wisdom of its predecessors and discard their failures to uphold the ideals of liberal equality for the common good.

The first part of the book examines the sources of constitutional law. Chapter 1 begins with a description of complex societies governed by impartial laws. It then examines whether the basis of legitimate authority lies in the text of the Constitution, the highest law of the land. I conclude that the written document embodies social mores that are broad enough to address novel situations that were unforeseeable to the framers. Legitimate authority comes from the people who retain general rights and establish institutional structures into the Constitution and then work out details through the operation of government, social group pressure, and a variety of other forms of deliberative governance.

Chapter 2 provides historical context to the two principle texts of constitutional purpose. The Declaration of Independence established normative and aspirational values of nationhood. It sets the parameters for securing inalienable human rights and guaranteeing that politics will be representative of the will of the people. Its terms for independent nationhood laid the foundation on which the institutions of government, as they are set out in the Constitution and various statutes, must be predicated.

Chapter 3 takes the Declaration beyond its historical setting. In it, I explain the Declaration's constitutional relevance. The document is not solely a product of its time but also a statement of principle. Courts and scholars have too often neglected the Declaration, even though it offers a wealth of information about the normative foundation of national obligations to individuals and communities. Its guarantees of representative government and inalienable rights are an inspiration to social movements and a framework for the advancement of civil and political entitlements against which the legitimacy of state and federal actions can be evaluated. The congressional authority to uphold the fundamental rights secured by the people for all of the nation's inhabitants by the Declaration of Independence was incorporated through the three Reconstruction Amendments.

From the Revolutionary Era until the present day, social groups have found the Declaration to be an invaluable tool for interpreting the Constitution. The Declaration's statements about equal inalienable rights establish core commitments of US representative government and federalism. The retention of sovereignty in the hands of the people has significant implications for the functions of government and its policies. The Preamble to the Constitution, which is the subject of Chapter 4, provides more guidance for the collective right of the people to enjoy justice and safety. While the Declaration is a statement of innate rights retained against government intrusion, the Preamble is a statement of the government's ultimate responsibility to create policies that positively impact the people's general welfare. Its statement of national purpose complements the Declaration. Both guarantee representative democracy. Together they form a synthetic statement of the people's retention of human rights in a nation of equals, with each able to pursue individual happiness, with powers entrusted to government to provide for the common good of the whole, rather than arbitrary preference for any segment of the polity.

Persons in a society gain personally from the protection of procedurally neutral but substantively value-laden policy decisions. Fair rules, not favoring any particular group or individual, must provide citizens with equal access to elected politicians and courtrooms to vindicate their rights and to lobby for change. The constitutional obligation to equal treatment implies a normative undercurrent of representative democracy, one that treats each person with dignity while facilitating the welfare and safety of the community.

The second part of the book reflects on the nature of ethos and maxims. It demonstrates the importance of principle as a predicate to constitutionalism. Chapter 5 discusses how constitutional ethos plays a role in policy making and adjudication. Constitutional principle is essential for maintaining a stable polity, yet context, not merely formality, also plays a role in resolving social disputes. Specific statutes and judicial holdings are legitimate insofar as they stay within the general confines of national ethos.

Chapter 6 explains the relevance of normative principles to adjudication and fair administration of government institutions. I call public principles that are both aspirational and legally mandatory "maxims," which describe constitutionally enforceable entitlements and establish the limits of governmental authority. Besides setting limits on power, maxims lay the baseline principles for the exercise of public obligations.

Constitutional construction requires public officials to enforce policies in harmony with the constitutional maxim of liberal equality for the common good. Chapter 7 provides the core analytical construct of constitutional interpretation. In it, I develop the framework of maxim constitutionalism, which involves a balance of private and public goods. I parse the raison d'être of American law to be government's obligation to safeguard individual dignity and to develop policies likely to conduce to the public good, which the American people have adopted into the Declaration of Independence and Preamble. A constitutional framework with a unified overarching purpose creates positive and negative obligations on government toward individuals who compose the national community. Deliberative process enables the people and their representatives to react to contemporary dilemmas but not to abrogate the central purpose of government. Constitutional law should be understood synthetically to address collective and individual concerns.

The final part of the book considers the constitutional maxim in the context of other interpretive theories. It also discusses the maxim of constitutional governance in the context of several contemporary dilemmas. Chapter 8 discusses several competing theories on constitutional interpretation—focusing on originalism, living constitutionalism, and proceduralism—in an effort to explain why a maxim-based approach offers a more comprehensive and synthetic picture of constitutional meaning. The chapter closes with a critique of process-based schools of thought.

Chapter 9 concludes the book with an eye to contemporary structural issues to which the maxim-based approach is relevant; to whit, representative democracy, healthcare, sovereign immunity, and state action.

Representative democracy is advanced by cooperative deliberation about rights and social welfare. Social, historical, cultural, and legal analyses are critical to the resolution of contemporary public issues. A principled constitutional foundation, mandating government to safeguard individual liberties and advance the general welfare, provides the stability essential to an evolving national community of equals.

PART I

SOURCES OF CONSTITUTIONAL LAW

1

Principled Constitutional Discourse

Individual rights and the general welfare have been in American conscience since the Revolution. In a speech delivered before the Pennsylvania constitutional ratifying convention of 1787, one of the most influential proponents of constitutional ratification, James Wilson, connected rights with the welfare of the nation: "I have said before, no government, either single or confederated can exist, unless private and individual rights are subservient to the public and general happiness of the nation."[1] In his view, which other prominent founders, like John Adams, shared, equality consists of citizens' duties and rights.[2] Wilson's vision for America reflected the widespread belief that the Constitution would establish a national community from what had been 13 divergent British colonies.

All states and federal powers derive from the will of individuals. Legislative representatives, Wilson explained, are to work for the common good and public interest.[3] By 1787, citizens of the newly formed country already shared certain values, first set out by the Declaration of Independence, and soon to be safeguarded through constitutional ratification. Unlike England, where the monarch granted rights, Wilson and other Americans considered rights to be natural entitlements, better protected (but certainly not created) by written constitutional guarantees than solely by the common law or executive grants.[4]

Wilson knew well the relation of written text to natural entitlements, having been one of the most vociferous participants of the Philadelphia Convention, which drafted the original Constitution. Eleven years prior, Wilson had been the Pennsylvania delegate to the Second Continental Congress when that body adopted the Declaration of Independence. He viewed the 1776 document as a guarantee of private and social interests. The American people, he argued, had gained independence from colonialism and constituted the federal government to preserve their inherent and unalienable rights.[5] Wilson further explained his meaning in a widely printed and disseminated Pennsylvania ratifying convention speech. Society, which he as most others of his generation viewed through the lens of a social compact, does set some restraints on natural rights because "it is evident that" each person "gains more by the limitation of the liberty of others than he loses by the limitation of his own—so that in truth, the aggregate of liberty is more in society, than it is a state of nature." The interplay of individual and community interests directing the course of government is implicit in both of the documents he signed.[6]

Complex representative democracy is made up of individuals who, unlike populations of totalitarian regimes, are not obligated to renounce their separate points of view and unique pursuits. Law provides a means of resolving conflicts. A community of diverse equals requires some unifying ideal to interpret the many broad statements of the Declaration and Constitution. Both documents establish an inclusive ethos for a pluralistic society. They set out not merely a dialectical system that has no force in contemporary society but one that is connected to day-to-day governance and policy making. Their parameters for enacting practical legal schemes are meant to advance human dignity and general welfare; and when they fail to do so or are contrary to that synthetic aspiration, amendment is in order.

Our contemporary understanding of the Constitution is an evolutionary reality that reflects the collective will, moral sensibilities, and effects of history. Interpretation is not merely theoretical but relevant to practical application. Without knowledge of the moral community's commitments and its past practices, the Declaration and Constitution would be historical artifacts.

A. Complex Society

Wilson's social compact theory of government was widely accepted by framers of the Constitution. He explained that people form a civil society for "their preservation, their security, their improvement, their happiness." A social compact allows the individual to engage "with the whole collectively, and the whole collectively [to] engage with each individual."[7] While a jurist and more articulate about law than the average American, Wilson, who eventually became Associate Justice of the US Supreme Court, expressed a view accepted in all corners of the newly founded country: Civil society is meant to secure general happiness, granting all citizens equal constitutional rights.[8]

The collective community of the United States has a federalist character because it is composed of state and national sovereignties, each with a separate sphere of authority. Matters like estate formation and administration, land surveys, marriage licenses, elections of local officials, and many other ordinary legal matters were left to the states. The overarching scheme of a unified government, as Wilson and his fellow founders envisioned it, was established to protect natural human dignity.[9] Natural rights were thought to be intrinsic to human beings as residents of states and citizens of the country.

The revolutionary generation firmly believed in the existence of inalienable rights, although prejudices blinded them to the equal humanity of all Americans. Blacks and women were kept from enjoying the tranquility and safety for which the Revolution was fought. Nevertheless, from the beginning the seeds of equality were sown. Albeit revolutionaries often sought their own interests rather than abiding by the ideals they had planted.

Unlike simple organizations, the union of the 13 states, each with its unique colonial history, was a complex group that required written rules. Foremost of these was the Constitution, which dealt with a breadth of topics, but most of its provisions were too broad to apply to specific situations without further elaboration. When ratified, it set rules empowering political and judicial officeholders.

The document is not simply a statement of purpose but a basis for action. Mechanisms are required for the exercise of power. The compact is not, however, solely concerned with structure nor process. Several clauses of the Constitution authorize governance, while others place limits on the uses of power to prevent overreaching. Ex post facto laws are among those that are prohibited, while the right to petition for habeas corpus is preserved. When amendments were later adopted, they continued in this dual tradition. The Bill of Rights and the Reconstruction Amendments enumerate the people's retained prerogatives, while the 11th Amendment places limits on judicial diversity jurisdiction. Mechanisms for the formal resolution of conflicts—including judicial rules of fairness, legislative devices for setting policies, and, in the most extreme circumstances, declarations of war—also figure into the making of constitutional law. In all respects these provisions must be understood as public-directed in the sense that the ultimate function of government is the betterment of the people rather than simply the empowerment of governmental bodies. In the words of Chief Justice John Marshall, delivered in an often-cited 1819 decision, "the constitution acts directly on the people, by means of powers communicated directly from the people."[10] His statement about the sovereignty of the people over federal and state actors remains as true today as it was then. The Preamble's opening words, "We the People of the United States, in order to form a more perfect Union . . . establish this Constitution for the United States of America," clearly indicate that the people—not the states nor any other unit of government—remain the deciding force of constitutional governance.

Since the Constitution's adoption, US culture has changed, often dramatically. For one, the racial and ethnic demographic of the nation's population has changed significantly. Over the centuries, the steady stream of immigrants from all over the world has made the United States a more multicultural society than it had been at its founding, when, for the most part, the colonial population was European, primarily composed of British colonists and expatriates. Other forces were at play even then, reflecting the influences of Native American contacts, forced African migrations, as well as Spanish and French and, to a lesser degree, Dutch and Swedish efforts at colonization. With the passage of time, various waves of mass migration would test the authenticity of the country's stated commitments, but they would also inform and broaden their meanings. People from more diverse cultures now make up the ever-shifting complexion of American pluralism.

The Constitution of the United States defines the parameters for order in a country that has evolved into a complex society of integrated, entangled, and diverse cultures, religions, and ethnicities. Under the circumstances, tolerance is indispensable for the maintenance of domestic tranquility.

Self-identity derives, in no small part, from the culture of one's family or social group. A pluralistic constitutional scheme must respect this diversity of identities while also providing the legal and cultural contours of toleration. Government's duty to a diverse citizenry entails the creation of laws, such as those prohibiting nationality discrimination, that will provide the breathing space for individuals to exercise their intellectual, economic, or entrepreneurial abilities. The understanding of equality must be broad enough to facilitate cross-cultural discussions, empathy, understandings, and common grounds for mutual support and empowerment. Inevitably there will be interpersonal frictions. The dilemma for constitutional scholars and public officials of the 21st century is how to accommodate all of these diversities, while maintaining the generic principle of representative governance.[11]

The Constitution should therefore be understood to protect individuals in the social context of, and to establish correlative limits for, a tolerant society. While people are free to choose their own paths in life, their choices are limited by the constitutional rights of others to be treated as equal members of society.

B. Discursive Pluralism

The constitution of a heterogeneous society should provide the core of a shared legal ethos that is tolerant to the diverse groups composing it. That ethos is not set in stone. The history of United States, as one scholar comprehensively characterized it, "is best understood as an ongoing struggle over our collective constitutional identity."[12] The precepts of a multiethnic culture are partly derived from the limits of its constitution. But the institutional actors are not the sole sources of community identity; indeed, the people must breathe spirit into the words of the Constitution and empower officials to legislate, adjudicate, and enforce laws.

The public voice should be heard in the making of laws and in the assessment of their outcomes in so far as it dictates decisions consistent with norms of representative governance. Robert Post has described the relationship of democratic government to its constituents: "Constitutional law and culture are locked in a dialectical relationship so that constitutional law both arises from and in turn regulates culture."[13] Others, like Jürgen Habermas, Cass Sunstein, Frank Michelman, and Amartya Sen have also explained the importance of discourse and deliberation. These authors have their differences (for instance, as to the appropriate numbers of arenas for deliberation and whether the principal forum should be the legislative or judicial branch), but all of them agree that decision makers should receive feedback from interested parties who want to engage in the discussion of pertinent ideas. Inevitably, in a pluralistic society there will be many disagreements about the text's meaning. Not only do differences arise between groups but intragroup disagreements about policies are also common.

The discursive process provides citizens with the opportunity to debate proposals for resolving social, political, and economic problems. The legitimacy of public policy hinges on relevant constituencies having fair notice and opportunity to comment prior to enactment and, later, on agencies' impartial administration of it. Constitutional evaluation concerns itself with the likely effect of legal restraints on both the individual and community. The congruence of duties and benefits places restrictions on persons commensurate with the needs of a complex community of equals. Without the ability of its members to participate in the development of legal norms, citizens cannot be said to be free and equal. Representative democracy, at least in theory, prevents the exercise of power without first giving all affected groups the ability to voice their desired course of action and to criticize competing proposals.

The social contract between states and citizens presupposes that the winners, losers, and wilful non-participants will be required to abide by fairly enacted legal decisions. Once a decision has been codified into a statute, the means of recourse, except in extreme cases of tyrannical oppression—when popular uprising might be justifiable—is to pursue legal claims in court, challenging its application or facial validity, or to seek the law's repeal through legislative means.

A variety of forums can be used to enhance the discursive feedback regulators receive through meetings, public hearings, lobbying, and litigation. The written constitution is an important facilitator for negotiations between lawmakers and lobbyists, but so too are the country's traditions, history, sensitivities to contemporary concerns that past generations overlooked, and pragmatic evaluations. Rational input is open to any relevant school of interpretation. A secular society cannot punish the expression of non-harmful thoughts even when they are contrary to accepted views. Freedom of expression is the right of all persons both because it is a personal liberty and because of its value to social and political dialogue.

But deliberation is not the end-all of popular governance. Dialogue is rather a means to substantive aims. Debates on any relevant public subjects from the domestic budget to foreign policy not only allow individuals to flesh out views but also to enrich public thinking. A constitution offers common ground for conflicting parties but by itself it provides few concrete solutions. Answers to pressing questions about everything from powers of government to regulate environmental pollution, education, interstate travel, to a slew of other issues are not found in constitutional text. Those topics require normative solutions. Efficiency theory alone looks only at part of the input relevant to deciding complex social quandaries. More context is necessary as to how policy affects both individuals and their communities. Free and open communication helps resolve conflicts with the input of ordinary citizens, who speak from their quest for personal benefits in their communal capacity as civic actors. No written text, neither constitutional nor statutory, can account for all of the interpersonal and intergenerational contingencies relevant to any one decision, much less to an enumerable number of public choices.

Steady changes do not imply complete alteration of principles nor an evisceration of written clauses. To the contrary, popular movements often rely on the words of the Constitution in their advocacy, as when they debate whether the Second Amendment protects an individual's or only the militia's right to bear arms or whether the death penalty is a cruel and unusual punishment under the Eighth Amendment.

Despite the ambiguity of text, judges and other officials must consult the Constitution in novel and mundane circumstances. Though the document establishes the terms of offices for high-ranking public officers, the three branches of governments enjoy powers well beyond the written instrument. It would be too stifling for text to constrain the creation and liquidation of agencies, duties, and offices given the broad array of bureaucracies that compose the executive, legislative, and judicial branches. Moreover, many details about the relationship between state and federal governments are not defined by the Constitution. Even the claim to sovereign immunity is not explicitly mentioned there, even though the Supreme Court has read it into the 11th Amendment.[14] Neither does it say anything about major operational issues such as what percent of the federal budget should go to defense appropriations and what real properties federal courts should occupy, nor does it address more routine matters such as what furniture is appropriate for congressional offices. The answers to these subjects will vary from one official to another, from one administration to another, and from one generation to another. The Constitution's silence on these and many alternatives faced by the government can be explained on a variety of grounds.

Public officials must be given the latitude to make decisions that stay within the parameters of their office. The lack of constitutional answers about these and a countless number of other big and small functions of government also enables differing groups to influence decision making by raising fiscal, administrative, and other concerns.

Constitutional issues arise not over the minutia of legal proceedings but about matters of whether government is functioning in a socially conscious manner that is consistent with certain parts of text and their underlying meanings. Evaluation of these fundamental concerns should be done through the prism of clauses that either provide government power or guarantee the public rights.

Text alone, however, does not suffice for policy makers to balance interests that go into public decisions. Judicial interpretation must often fill in missing details. Even something so elementary to democracy as franchise is not exhaustively described in the Constitution. The 15th, 19th, and 26th Amendments provide explicit lists of constitutionally protected traits (race, sex, and the like) against the arbitrary exclusion of voters, but the Court has also found it necessary to extend the definition of the Equal Protection Clause of the 14th Amendment—which the original framers did not intend to apply to franchise—to voter suppression cases.[15] The Court has, for instance, found that malapportionment hampers citizens' ability to participate equally in state and federal elections. As the majority of justices put it in a leading case, the Constitution's guarantee that the people choose members of the US House of Representatives "means that as nearly as practicable one man's vote in a congressional election is to be worth as much as another's."[16] The "one person, one vote" principle also holds for state elections.[17] The justices did not derive this test from any explicit statement in the Constitution nor from its original meaning (as at the time of the founding voting equality was conceived in the context of propertied white men) but from the general principle that in a representative democracy all eligible adults have the right to engage in deliberations about social policies and then to effectively vote for policy choices. Just as apportioned voting is not textually defined, so too protections of privacy rights derive from a principled reading that is only tenuously connected to the actual language of the 14th Amendment's Due Process Clause.[18] In a seminal privacy case, Justice William O. Douglas listed the rights to association, parental decision about whether to educate a child in public or parochial schools, and other choices that are not explicitly mentioned but certainly implicitly constitutional.[19] Both the demands to equal franchise and privacy are rights retained by the people on a more extensive basis than what is specifically mentioned in the Constitution.

The analysis of how to address citizens' opposition to government requires the formulation of constitutional structure crafted to prevent the arbitrary uses of power. A constitution that is excessively detailed renders it more difficult to abandon old stereotypes and experiment with fresh ideas. Abstract statements of law often provide added flexibility. The Due Process Clause, for instance, has become a judicial favorite for a variety of rights connected with personal privacy. In a series of non-textual decisions the Court initially found that the Clause protects the right of procreation, then extended the definition of privacy from marital to non-marital contraception, and later still to doctrines supporting gay and lesbian rights. These holdings were not logically entailed by any literal definition of "due process," neither contemporary nor historical; rather, the holdings were products of long, cultural assessments of what constitutional liberties are fundamental to free and equal citizens.

Going beyond the text requires looking outside the handiwork of the authors of the Due Process Clause–or any other provision–to the underlying principle of constitutional unity. That does not mean text is irrelevant but that it is the starting point from which precedent, history, tradition, and contemporary sensibilities should inform progressive judgment. Stagnation is no solution, particularly when it impedes a contextual balancing of private and public interests. Yet balancing with no fulcrum for judging whether government action is fair is too prone to manipulation.

As the ultimate sovereigns of national government, citizens explore mores through social organizations, community discussion groups, one-on-one conversations, and introspection. Individuals are thus tied to various communities in working out political institutions like self-rule. They are not secluded islands but members of an interlinked archipelago. In this regard, Aristotle was certainly correct to say, "Man is by nature a political animal," but I think it dubious for him to also argue that "the state is by nature clearly prior . . . to the individual";[20] in the order of priorities, society is a compact between individuals who create a constitutional order to place certain limits reasonably likely to better the common good. The people can alter original agreements through amendments or add nuance to them through lesser legal vehicles, such as judicial opinions.

The upshot of this section is that the written Constitution is not by itself the source of legitimate authority. In the broad sense of the term, "Constitution"— as it is used by courts and citizens—can refer to text, its principle, aspirational value, tradition, interpretation, and elaboration. What is ratified as "the Constitution" is the document, but Americans understand much more to be at stake safeguarding their constitutional rights including equal voting apportionment, old age social security, and the right to sue officials who violate their rights under color of state law. These statutorily based rights are subject to change but so too is our interpretation of general clauses of constitutional text.

Even the explicit functions of governmental found in the written instrument— such as taxation, adjudication, commercial regulation, and military command— are only binding because the people have acquiesced to be governed by institutions. They can add to those functions, modify them, or try something new without destroying the nation. What is unchangeable, short of carrying out another revolution, is the maxim that government's ultimate commitment is to the execution of policies for the betterment of the social individual. The preservation of rights and the establishment of laws conducive to the happiness of the people benefit the whole, where the totality of welfare is measured by the ability of each member to pursue his or her well-being. In keeping with the public trust, before enacting a law officials must analyze how it is likely to affect civil liberties and inter-social relations among equals. Relying on the literal wording of the Constitution will not get officials very far. Normative evaluations are indispensable to the fair operation of government institutions. A commitment to the well-being of a pluralistic community must inform the interpretation of constitutional clauses. While the living ethos of constitutional law is indispensable, the text provides parameters for cultural growth. On the other hand, it would be wrong to discount constitutional text. In the next chapters we turn to the textual authorities of constitutional policy. Before further fleshing out the underlying ethos of American constitutionalism, it is important to parse two statements of constitutional governance, the Declaration of Independence and the Preamble to the US Constitution, that should inform interpretation of more specific clauses.

‖ 2 ‖

Declaration of Independence
in Historical Relief

We have seen that text alone is too narrow to identify the ideals and deliberative nature of constitutional justice, but we have just begun to explore why constitutional ethos is necessary for fair governance. A tension exists between the
need for a written compact sufficiently robust to prevent the arbitrary use of
power and a socially recognized set of quasi-constitutional principles to check
extreme interpretations of text. As stated in the Introduction, the Declaration
of Independence and the Preamble to the Constitution are authoritative statements that provide the baseline for stable representative governance. They
jointly establish a maxim of governance that is as binding on all three branches
of the federal government as it is on state governments. This chapter parses the
earlier document. Part II will unpack the details of normative constitutionalism,
but we must first explicate their textual groundwork.

The Declaration is not merely a statement of ancient grievances against Great
Britain by newly independent states but overarching mandates for the legitimate
exercise of public powers. It contains many of the components of constitutionalism, including the people's sovereignty, equality of political representation, and
an inexhaustive set of rights protected against the abuse of power. The founding
generation thought of the Declaration's statements about innate human rights and
representative government to have universal application. The framers believed
that the Declaration expressed eternal principles while the structural parts of the
Constitution concerned administration and could be altered as needed for efficient government operations. The Declaration informs the normative parts of the
Constitution, such as the Bill of Rights, and also places limits on what amendments can be passed to enhance people's ability to enjoy inalienable rights such as
free speech in a civil society, making clear that their complete abridgment would
violate the mandates of the Declaration. There is therefore no formal mechanism,
short of a new revolution, for amending the Declaration of Independence, making it an even more stable statement of national ethos than the Constitution.

This chapter begins by examining the early American understandings of the Declaration of Independence. The subsequent chapter will use this background to demonstrate that the Declaration remains an authoritative assertion of human rights and a guarantee of the people's will to participate in deliberative democracy. The Declaration contains the starting point for legal and cultural evolution within the confines of a prudentially acceptable framework of relationships between rulers and the people.

A. Identifying Foundational Theory

Foundational theory runs counter to views of scholars like Judge J. Harvie Wilkinson, who counsels against pursuing a unified constitutional framework.[1] He argues against judicial reliance on any one theoretical method of constitutional interpretation. Wilkinson is critical of originalism, living constitutionalism, and pragmatism, theories that I will address later in the book. He writes that "cosmic constitutional theories" are misguided because they "suggest simple answers to intractable problems, thereby abetting judicial hubris." The Constitution is rather "designed to resist answers and incorporate tensions rather than yield its secrets to a single or comprehensive viewpoint."[2] It is therefore an act of puffery to develop much less judge on the basis of a grand theory.[3]

Wilkinson presents his project to be aimed at judicial restraint. A judge's task is to find "a role for reason within the rule of law" rather than "idiosyncratic preference."[4] Within this broad framework, he counsels judges to apply "impersonal principles of law to varying acts."[5] His main qualm is with the reliance on abstract theory in adjudication.

Wilkinson's affinity to judicial modesty is laudable for seeking to prevent politicized adjudication under the veneer of methodological consistency, but his claim that foundational theories oversimplify problems and leave judges with too much latitude is mistaken. Wilkinson's dismissiveness provides no alternative framework other than simple civility for determining whether a holding or statute is constitutionally legitimate. For instance, he sets out no way to decide the validity of his own critiques of cases like *Roe v. Wade*[6] (finding a privacy right to abortion) and *Bush v. Gore*[7] (putting a stop to a presidential ballot count during the 2000 election). One must either agree with him or not, without any way of determining whether the conclusions are based on constitutional standards. He leaves readers with no coherent structure for adjudicating constitutional cases nor for formulating constitutionally conforming policies. Without any framing order for analysis, powerful actors can more readily force their will on persons with less training, financial support, and retinue.

Similar skepticism about comprehensive theory by writers like Suzanna Sherry and Daniel Farber[8] has led to widespread academic and judicial neglect of the Declaration's and Preamble's statements of national principle. The Declaration of Independence is a substantive statement of rights and of anti-autocratic representative democracy. Put another way, the Declaration establishes the principles of national government—protecting individual rights and the pursuit of happiness in a representative democracy—while the Constitution sets out a structure for fulfilling the earlier document's purposes. The Preamble to the Constitution is likewise typically thought to be unenforceable, despite its overarching statements of national purpose and governmental obligation. The expression of the people's will requires all three branches of government to protect rights for the common good. Both the Declaration and the Preamble contain a unified guiding principle about governmental powers and limitations. Despite the Supreme Court's relative inattention to those documents, throughout American history—as I have shown at length elsewhere[9]—movements have incorporated them into their demands for social change.

B. Place in History

From its founding, the United States adopted a declaration of intents that prominently identifies one of government's purposes to be safeguarding equal individuals' right to pursue happiness. Members of the compact can pursue their individual life projects without state interference, but their liberties are not absolute. The sovereign nature of representative government enables it to pass laws born of public deliberations.

The Declaration of Independence's statement on the equal human right to pursue happiness stands in sharp relief from constitutions, such as the Confederate Constitution of United States and the 1857 Oregon Constitution, which expressly exclude certain groups from full enjoyment of legal and social safeguards.[10] The Second Continental Congress adopted the Declaration of Independence to differentiate itself from autocratic sovereigns. The United States broke from the British monarch and began developing the skeletal outline of a system averse to aristocratic privileges. Some of the document's paragraphs accuse King George III of failing to pass "laws for the accommodation of large districts of people, unless those people would relinquish the right of representation in the legislature" and dissolving whole legislative bodies. Other paragraphs accused the king of refusing to respond to colonial petitions opposing tax measures like the Stamp Act of 1765 and the Townshend Duties of 1767 that colonists sent in the decade prior to the American Revolution. These are statements about the historical conflict between the Mother Country and her colonies. But there is more to them: They contain kernels of wisdom about representative government.

Most important for posterity, colonial representatives adopted the statement that "all men are created equal, that they are endowed by their creator with certain unalienable Rights, that among these are Life, Liberty and the Pursuit of Happiness." Thomas Hartley, like James Wilson a member of the Pennsylvania ratifying convention, held a rich understanding of the Declaration:

> As soon as the independence of America was declared in the year 1776, from that instant all our natural rights were restored to us, and we were at liberty to adopt any form of government to which our views or our interests might incline us.—This truth, expressly recognized by the act declaring our independence, naturally produced another maxim, that whatever portion of those natural rights we did not transfer to the government, was still reserved and retained by the people.[11]

Contemporaries of the Revolution often restated the hope of building a country from the bottom up where institutions would be committed to advancing human happiness. An anonymous author expressed the opinion that "if universally embraced, . . . the maxim, that 'all men are born free, equal, and independent'" would "render the human race secure and happy."[12] These assertions were indicative of the early understandings of how the Declaration should impact constitutional democracy. Every generation since then has also put effort into explaining and defining the document's meaning, reminding itself at every Independence Day of the founding principles.

Even before ratification of the Constitution, the new nation's adoption of the Declaration committed it to exercising "just powers" derived "from the Consent of the Governed" to secure equal liberty for all Americans. The decision to place limited powers in a unified national government, rather than fracturing into 13 separate countries, was to establish safeguards for inalienable rights that the document expressly acknowledged to be the birthright of all people. The Declaration expressed the normative maxim of peoplehood, not beholden to the special concerns of the newly formed states. An author in the late 1790s expressed a sentiment in accord with the ideal of the Declaration that class differences were anathema in the United States, where "liberty and equality well explained and understood" are "a maxim worthy of the dignity of man."[13] Equal social status was a criterion for the equal enjoyment of freedom.

Despite the validity of this sentiment, framers were not above other forms of prejudice and chauvinism of their time. First-wave feminists of the mid-19th century understood that the ideals America espoused from its inception included people of both sexes, in spite of the actual inequality women suffered. Therefore, Elizabeth Cady Stanton expanded Thomas Jefferson's original formulation of the Declaration of Independence in her Declaration of Sentiments of 1848 to: "All men and women are created equal; that they are endowed by their Creator with certain inalienable rights; that among these are life, liberty, and the pursuit of happiness." Stanton took Jefferson's statement of human equality and spelled out its logical conclusion. Neither the framers intent nor the meaning of those words in their day, but its logical meaning, guided her understanding of the ethos they identified. She needed no court to tell her the authentic, universal meaning of the Declaration.

Several historians, like Jack Rakove and David Armitage, have mistakenly claimed that the Declaration of Independence was almost exclusively concerned with the British tyranny rather than universal equality.[14] The Declaration is a cornerstone of representative democracy in the United States. Rakove's and Armitage's claims are belied by contemporaneous statements like those by James Wilson, who asserted that the proclamation of equality and inalienable rights found in the second paragraph of the Declaration of Independence provided the "broad basis on which our independence was placed." In that context, he stated that the Constitution was built "on the same certain and solid foundation."[15] On this reading, the Constitution's specific grants of power were predicated on the principles adopted into the Declaration of Independence.

From the country's founding, the joint interest of protecting inalienable rights was intertwined with putting an end to monarchical privilege. The revolutionary generation made clear the enduring value of the Declaration. They did not define it for all times, but their speeches and pamphlets provide excellent starting points for understanding the norm on which the nation built its constitutional edifice. Speaking in retrospect, John Hancock, who had earlier signed the Declaration in his capacity as President of the Continental Congress, asserted that American federalism was "founded in the ideas of natural equality," best suited for all its members "to seek their own happiness as a community."[16] This was a clear vision of a society of equals, suited for the betterment of the whole. It was grounded on the common 18th-century view of self-interested, autonomous persons joining to better safeguard their interests than they could in a state of nature. Samuel Adams, at one point John Hancock's Lieutenant Governor of Massachusetts, later the Governor of that state, and a signer of the Declaration, was more specific in explaining how the Declaration helped frame US social ethics. As acting governor for the state of Massachusetts, he asserted in a 1794 speech that human equality was the political principle of the United States.[17] By approving the Declaration of Independence, the country adopted "the doctrine of liberty and equality" to be the "political creed of the United States."[18] Adams explained that Americans "declaration of their Independence" was the first step taken to retain natural rights, such as the ownership of property and the pursuit of happiness.[19]

By "equality," authors of the day meant parity in citizens' rights, not of material station or talents. Regulations were needed to preserve the general welfare against licentious abuses of legal privileges.[20] The Declaration acknowledged that equality was universal, but also recognized the need to limit indiscriminate endangerment to the public safety. The benefits of equal community membership implies a reciprocal obligation of social responsibility—a uniform law against committing murder is the most obvious restriction on liberty—requiring persons to make sacrifices for the sake of social tranquility. As an author put it in 1770, preventing "clashing interests and violence" to destabilize "important . . . rights of mankind" requires civil governance.[21] The philosophical belief in natural rights went hand-in-hand with the compact theory of government, which required the people's representatives to place reasonable limits on conduct for the greater good of community well-being. Authors of the day linked individual interests with the needs of others to maintain their equal access to common goods, judicial process, and personal well-being.

C. Antislavery

Many revolutionaries recognized slavery's incompatibility with the widely accepted political philosophy of natural equality. The antislavery movement was quick to seize upon the Declaration and the civic morality it established for the newborn nation. While the sentiments of the movement were not shared by everyone, they offer the quintessential example of how the universal ideals of the Declaration readily lend themselves to advocacy for social betterment and rational integrity to the values espoused in the nation's statement of collective purpose. One anonymous poet, who chose the pseudonym "American in Algiers," wrote provocatively that whites have no more right to enslave Africans than Africans have to enslave whites. The Declaration of Independence, which that author called "the fabric of the rights of man," condemned slavery by the document's own terms about "the rights of man." He further mocked those who celebrated "the Rights of Man," while continuing to keep others in bondage.[22]

Several of the greatest visionaries of the document's equality clause were Quakers. Arguably the greatest luminary of the Friends, Anthony Benezet, wrote in 1778 that the guarantees of human equality pertain to all inhabitants, irrespective of their race or class. The Declaration's statements about the people's right to separate from Great Britain, he wrote, "apply to human nature in general, however diversified by colour and other distinctions."[23] Nationhood, Benezet believed, was to benefit everyone, not just white men. Just two years after the Continental Congress adopted the Declaration of Independence, Benezet expressed his belief that its statement about "all [m]en [being] created equal" with the inalienable rights of "Life, Liberty, and the Pursuit of Happiness" placed certain moral demands on the United States. The document's binding recognition of rights and its statement against political oppression were also a forceful condemnation "against the slavery of the Negroes."[24] In the same year, Jacob Green, a pastor and physician with close ties to Princeton University (then the College of New Jersey), delivered a sermon in New Jersey. Like Benezet, Green expostulated about the incompatibility of the Declaration's statements of human equality and entitlement to liberty with the retention and promotion of slavery.[25] Contrary to the claims of Rakove and Armitage, these men and their many students had no doubt that the principles of the Declaration were of richer significance than national sovereignty and created obligations driven by social morality.

During the succeeding decade, speakers and writers continued to rely on the Declaration to buttress their advocacy for social justice. In a side-by-side presentation, in one column New Jersey Quaker David Cooper drew readers' attention to the Declaration of Independence's statement of rights and obligations, while in the other column he wrote:

> If these solemn truths, uttered at such an awful crisis, are self-evident: unless we can shew that the African race are not men, words can hardly express the amazement which naturally arises on reflecting, that the very people who make these pompous declarations are slave-holders, and, by their legislative conduct, tell us, that these blessings were only meant to be the rights of white men not of all men. . . .[26]

Cooper's address drew attention to the grave contradiction between slavery and the Declaration's statements about human equality and the perpetration of hereditary.

He believed that "holding thousands and tens of thousands of their innocent fellow men in the most debasing and abject slavery" was not only harmful to the victims but to the American freeholders, whom the institution made more callous and prone to despotism. Having shed monarchical rule, slaveholders perpetuated despotism against men with the same inalienable entitlements as whites. To his mind, while the tyranny against blacks was deplorable, it did not undermine the ideal of liberal equality; to the contrary, contemporary injustices were an affront to the very ideal of freedom, the pursuit of happiness, and representative government to which the Americans had agreed. Cooper's reasoning condemned slavery as an abomination against the terms of national sovereignty. The framers generally understood that the logical implications of the

Declaration's promises were universal and untethered to any race. All men, irrespective of background, "are equally entitled to life, liberty and property . . . and have never ceded to any power whatever, a right to deprive us thereof."[27]

Outside the religious dialogue, in a speech before the American Philosophical Society, George Buchanan quoted the Declaration of Independence to demonstrate that its principles were incompatible with the oppression of the "[u]nfortunate Africans."[28] By no means all Americans held these antislavery views, but they demonstrated that from the founding, a variety of visionary thinkers regarded the Declaration to be an ethical statement committing the national government to policies for protecting intrinsic human autonomy on an equal basis. Those who understood its broad significance to all elements of the population had the foresight to look beyond the prejudices of their generation to a universal understanding of inalienable rights and equality. And these early antislavery sentiments set the stage for post-Civil War constitutional amendment, which granted Congress the powers necessary to better fulfill the Declaration's promises of a government instituted to secure unalienable rights.

D. Popular Government and the Common Good

The purposes for issuing the Declaration were to declare sovereignty; establish a representative system of government in the Continental Congress even before the passage of the Articles of Confederation, which was to become the nation's first, albeit short-lived, constitution; assert the existence of intrinsic human rights; and adopt a political philosophy for the country, committing it to the betterment of the people as opposed to a monarch or aristocrats. Writing in a weekly Philadelphia newspaper, a contributor stated that the same "sages, who penned the Declaration of Independence, laid it down, as a fundamental principle, that government derives its just powers from the *consent of the people* alone."[29] Years after drafting the Declaration, Thomas Jefferson explained in a letter to a friend that he had not tried to present any novel argument for government. The document "was intended to be an expression of the American mind."[30] In harmonizing the sentiments of the day, Jefferson was able to capture the will of the people. Counter to the recent claim of two authors, popular opinion did not follow Jefferson's lead;[31] in fact, he professed to be distilling the sentiments of the people, the members of the Continental Congress, and American pamphleteers. Prior to the ratification of the Bill of Rights and much later the Reconstruction Amendments, the Declaration was the only authoritative directive for government to safeguard liberty and equality.

Echoing the sentiments of the Declaration, an author calling himself simply "A Ploughman" wrote in another Philadelphia newspaper, "It is a general maxim that government was instituted for the protection and happiness of the people."[32]

These were not presented as utopian ideals but a mandatory ethos of a just society whose founding document committed its entire structure of government to the preservation of universal human rights.

The revolutionary generation thought quite differently of popular governance than we (taking for granted the political exclusion of women, minorities, and unpropertied men that violated the very principles they laid out), but the shortcomings of their conduct do not gainsay the normative values of the Declaration. Violation of rational norms does not undermine their validity but is a sign of unjust conduct. That was as true in the 18th century as it is in the 21st. The colonists had likewise robbed, misappropriated, and encroached on Native American lands (from tribes like the Mohegans, Cherokee, Assateagues, Susquehannas, Wicomisses and many, many others),[33] but those unconscionable thefts do not indicate some analytical problem with their concept of freehold estate. To the contrary, the colonists' views about the sanctity of property condemned their practices of encroaching on the communal lands of aboriginal peoples without providing them with due process. So too the ideals of the Declaration imputed the wrongheadedness of the framers' class and gender privileges but not the abstract ideals they espoused.

The founding document created a framework for just governance. Constituting a government, the Declaration stated, would allow voters to make political decisions to positively affect their "safety and happiness." With each person having an equally inalienable claim to liberty, the Declaration's abstract statements would not be enough. Specific laws were necessary to resolve disputes and establish enforceable solutions to private and public controversies. A contemporary, echoing Wilson's sentiments, regarded it a "fundamental maxim" of lawmaking "that a part of our liberty must be given up for the security of the rest."[34] Without such limits on liberty, equality could not be secured because the strong would exert their will against those with less resources and power. Each person could exercise liberty to the full extent until it harmed another, at which point government had a legitimate interest to step in to preserve domestic tranquility. Natural liberty, as Samuel Adams explained, could be "abridged or restrained, so far only as is necessary for the great end of society."[35]

By being free to participate in elections and deliberative politics, winners and losers give their tacit consent to the resulting law. No one is guaranteed the enactment of their desired policies. According to this model of liberal equality for the common good, legal limits provide the preconditions necessary for each person to be able to live a fulfilling life. For instance, property rights create norms for acquisition, use, and control of chattel and real estate. These limits, in turn, set a reciprocal obligation, enforceable by state authorities, on each member of society with respect to the possessions of others.

A representative republic's ultimate goal is to provide laws conducive to socialized well-being and individualized happiness. John Adams, in his *Thoughts on Government*, composed the same year as he became a member of the committee responsible for drafting the Declaration of Independence, expressed an oft-stated theme that "happiness of society is the end of government."[36] John Dickinson, another member of the Second Continental Congress whose fame was widespread throughout the colonies, thought the "right to be happy" was attainable only in a free society.[37] Indeed, where a government did not promote the welfare and happiness of the people, it was their right to "amend, and alter, or annul, their Constitution, and frame a new one."[38] Years before the Revolution, James Otis Jr. eloquently described the government's duty "to provide for the security, the quiet, and happy enjoyment of life, liberty, and property. There is no one act which a government can have a right to make, that does not tend to the advancement of the security, tranquility and prosperity of the people."[39] The luminaries of American independence therefore conceived a government made by the people for their benefit. This was a vision of negative and positive powers to protect liberties and expand opportunities to enjoy them.

On a structural level, the Declaration established several key components of constitutional governance over a decade before the Philadelphia Constitutional Convention. The Declaration's recitation of reasons for independence made clear that the new government would need to separate the responsibilities of the executive and judicial branches of government and the executive and legislative branches.[40] The separation of the legislative and judicial branches would come later, in the text of the Constitution. But the ideal of separating the function of the three branches came even before July 4, 1776, with some in the popular press going so far as to call it a maxim of governance. Recognizing separation of powers to be fundamental for government, a citizen from Pennsylvania wrote that, "It is a determined maxim in politics, that the legislative and executive powers of government should be carefully kept separate and distinct."[41] James Madison likewise took the "political maxim that the legislative, executive, and judiciary departments ought to be separate and distinct" to be essential for constitutionalism.[42] The Declaration accused King George of interfering with the judicial branch and of preventing the people's legislative representatives from meeting to conduct the people's business. In 1787, the Constitution added the details about institutional function that were necessary for the operation of the multi-branch government that the Declaration accepted.

The Declaration of Independence set a baseline expectation of representative governance. The document was still a rough sketch with much need of elaboration. Professor Jack Balkin has similarly asserted, "American constitutionalism is and must be a commitment to the promises [of] the Declaration."[43] The document declared the rights of the people, not the states. It is mistaken to argue, as one prominent legal theorist puts it, that some clauses of the "Declaration of Independence . . . refer to grievances that the States as States had against the king, such as the dissolution of their legislatures or the excessive use of the royal negative against state laws."[44] That view follows the historically unsupported claim of the Confederate States of America that the Declaration was created by the states rather than being the people's statement of national ethos and grievances against the king.[45] I do not think that any of the clauses were specific grievances against the states. For one, state entities did not yet exist at the time of the Crown's maladministration. A further reason for believing that the grievances were against the people rather than the states is the wording of the following two paragraphs of the Declaration: "He has dissolved Representative Houses repeatedly, for opposing with manly firmness his invasions on the rights of the people," and "He has refused for a long time, after such dissolutions, to cause others to be elected; whereby the Legislative powers, incapable of Annihilation, have returned to the People at large for their exercise; the State remaining in the mean time exposed to all the dangers of invasion from without, and convulsions within." The first of these clearly speaks of legislatures (Houses) as representatives of "the rights of the people," not simply as beacons of state administration. Thus, it points to a violation of the people's rights prior to the Revolution, when they were citizens of Great Britain. The second is also about representative governance because it speaks of elections, which might have brought to power new representatives of the people—rather than the state's—will. The lack of legislatures, then, required legislative power "to the People," not the states or colonies. Details of how the Declaration's visionary statements might be carried into effect would come first and foremost from the Constitution, which defined the powers of government and proclaimed its purpose to be the protection of liberty and the promotion of the general welfare.

Even more important than any contemporary understanding of the Declaration of Independence and its passages on equality and natural rights is their implication to the nation's trajectory. The Declaration of Independence laid the constitutional foundation for the evolution of thinking about equality, making later transformations about the Reconstruction Amendments possible. The statements, which were inclusive, led not only abolitionists but women suffragists, labor activists, agitators against debtor prisons, and many more to adopt its progressive vision. Their calls for reform were made in the context of the Declaration's statement of national purpose. This commitment to safeguarding equal human rights created abundant opportunity for later cultural transmutation without the violence of repeated revolutions. Through more than two centuries since the Declaration's signing, the people's attitudes toward civil rights and civil liberties have significantly changed as have their structural commitment to federalism. Following the Civil War, the New Deal, and then the Civil

Rights Era, the federal government's powers were incrementally augmented to meet national needs of a people with more access to commercial exchange and communication than the founders could have fathomed. Nevertheless, the Declaration remains vital for introspective reflections on the public policies affecting individual rights and the common good. The constitutional maxim connecting rights and general welfare is the root of constitutionality in the United States. It is essential for defining the limits of legitimate political dialogue about the thorniest problems of our day.

3

Declaration of Independence and the American Dream

Martin Luther King, Jr., one of America's most beloved civil rights leaders, expressed the tenet that the Declaration of Independence created a public obligation to safeguard individual rights on an equal basis for all. At his 1963 speech at the Lincoln Memorial, he told the quarter-million strong audience that his hope for social justice was "deeply rooted in the American dream . . . that one day this nation will rise up and live out the true meaning of its creed: 'We hold these truths to be self-evident, that all men are created equal.' "[1] He realized the racial, religious, and socio-economic reality of his day significantly departed from American aspirations. The "American dream," which King linked to the "majestic words of the Declaration," is steeped with "an amazing universalism" signaling the way out of existing inequalities.[2] This social striving, unjustifiably postponed but never erased from the nation's conscience, stayed with King to the end of his life, even as he traveled the country and experienced firsthand the nightmares of poverty and racism. He remained steadfast in his conviction that no one could "in all good conscience obey . . . unjust laws and abide by the unjust system," even as he pressed for a society where the dignity of individuals is respected and they "live together as brothers."[3]

The Declaration of Independence, where this American dream was first formally set out in writing, is not merely a statement of a bygone revolutionary era but a normative proclamation and an interpretive instrument that imbues constitutional democracy with an abiding value, constant through the centuries of fluctuating statutes, doctrines, and customs. The document is both an abiding statement of inclusiveness and of the values on which general welfare can be achieved. It is an assertion of the country's normative commitment. The "self-evident" truth that "all men are created equal" has served as a standard against which public behavior has been judged and according to which transformative policies have been developed.

Shortly after setting down the country's values in the Declaration, the people granted the authority to carry them out in the Articles of Confederation and then modified the terms of federalism in the Constitution. Despite the idealistic beginnings, pragmatic compromises at the Constitutional Convention of 1787 codified several nefarious provisions—especially the Importation, Fugitive, and Three-Fifths Clauses—that buttressed the badges and injustices of slavery. The national ideal was also swept to the side for decades by universal restrictions against women's political involvement, prohibitions on non-white naturalization, and restraints on collective bargaining. This chapter discusses the founding ideal of liberal equality[,] and how amendments to the Constitution were needed after the cessation of the Civil War to provide Congress with the power to pass legislation in keeping with the nation's founding promise to secure the inalienable rights to life, liberty, and the pursuit of happiness.

King's faith in the ideals of the Declaration of Independence and their significance to disempowered groups stands in stark contrast to a pessimistic view popularized by political scientist professor Rogers Smith. He argues that US constitutional tradition is exclusionary, or "ascriptive" as he calls it.[4] While Smith is correct that prejudice has tainted the annals of US history, his pessimism is overblown. The historical record is indeed replete with injustices perpetrated against women, blacks, Native Americans, Jews, Catholics, Irish, Japanese, Chinese, Filipinos, and others. However, these were deviations from, not manifestations of, the core American commitment. Even during the darkest decades of racism, chauvinism, and other forms of intolerance, reform leaders and groups often linked their efforts to the statements of universal rights and equality found in the Declaration.

The founding ideal of liberal equality for the common good has been a beacon shedding light on the United States' strengths, shortcomings, and possibilities. What's more, the foundational principle of representative democracy found in the second paragraph of the Declaration is a statement of the ultimate ends of governance. Some of the nation's greatest civil rights achievements, such as the Civil Rights Act of 1964, the Age Discrimination Employment Act, and the Americans with Disabilities Act, are examples of government functioning to protect equality, empower individuals, and benefit the public as a whole.

A. Declaration of Principle

Normative statements of the Declaration of Independence set a foundation for constitutional structure and interpretation. As Professor Charles Black points out, the Declaration is the American document "where the rights of humankind are set out[,] . . . [It] commits all the governments of our country to 'securing' for its people certain human rights."[5] The Declaration's statement of "self-evident" truth commits the country to vindicating "unalienable rights," including "life, liberty, and the pursuit of happiness." Its promises, in the words of one of the most popular and influential politicians of the nineteenth century, Daniel Webster, provides "the title deed for [Americans'] liberties."[6] In more recent times, King similarly asserted that the Declaration and Constitution are jointly written promises to Americans of all generations, not only to those alive at the time of the Revolution.[7]

Americans first wrote their vision of representative governance into the Declaration of Independence. As a contemporary put it in a speech delivered at a 1790 Boston Independence Day celebration: "The declaration of Independence spoke the united sentiments of the people" about the unalienable birthright of humanity.[8] Only later did they set up constitutional structures and powers. The Declaration reflects universal principles and lists colonial grievances.[9] It declares a national commitment to safeguarding innate rights (or in 18th-century language "unalienable rights"). They are inborn and not grants of government. The dignity interests of individuals therefore precede the written Constitution and, indeed, even governmental sovereignty.

The Declaration states that the Revolution was waged "to secure these rights," not solely to raise a new nation. Government derives its "just powers from the consent of the government." The people grant institutions powers to pass regulations conducive to their living self-directed lives in a community of equals. The founding document's statement of formative sentiments has informed countless reform groups, who, like abolitionists and suffragists, demanded the liberties of personal uplift and social betterment. For more than two centuries, its inspirational statements have brought together persons of differing backgrounds and classes into big tents with others struggling for just causes. Justice Arthur Goldberg of the US Supreme Court memorably summarized the function of the document: "The Declaration of Independence states the American creed." The manifesto of universal rights located in its second paragraph makes the country accountable to ordinary citizens. Reformers found in the document much more than empty rhetoric. But in the early Republic the Declaration proved inadequate for eradicating the country's worst evil, slavery; nor, yet, less severe forms of racial and other forms of discrimination. A major restructuring of the Constitution took place during the post-Civil War reconstruction of the mid-1860s through the mid-1870s. Even after these changes, the Declaration's unifying principle remained intact and should continue to add to our evolving legal understanding, dialogue, and judicial review of substantive rights.

By adopting the Declaration of Independence, the country committed itself to governing according to the will of the people. The Declaration's statements on legislative representation differ from the Guarantee Clause of the Constitution, which commits the federal government to intervene against state disruptions of representative governance.[10] The legitimacy of the government requires the people's consent to its policies and enactments. Professor Frank Michelman describes the representational process to establish norms "through public dialogue" that are later "expressed as public law."[11] His explanation of the constitutional integration of principles and individual rights is likewise applicable to the Declaration of Independence: "Subjective rights reflect norms governing the state's immediate treatment of persons, while objective principles point to more comprehensive states of social affairs—'equality,' for example—which the constitution commits the state to pursue and uphold." The general principles of the Declaration state the objective and equal human interests in liberty, life, and happiness, but they also indicate an individual's unique interests that are not mixed with the general public's. The practical judgment that Michelman explains in detail as associated with "endorsement of both a general standard and a specific application" also requires cognizable public morality as it is stated in general, promissory terms by the Declaration of Independence. The representational process of democratic politics can identify general ideals applicable to the protection of individual safety and equal status.

B. Declaration and Constitution

As we saw in the previous chapter, a careful study of pamphlets and newspapers demonstrates that some visionary thinkers in the early United States regarded the Declaration along the same lines as did Martin Luther King, Jr.: as a promissory note between the people and their government. The historical record debunks the claims of those contemporary scholars who question the premise that even after ratification of the Constitution, the Declaration of Independence continued to influence political philosophy and constitutional thinking. One such argument denies that the Constitution adopted the Declaration's rights-based logic. One prominent southern political scientist writes that the Declaration was no more than a statement of states' sovereignties, lacking all the rights guaranteed by the Constitution.[12] That perspective overlooks the extent to which the general principles of the Declaration became more concrete, first through the Constitution; then by the Bill of Rights; various Amendments (especially the Reconstruction Amendments); as well as by statutes and regulations.

Some of the original 10 amendments to the US Constitution, collectively known as the Bill of Rights, are clearly related to the Declaration. Take for instance, the Declaration's condemnation of the king for depriving Americans "of the benefit of trial by jury." The Sixth Amendment takes this statement of principle and puts it in affirmative terms, providing that criminal defendants "shall enjoy the right to a speedy and public trial, by an impartial jury." The Declaration condemns the king for "quartering large bodies of armed troops among us," and the Third Amendment of the Constitution turns it into an injunction against the quartering of soldiers in any house at a time of peace without an owner's consent, "nor in time of war, but in a manner to be prescribed by law." The Declaration presents the people's mandate to their representatives and statement of sovereign purpose, the Constitution provides the structural mechanisms for carrying them out.

The Declaration accuses Great Britain of dissolving and suspending American legislatures, preventing the people from governing their affairs, and passing parliamentary laws without consent of the governed. King George III is condemned for preventing Americans to pass laws "most wholesome and necessary for the public good." Among other grievances against self-rule, the document also states that the king has demanded that the people "relinquish the right of representation in the legislature." The Declaration further accuses the Monarch of not holding regular elections after dissolving legislatures, causing the people for a time to remain "to all the dangers of invasion from without, and convulsions within." To prevent the same from happening in the United States, the Constitution proclaims that government is established to act in the "general welfare." To avoid the king's recalcitrance to seat the elected representatives of the people, which the Declaration listed, the original Constitution guaranteed "to every state in this union a republican form of government" composed of elected legislators. Article I sets a specific time for electing the representatives and senators, and Article II sets a similarly enforceable mechanism for presidential elections.

It would be formalistic to discount the Declaration's interpretive value because it did not list the full panoply of fundamental rights. The Declaration was the foundational document on which later generations could build to establish a "more perfect union" where the people could "secure these rights," which are recited in only general terms both in the Constitution and the Declaration. Rules, standards, conventions, and judicial interpretations were needed to reasonably define the boundaries of their general principles. The people could all share the belief that government must secure their pursuit of happiness, due process, and equality, but the details needed to be chiseled out in statutes and judicial opinions. Equality was explicitly adopted into the Declaration and the 14th Amendment to the Constitution, but those statements, also like the Declaration, required further details such as those provided by the Civil Rights Act of 1964 and *Brown v. Board* to become enforceable realities. The core ideals were there, but it took cultural shifts, political determination, constitutional amendments, statutory innovations, and judicial commitment to vivify them.

The historical tragedy was the failure to put the ideals into practical laws sufficiently robust as to protect individual rights for the common, equal good. While at the time of the founding discrimination was practiced against a variety of groups, the Declaration established a universal norm in the nation's core legal structure, in contrast to actual laws and customs. Even before the ratification of the Constitution, the Declaration had become (and would afterward remain) the binding statement of national purpose, popular sovereignty, and government responsibility. The Declaration of Independence announces that it is the people's "right, it is their duty, to throw off such government, and to provide new guards for their future security." In its place, they can structure sovereign offices to be responsible for fulfilling the people's will to best "effect their safety and happiness." The original Constitution added detail to carry out that mandate of independence, and later amendments have further advanced it.

Several portions of the Declaration influenced later changes to the Constitution. For instance, the document clearly stands for the principle that voting is essential for self-government. Its general terms speak of "governments [being] instituted among men, deriving their just powers from the consent of the government," and some of its specific terms condemn King George III. A nation that does not provide its citizens with representational government is illegitimate because it lacks the necessary channels to advance popular petitions and policies. Prohibiting the colonists from participating in parliamentary debates and votes catalyzed Americans to assert their right to self-determination. The right to vote, then, is an enduring principle that, as a matter of constitutionality, stems from the nation's first legal document, the Declaration of Independence.

The Declaration failed to achieve universal adult franchise but so did the original Constitution. The racist and chauvinistic aspects of state and federal practices were only eliminated when the 15th Amendment was ratified in 1870 and the 19th Amendment in 1920. Even after ratification of those amendments, many hurdles remained to full voting participation, requiring the additional details of the Voting Rights Acts of 1957; on an even grander scale, the Voting Rights Act of 1965; and Supreme Court cases like *Wesberry v. Sanders* and *Reynolds v. Simms*, which established the one-person, one-vote doctrine of equipopulous legislative districts.

Setting the stage for these accomplishments, the Declaration's condemnations of the British Monarch logically require equal, universal suffrage. The Declaration denounced King George III's decrees preventing colonial governors from executing laws "of immediate and pressing importance" to the people. Repeated dissolution of "Representative Houses ... [that] oppos[ed] with manly firmness [the king's] invasions on the rights of the people" made

it impossible for the people to influence the course of legislation. These grievances were as much accusations against the king as negative statements against
which American constitutionalism was and should continue to be judged.
Arbitrary limits based on race, sex, and class were despotic and noninclusive, as
had been George III's measures against representative government. The passages
denounce the British government for being unresponsive to the people and provide a negative model against which the new country's commitment to a unified
maxim guaranteeing individual rights and representative sovereignty should be
measured. The Declaration was relevant to the drafting of the Constitution and
continues to be relevant to its interpretation.

C. Ethical Standard

The national ethos of individual equality in a just political community is not
the product of judicial doctrine. For one the people, not their judges, are the
ultimate sources of power. Their sovereignty extends to the ability to engage effectively in developing mechanisms for resolving conflicting individual and social needs. Whereas the Supreme Court has asserted its supreme authority to
interpret the Constitution, the justices have said nothing of the like about the
Declaration of Independence. Indeed, the Court has rarely said much about the
Declaration outside passing references to the document's statements on judicial
review,[13] jury trials,[14] and popular sovereignty.[15] But the Declaration's value to
constitutional thought is far broader than that. Where the Supreme Court has
left doctrinal holes, it should be up to social advocacy groups, political organizations, and legislatures to develop a body of legal understandings for the application of the Declaration's principles. Indeed, progressives have often relied on the
document to advance causes against arbitrary inequalities.

The Declaration spells out the purpose of government, and the Constitution
provides the mechanisms for carrying it out. Justice William O. Douglas voiced
the same idea in one of his dissents: "The ideas of 'life, liberty, and the pursuit
of happiness,' expressed in the Declaration of Independence, later found specific definition in the Constitution itself, including of course freedom of expression and a wide zone of privacy."[16] Abraham Lincoln likewise believed the
Constitution to be the framework for the Declaration's principles.[17] Quoting
from the *Proverbs* of the Bible, Lincoln likened the "fitly spoken" words of the
Declaration of Independence to "apples of gold" fitted into Constitution's "picture of silver": "The picture was made, not to conceal, or destroy the apple; but
to adorn, and preserve it. The picture was made for the apple—not the apple
for the picture."[18] While the Constitution is precious, he seemed to say, the
Declaration is of even higher worth.

It will come as no surprise that this is not the only way to understand the document. Some scholars, such as Carlton Larson, have interpreted the Declaration of Independence more narrowly, as a statement of national sovereignty rather than one primarily written to identify national principle. Larson raises theoretical concern about treating the document as primarily a statement of rights. "Lacking specificity," he writes, "the passage could be used to support almost anything."[19] But surely he does not believe that the Declaration could, in any authentic manner, support autocracy, racism, or sexism. The logical meaning of its republican government maxim for the establishment of government committed to individual and social well-being simply does not logically lend itself to arbitrary suppressions of equality or overall well-being. If we assume Larson means that the general statements can support conservative and liberal causes, that is true of any general constitutional statement, such as the Due Process and Free Speech Clauses.

Saikrishna Prakash is even more emphatic than Larson, claiming that "the Declaration has little more substance" than the constitutional preamble telling us "nothing concrete."[20] Larson and Prakash are not merely making linguistic points. They are concerned that judges might abuse the ambiguous words of the Declaration to advance their own political agendas. Justice Antonin Scalia shares their concerns: "The Declaration of Independence . . . is not a legal prescription conferring powers upon the courts."[21] These treatments of the Declaration overlook its value to the people, not merely the judiciary, as a rallying point for expressing pluralistic aspirations. Arguing that abstractions are constitutionally meaningless can lead to the absurd devaluation of all general portions of the Constitution, including Search and Seizure, Establishment and Free Exercise of Religion, Cruel and Unusual Punishment, and other clauses. In the abstract, these passages are indeed subject to manipulation, but their words come alive in specific contexts. As with other general, constitutional statements, Douglas's, King's, and Lincoln's views on the constitutional value of the Declaration should be applied to specific cases, balanced against other pertinent values, and taken to their logical conclusion and controversies.

Even prior to the ratification of the Constitution, the second paragraph of the Declaration of Independence placed sovereignty in the hands of the people, asserting that representative government received its "just powers from the consent of the governed" in order "to secure" the rights of "life, liberty and the pursuit of happiness." A close scrutiny of other parts of the Declaration indicates that Larson is too narrow in stating that the Declaration's charges of regal obstruction "do not directly abridge any individual's life, liberty, or the pursuit of happiness, but they do interfere dramatically with the people's right to self-government." More accurately, passages of the Declaration connect the British abridgement of self-government with the constitutional principle against legislative and executive curtailment of the people's civil and political rights.

The founding document enumerates a variety of grievances to explain the reason for establishing a republic better capable than England to advance the people's "safety and happiness." Whenever leaders are completely unresponsive to citizens' lobbying efforts, the Declaration justifies altering or even abolishing existing institutions and organizing anew under principles for the betterment of the populous. Any authoritarian power that prevents the people from legislating on their own behalf can be "throw[n] off." Listed indictments against King George III help to explain why Americans value personal autonomy and protest against autocratic privilege. The accusations Jefferson drafted and the Continental Congress adopted are not only statements against the British monarch nor are they simply explanations for disentanglement through independence. They are also negative accounts of government against which the deeds of a nascent representative polity could be judged.

D. The Declaration and the Structure of Government

The American people adopted representative structures that safeguard rights against majoritarian whim. The schematic notion is that people voluntarily submit to just laws designed to advance their health and safety without sacrificing dignity to majoritarian oppression nor to autocrats. While we can join American constitutional scholar Akhil Amar in saying that "popular majority rule in making and changing constitutions" was one of the "bedrock principles in the Founding, Antebellum, and Civil War eras," this statement should be further refined.[22] Unchecked majorities can run roughshod over the very interests guaranteed by the Declaration and Constitution. Thus the guarantee of unalienable and enumerated rights limits majoritarian rule. General welfare should not be defined by a numerical majority but by the extent to which everyone—members of majority and minority groups—benefits from a polity of equals.

The Declaration's ideals for representative government informs popular governance and limits its reach. Majorities cannot, for instance, be permitted to undermine the explicit protection of unalienable rights, which is imbedded in the structure of national ethos. The Supreme Court has therefore placed significant limits on majorities' abilities to alter congressional districts in order to prevent dilution of minority votes. The ideal of individual rights for the common good requires nearly exactly equal representation allotted to the eligible members of the polity. Malapportionment detrimentally affects those individuals who do not enjoy equal voting power and balkanizes societies rather than advancing the common good. The Supreme Court has required parity in voting by establishing the one-person, one-vote doctrine, which orders nearly numerical equality in voting districts.[23] The Supreme Court has linked the origins of the one-person, one-vote doctrine to the Declaration as it made its way into constitutional law, "The conception of political equality from the Declaration of Independence, to Lincoln's Gettysburg Address, to the Fifteenth, Seventeenth, and 19th Amendments can mean only one thing—one person, one vote."[24] Currently this doctrine applies differently to state and federal elections, with more latitude given to disproportionate representation in state elections.[25] But such a distinction in constitutional doctrine is not sensible. Both state and federal governments must abide by the equal representative vision of the Declaration.

The framers of the Declaration believed that rights need special protection. They consequently built anti-majoritarian measures into the Constitution. This is the case with the US Senate, which gives states with small populations like Delaware or Wyoming the same number of votes as those with large populations like California or New York; the Electoral College, which allows only for indirect voting for the President; and even Separation of Powers authorizes the judiciary to prevent congressional majorities from achieving ends that might otherwise harm fundamental rights. Whether these institutions actually achieve their beneficent end is not a purely theoretical matter but should be judged by whether officials translate them into practice. Even though many scholars, most effectively Sanford Levinson, have taken a negative stance against these institutions as being contrary to popular governance, they are arguably meant to protect individuals against majority exploitation.

Thus even though the Declaration sets the baseline representative structure, the Constitution and Supreme Court doctrine further flesh it out—in some ways limiting it but also maintaining enough protections against the will of tyrannical majorities to uphold the Unalienable Rights Clause of the Declaration of Independence. Indeed, even after ratification in 1789, the Constitution remained a flawed instrument that through amendment; political and judicial self-reflection; and, most terribly, the scourge of the Civil War has, through more than two centuries, become truer to the mandate of independence: A state empowered to guarantee liberty against discrimination in order to better the lives of everyone regardless of their ethnicity, race, religion, gender, sexual orientation, age, class, color, nationality, or any other characteristics irrelevant to the dignity of pursuing, and, verily fashioning, one's destiny.

A legal structure is needed to deal with the inevitable conflicts of interest. Constitutional text provides elaboration on legal norms, but it cannot explicitly resolve most specific debates. Unlike the philosopher Ronald Dworkin, I'm unconvinced that there is one correct, idyllic answer that can guide judges in resolving each dispute.[26] By this Dworkin is not expecting any particular judge to identify that right answer; rather he means that the ideal, Herculean judge, would be able to reconcile all seeming value disputes into a coherently reasonable judgment. Judges certainly must seek the correct answer, even though it will often be out of their reach.[27] While the desire for idyllic construal is admirable, it misses the important role of other social actors—both officials and ordinary citizens—in the evolution of legal standards about rights and general welfare. Firm principle is of central importance, but that does not imply that officials should discount all forms of interpretation except those that come from the bench. While the Supreme Court is the final arbiter of constitutional meaning, its legitimacy comes, in part, from the ability to stay relevant in a world of expanded meaning, as it appears in statutes, popular opinion, and legal advocacy.

Finding the right application of constitutional principle requires an assessment of culture, judicial precedent, constitutional structure, relevant rights, predictable outcomes, factual and contextual circumstances, and ethical inputs and implications. The relevant combinations and factors will vary from case to case, but the anti-authoritarian foundation of the Constitution, as it is expostulated in the Declaration, will guide determinations and outcomes. Both documents create a structure for the just treatment of individuals and a balancing of social values, but solutions are fact-specific and will inevitably be influenced by the unique perspectives and background of decision makers. The structure of interpretation will often establish several alternative correct answers that will help civil society advance the "integrated understanding of our moral responsibilities," to which Dworkin understandably aspires. The discretionary role of the judge is to choose among a set of right answers, competing alternatives suggested by precedent, history, tradition, legislative choices, and litigants' advocacy. Given that judges remain fault-prone humans, even when rendering decisions to the best of their ability, at objectivity, we can anticipate that some difficult cases will have more than one reasonable choice of resolution.[28] Whatever the decision, judges must stay true to the central purpose of representative democracy (protecting individual rights for the common good).

Interpretive framework is not the end of the matter. Good policy making must also reflect the specific circumstances of a dispute requiring formal resolution. The Declaration provides the overarching structure and purpose for nationhood. It sets essential features of federal sovereignty, much as do the macro features of the Constitution, such as the guarantees of free speech, religion, and equal protection. These are essential facets of nationhood, but when it comes to deciding between competing claims, the devil is in the detail. That is not, however, a weakness; rather, the generality of constitutional principle empowers each generation to develop pluralistic legal protections.

E. Declaration of Independence, Constitution, and the Reconstruction Amendments

Besides analytical arguments indicating that the framers, later social groups, and some of the Supreme Court justices understood the Declaration of Independence to be the background condition for constitutional interpretation, there is also reason to believe that the document's principle of human dignity was formally adopted by amendment into the text of the Constitution. For one, the original Constitution clearly elaborates, without superseding, the Declaration's earlier statements. One need not agree that specific paragraphs of the Declaration continued to have constitutional value even after ratification of the Constitution, to agree that its overarching value of protecting equal liberty to pursue happiness remains pertinent to understanding the structure of constitutional clauses and the limits of federal power. To argue otherwise would be to purport that the Declaration's assertions about the universality of human liberty and equality, as well as its characterization of representative democracy, are things of the past, which in the United States would be untenable.

1. Declaration of Independence and Constitutional Meaning

On a structural level, the Declaration of Independence established several key components of constitutionality over a decade before the Philadelphia Constitutional Convention. The Declaration's recitation of reasons for independence made clear the need for separating the executive and judicial branches' responsibilities. The Constitution would later add separation between legislative and judicial branches: the recognition of a necessary division of labors was tied to ideas circulating in the colonies prior to 1776. In the year of independence, official instructions for the delegates of Boston asserted that it is "essential for Liberty, that the legislative, judicial and executive Powers of government, be... independant [*sic*] of, and separate from each other."[29] The need for separate executive, legislative, and judicial powers was shared throughout the United States.[30] These sentiments were not sectional. The Virginia Declaration of Rights of June 12, 1776, which was drafted by George Mason, made clear "[t]hat the legislative and executive powers of the state should be separate and distinct from the judicative." James Madison of Virginia likewise held to the notion that republican constitutionalism necessarily required inter-branch checks of government.[31] The Declaration, then, adopted the accepted principle of representative democracy.

Besides representational democracy and separation of branches, another element of constitutionalism that migrated from the Declaration into the Constitution is the requirement that the polity be beholden to the people's will.

Both documents are rooted in an older concept that the wisdom of governance resides "in the body of the people."[32] The Declaration makes clear that a representative government must respond to political petitions, condemning the king for failing to answer to the colonists' entreaties, and the First Amendment of the Constitution prohibits government from abridging "the right of the people . . . to petition the Government for a redress of grievances."

This is only a short catalogue of overlaps between the Declaration and Constitution. There are many others worth mentioning: Article III of the Constitution secures the power of the judiciary, while the Declaration condemns the British monarch for "refusing his assent to laws for establishing judiciary powers." Both provisions speak to judicial independence, a deeply held principle of US constitutionalism. Likewise, Article III prohibits removal of federal judges during good behavior and forbids the diminution of judicial compensation. The Declaration rejects judicial dependence on the will of the executive "for the tenure of their office" and on the amount and payment of their salaries. The Constitution grants power over the military to civilian leadership; making the president the commander in chief and putting declaration of wars exclusively in the hands of Congress. The Declaration rejects making the "military independent of, and superior to the civil power." The Third Amendment to the Constitution prohibits quartering of soldiers during peacetime in "any house" without the owner's consent, while the Declaration asserts the evil of "quartering large bodies of armed troops among" the people. On the subject of immigration, the Declaration accuses the executive of "obstructing the laws for naturalization of foreigners," while the Constitution grants Congress the exclusive power of a "uniform rule of naturalization." Another congressional power granted by the Constitution is raising and supporting armies; this is partly in response to the Declaration's dissatisfaction with the monarch maintaining armies during peacetime "without the consent of our legislatures." So too the colonists upbraided Great Britain for raising taxes without the people's consent, while the Constitution put the power of taxing for the general welfare in the hands of the people's representatives in Congress. The list could be expanded, but these complimentary provisions in the two documents should give a representative sense of how much the Declaration informed the drafting of the Constitution. Just as after ratification of the Constitution, the details of the Declaration remained relevant to comprehending the nation's constitutional structure, so too its maxim of liberal equality for the common good continues to be the maxim of the land.

2. The Wisdom of Reconstruction

Besides its textual congruity with the Constitution, many framers' expectations of the Reconstruction Amendments also testify to the interpretive value of the Declaration of Independence. They often broached its meaning during debates preceding the amendments' passage. A century after ratification, Justice Clarence Thomas spoke of the extent to which the 14th Amendment broke with the nation's initial failure to abide by "the principles of equality, government by consent, and inalienable rights proclaimed by the Declaration of Independence and embedded in our constitutional structure."[33] Likewise, the 13th and 15th Amendments reoriented the country toward its nascent ideal, away from its former compromises with injustices and racial oppressions. All three were ratified less than a decade after the Civil War and extended federal power well beyond its original boundaries.

To begin, the driving political force behind the 13th Amendment, which in 1865 was the first of the three Reconstruction Amendments to be ratified, was to abolish slavery and any institutions and customs connected to it. During congressional debates prior to its passage, orators regularly quoted and referred to the Declaration. They did so in the context of a progressive vision of what laws federal government would pass and the claims to freedom individuals would make to better civil society. Radical Republicans, whose wing of the party briefly dominated the political agenda at the end of the war, repeatedly explained the amendment's scope of power. They commonly regarded the amendment to be a logical offshoot of the Declaration. Contemporaries shared a sentiment expressed long after the war by a 20th-century scholar: "The Thirteenth Amendment had lain latent in the Declaration of Independence."[34]

In 1864, during the first House debates on its passage, Representative Godlove Orth condemned the country for allowing the despotism of slavery to flourish for 80 years after the founding. During that time the manifold injustices associated with the institution were allowed to "ruthlessly trampl[e] upon every principle of the Declaration of Independence." Orth and his fellow Republicans invoked the Declaration of Independence both for its rhetorical force to the congressional debate and to demonstrate the need for constitutional change to fully adopt the aspirations of the founding document. Ratification of the amendment, Orth predicted, would "be a practical application of that self-evident truth, that all men are created equal; that they are endowed by their Creator with certain inalienable rights; that among these, are life, liberty, and the pursuit of happiness."[35] Radicals often wove the framers' natural rights philosophy into their speeches, believing the amendment would secure personal liberties integral to civil welfare. Simply breaking off the bondmen's chains would not be enough to secure the promises of liberty. As Congressman M. Russell Thayer of Pennsylvania rhetorically asked:

> What kind of freedom is that which is given by the amendment of the Constitution, if it is confined simply to the exemption of the freedom

from sale and barter? Do you give freedom to a man when you allow
him to be deprived of those great natural rights to which every man is
entitled by nature?[36]

The implication was clear, Congress would need to pass laws even after slaves
were set free to prevent continued abuses against their integration into a society
of equals.

Shortly after Congress passed the 13th Amendment onto the states for a
vote, the incoming Speaker of the House of Representatives, Schuyler Colfax,
addressed the House:

> [I]t is yours to mature and enact legislation which, . . . shall establish
> [state governments] anew on such a basis of enduring justice as will guar-
> antee all necessary safeguards to the people, and afford what our Magna
> Charta, the Declaration of Independence, proclaims is the chief object
> of government—protection of all men in their inalienable rights.[37]

The scope of congressional power to pass civil rights laws Colfax and the supermajority of Congress envisioned was broader than anything it previously
enjoyed.[38] More precisely, in the words of the Supreme Court, Congress has the
power "rationally to determine what are the badges and the incidents of slavery,
and the authority to translate that determination into effective legislation."[39]

The 14th Amendment further expanded Congress's enforcement authority,
granting it the necessary and proper power to safeguard life, liberty, and the pursuit of happiness for the common good. During debates on the amendment,
with the Civil War still fresh in the minds of participants, Vermont Senator Luke
Poland, speaking in the well of the Senate, recounted how the Declaration's statement of national aspiration had inspired the drafting of the 14th Amendment's
first paragraph, which contains the crucial Due Process, Privileges or Immunities,
Equal Protection, and Citizenship Clauses.[40] Speaker of the House Colfax also
heaped effusive praise on Section One of the 14th Amendment, identifying
it as "the Declaration of Independence placed immutably and forever in our
Constitution."[41] Also in the House, Representative John Farnsworth of Illinois
asked rhetorically how it was possible for anyone to "have and enjoy equal rights
of 'life, liberty, and the pursuit of happiness' without 'equal protection of the
laws?' "[42] Speaker after speaker expressed the belief that Congress would be able
to use its newfound authority to secure the amendment's guarantees of equal
liberty against states' interference.

Voicing support for the 14th Amendment's ratification, military veterans
at a Pittsburgh convention unanimously passed a resolution, asserting that
"henceforth [the] Constitution will be read in the interests of liberty, justice

and security, according to the lights of its preamble and the immortal declaration of independence."[43] The Enforcement Clause of the 14th Amendment granted Congress the power to protect every person's equal and inalienable right to enjoy the common good of the national community, irrespective of discriminatory state customs and laws. The amendment was partly an affirmative renunciation of the Supreme Court's *Dred Scott* opinion, which before the Civil War had severely hampered Congress's power to pass laws against racial injustices committed on US territory. By ratifying the 14th Amendment, the people reclaimed that authority and granted it to their representatives. They thereby empowered Congress to pass inclusive laws that would put into practical effect the Declaration of Independence's phrase "all men are created equal." The 14th Amendment's expansion of federal civil rights authority shifted power away from the states.

Like the 13th and 14th Amendments, the 15th Amendment also contains an Enforcement Clause, which empowers Congress to advance national norms. The 15th Amendment is specifically a prohibition against state and federal restrictions on voting that target parties' race, color, or previous condition of involuntary servitude. A member of the House of Representatives who directly linked voting with the Declaration's wording asserted:

> Without the elective franchise; without a voice in the making of laws by which he is controlled and to which he is amenable; without an option as to who shall administer them or how they shall be administered, what insurance has a man of his life, what security for his liberties, what protection in his pursuit of happiness?[44]

Other congressmen, like Senator Charles Sumner and Representative William Loughridge, connected the constitutional guarantee to vote to the Declaration of Independence's proclamation that the government's power to tax was subject to the people's right to political representation.[45] "No taxation without representation" had been a battle cry for the colonists, whose allegations in the Declaration of Independence against the King of England included and indictment "for imposing Taxes on us without our Consent." Voting was essential for participating in debates and influencing public policies as they affected the individual voter and society as a whole. What's more, some congressmen, like Senator Daniel Clark of New Hampshire, believed that voting was not a privilege for government to bestow, but "according to the Declaration of Independence" based on the "political equality of all men."[46] Behind these pronouncements was the perception that an explicit constitutional guarantee of suffrage was needed to be true to the Declaration's assertions that government must operate by consent of the people. Laws were only just, as Clark pointed out, if all those affected by and subject to them could participate in lawmaking to bring about change or protect the status quo.[47]

The three Reconstruction Amendments contained elements needed to strengthen the ramparts of the maxim to provide equally for the people's rights, by guaranteeing basic freedoms and due process under law, while advancing social interests, such as participation in national franchise.

3. Enforcement of the Ideal

The Reconstruction Amendments were part of America's awakening. Changing the Constitution, rather than simply passing statutes, was needed to eliminate the legal and social ramifications of the original Constitution's nefarious portions, such as the Three-Fifths and Fugitive Clauses, that had set at naught the inalienable-equality dictate of the Declaration of Independence.[48] Those clauses had violated the nation's founding principle of equal humanity, having the worst effect on blacks but also degrading social mores, creating economic and legal hierarchies, especially in the South but also nationwide, including in the nation's capital. The framers' decision to include them in the original Constitution may have garnered enough votes for ratification, but it ultimately led to hatred and distrust between individuals, politicians, states, and regions. Later attempts at inter-sectional tranquility, especially the Compromises of 1820 and 1850, increased the territory in which slaves could be kept and the Declaration enforced unequally. Contrary to Congress's desire, the compromises between North and South failed to forge lasting peace. And the sections eventually erupted into civil war.

Those post-bellum congressmen who spurred radical reform and reconstruction mocked the claim that the Declaration of Independence was no more than "mere rhetorical flourish without any practical meaning."[49] Such downplaying of the guarantee to free and equal citizenship was just as wrong, believed proponents of the Reconstruction Amendments, as would be dismissing the relevance of the constitutional clause that guaranteed republican government. Alterations to the Constitution augmented Congress's power to enforce the mandates of America's founding document. For a time, only a small minority in Congress continued to deny the relevance of the Declaration to constitutional interpretation, and this period of reawakening to the nation's first principles opened a window of opportunity for constitutional change.

The Reconstruction Amendments granted Congress the power to end any badges and incidents of slavery and involuntary servitude, lingering abuses of citizens' privileges or immunities, to safeguard persons' rights to due process, enjoin equal protection violations, and secure free elections without racial discrimination. The dominant opinion in Congress was that the enforcement clauses would allow the federal government to guarantee the fulfillment of the nation's design as first set out in the Declaration of Independence.[50] Grants of the necessary and proper powers of free and equal statecraft were predicated on, what Senator William Sprague, the son-in-law of Chief Justice Salmon Chase, called "liberal ideas" found in the "immortal Declaration of Independence." That well-spring of American constitutionalism "maintained that all men were created equal." The reformed Constitution was poised to become "an instrument for the protection of that liberty" that flowed from the people and was meant to apply to all rather than a privileged few.[51]

Outside of the Constitution, the Declaration of Independence also played an important part in statutory law guaranteeing state compliance with the Declaration's principles. In 1866, when Nebraska petitioned to enter the Union with suffrage restricted to free white males, initial congressional opposition to the state's admission stemmed from Nebraska's failure to comply with the Enabling Act. That law provided in part that admission into the Union was predicated on the adoption of a state constitution that guaranteed a republican government whose operation was "not repugnant to the constitution of the United States and the principles of the Declaration of Independence."[52] Opponents of Nebraska's original discriminatory proposal seized on this statutory requirement. They argued that no constitution granting voting rights exclusively to whites could be regarded as republican in nature. Senator Sumner forcefully asserted that the originally proposed state constitution was "repugnant to the principles of the Declaration of Independence."[53] Only when Nebraska altered the state constitution to include universal manhood suffrage did Congress vote to admit the state, later overriding a presidential veto and thereby finalizing the legislative decision.[54] In this struggle for admission, as was also the case in debates about the Reconstruction Amendments, the nation's founding document was far more than pro-forma. Moreover, states that have been admitted to statehood since the Civil War have included a similar provision requiring them to abide by the principles of the Declaration of Independence.[55] The implication is clear: All states must act in accordance with the public maxim of the Declaration of Independence.

Even more telling than the state enabling acts about the broad congressional powers of the Reconstruction Amendments' Enforcement Clauses were civil rights statutes passed pursuant to them. The second section of the 13th Amendment gave Congress the power to determine what federal statutes were necessary to protect the freedom common to all Americans—to life, liberty, and the pursuit of happiness—for the advancement of the common good. The individual is the principle part of policy evaluation, but the state can limit each person's liberties where they are used in discriminatory ways that harm our innate humanity.

Accordingly, shortly after the states ratified the 13th Amendment, Congress proceeded with a bill "to protect all persons in the United States in their civil rights and furnish the means of their vindication."[56] The Civil Rights Act of 1866 secured rights to contract, sue, give evidence, inherit, and purchase and alienate property.[57] The statute prohibited public and private discrimination, and remains law today in two sections of the United States Code.[58] The Act, as Minnesota Representative William Windom, who later became Secretary of the Treasury under Presidents James Garfield and Benjamin Harrison, jubilantly proclaimed was "one of the first efforts made since the formation of the Government to give practical effect to the principles of the Declaration of Independence." He meant that the statute would secure basic rights available to everyone, "high and low, rich and poor, white and black." Congressional authority to make freedom universally available to people in all states was essential in a nation that had professed from inception "the absolute equality of rights" but then "denied to a large portion of the people equality of rights."[59]

The Senate floor leader of the 1866 Act, Senator Lyman Trumbull, gave more concrete definition to the meaning of liberty and equality. He recognized that the 13th Amendment did not secure absolute equality in the possession of property but in the legal rights to conduct transactions, participate in court proceedings, and benefit from laws of wills and trusts. Trumbull relied on William Blackstone's enormously influential Commentaries to stress the intersection between individual freedom and the common good: " 'Civil liberty is no other than natural liberty, so far restrained by human laws and no further, as is necessary and expedient for the general advantage of the public.' "[60]

Trumbull also drew from Blackstone for the proposition that citizens are entitled to "natural liberty" and, therefore, the law can only restrain them insofar as it " 'is necessary and expedient to the general advantage of the public.' " Civil liberties " 'should be equal to all, or as much so as the nature of things will admit.' " In the context of civil rights bill debates, these quotes from Blackstone reflected a national perspective on individual rights and general welfare. Trumbull also quoted from James Kent, who like Blackstone wrote a legal treatise that broadly influenced US common law. Kent premised that among the interests included in " 'equal[] . . . rights . . . of a commonwealth' ' are " 'the right of personal security, the right of personal liberty, and the right to acquire and enjoy property.' " In Kent's treatise, Trumbull found further support for the proposition that inalienable rights are not limited to citizens but extend to all of the inhabitants of the United States.[61]

By passing the Civil Rights Act of 1866, Congress beneficently used the enormous 13th Amendment grant of federal power to enact legislation for the protection of fundamental rights. Ninety years after passage of the Declaration, this statute finally gave substantive federal backing for enforcing national norms as they were first spelled out at independence in the Declaration and later developed through radical reconstruction. The states' variegated policies on interpersonal behavior—familial and labor structures and the like—would remain but could no longer be used as barriers against federal civil rights laws. The 1866 Act was born of a determination to establish law that would "carry to its legitimate and just result the great humane revolution. . . ."[62] Moreover, most congressmen expected the law to be only a start with more of the same to follow, but the intransigence of President Andrew Johnson and the inability to garner supermajorities to overcome his threatened vetoes moderated and eventually stopped constitutional reconstruction long before Congress could complete its ethical dictates.

In the context of bringing the Declaration's ideals to fruition, it is also valuable here to examine the Civil Rights Act of 1875. Senator Sumner originally introduced the bill in 1870, but it did not make it out of the Committee on the Judiciary.[63] When he reintroduced the bill in 1871 as a rider to another proposal, its provisions included a misdemeanor charge for discriminating on the bases of race, color, or previous condition of servitude in providing public services. The bill guaranteed:

> equal and impartial enjoyment of any accommodation, advantage, facility, or privilege furnished by common carriers, whether on land or water; by inn-keepers; by license owners managers, or lessees of theaters or other places of public amusement; by trustees commissioners, superintendents, teachers, or other officers of common schools and other public institutions of learning. . .; by trustees or officers of church organizations, cemetery associations, and benevolent institutions incorporated by national or State authority.[64]

Not all of these provisions survived to the version enacted the year after Sumner's premature death in 1874.[65] Although he certainly would have been able to gain majority approval (at least in the Senate) for the original version of the bill, Sumner feared a presidential veto. Passage after that would have required a congressional supermajority, and he was uncertain whether enough votes could be mustered for a veto override. Thus the provisions against school, church, and cemetery segregation were taken out of the final version, compromising the final bill's value but still leaving it an enormous step forward for the national establishment of the human rights on an equal basis.[66]

In debates about passage of the law, Sumner explained that he regarded the 13th Amendment's enforcement clause to be the source of congressional authority: "Here is an amendment abolishing slavery. Does it abolish slavery half, three quarters or wholly?" he asked during the speech in the Senate well. "I say the article abolishes slavery entirely." What was the extent of Congress's power to end the "root and branch" of slavery? It was for legislators to "coordinate everything" to be "in harmony with the Declaration of Independence." Whenever civil rights are involved, Sumner asserted, "you must bring it always to that great touch-stone." He insisted "that the Declaration is the equal and coordinate authority with the Constitution itself" and "that the Constitution must be interpreted by the Declaration." Congress's power under the 13th Amendment, he exclaimed, was exercised with the passage of the 1866 act. That too was a law to advance the principles of the Declaration of Independence. The same constitutional authority gave Congress the right, drawing from Chief Justice Marshall's opinion in *McCulloch v. Maryland*, to pass any "necessary and proper" legislation for carrying out the government's constitutional functions. Only with a federal guarantee of equal access to public places could freedom be made complete, and advancement of civil rights required interpretation of the Constitution through the Declaration of Independence.[67] Sumner's opponents to the bill, like Senator Matthew Carpenter, poked fun at this argument, claiming that the Declaration had no substantive nor interpretive value. They accused Sumner of resorting to it in an effort to undermine constitutional federalism.[68]

In response, Sumner repeatedly asserted that he did not regard the Declaration to be a source of power; rather, he claimed the Constitution granted the federal government power while the Declaration "was a sovereign rule of interpretation."[69] Against a detractor who asserted that Sumner was being untrue to his oath to the Constitution by proclaiming his obligations under the Declaration, Sumner responded: "My oath was to support the Constitution as interpreted by the Declaration of Independence." The Civil Rights Act he proposed was born of his understanding of the Constitution "in favor of human rights."[70] An opponent to the proposal, Allen Thurman, saw things differently. To him, it was "a bill of despotism and not of liberty" that contradicted the white-only version of constitutional interpretation. Little did he comprehend the changes wrought by the Reconstruction Amendments.[71]

While Sumner believed legislative power to pass the Civil Rights Act was located in the 13th Amendment, others grounded it elsewhere. After berating Sumner, Senator Carpenter located the authority in the Privileges or Immunities Clause of the 14th Amendment coupled with the Enforcement Clause of Section Five. As he explained, the combination of these two provisions empowered Congress to put all US "citizens upon a common footing" whenever any state abridges "the right of a citizens."[72] Another Republican supporter of the civil rights bill, Senator Oliver Morton, looked instead to the Equal Protection Clause of the 14th Amendment to identify a "sufficient" source of power for the desegregation bill, but conceded that "the power to pass this bill can be derived from other sources."[73] Ultimately, these alternative views were, briefly stated, cogent, but not as thoroughly developed as Sumner's; he, after all, based his remarks on decades of abolitionist writings about the significance of the Declaration of Independence to the text of the Constitution, American culture, and Supreme Court doctrine.[74] As he understood it, the 13th Amendment was much more than freedom from bondage and even more than the specific provisions of the

Civil Rights Acts of 1866 and 1875. The amendment was an assurance of freedom secured by state power. More importantly the provisions embodied the maxim of liberal equality for the common good, which had first entered US law through the Declaration of Independence.

F. Judicial Rollback

Congress demonstrated its commitment to the protection of individual rights as a pragmatic demonstration of the changed society into which the United States entered following the Civil War. Passage of the Civil Rights Act of 1875 was a statement about the way forward and a legislative assertion. It became the final major act of legislative reconstruction. The statute's scope demonstrates just how far the nation's representatives were willing to move to establish societal norms on a national level rather than leaving civil rights to the states, which had exclusive power in this area of law prior to the war.

After it became law, all that was needed was for the Court to defer to Congress and the executive to prosecute cases. By narrowly interpreting congressional Reconstruction Amendment authority, the three branches of government could have become partners in ending oppression, empowering individuals to pursue happiness, and vastly strengthening a civilly egalitarian vision of the common good. Formal segregation might have ended in many licensed institutions in the 19th century, rather than—as turned out to be the case—in the late 20th century.

Instead, the Supreme Court proved to be a regressive institution. The 1883 decision in *The Civil Rights Cases*[75] shut the door to the liberal use of congressional authority, holding the 1875 act to be an unconstitutional infringement of state prerogatives. Thereby the majority beveled away at congressional powers designed to enforce the Declaration's guarantee of equality, inalienable rights, and representative government. The Court claimed for itself what the Constitution granted to Congress: The power to identify and enforce civil and civic rights.

In later chapters of the book, I will examine more recent uses of judicial supremacy to thwart broadly beneficial legislation. But first I turn to another source of textual authority for maxim constitutionalism, the Preamble to the US Constitution.

4

The Preamble
and General Welfare

The Preamble to the Constitution is even more broadly worded than the second paragraph of the Declaration of Independence. Both are critical to the construction of constitutional meaning. These texts jointly establish the overarching duties of representative government to safeguard inalienable rights and secure the general welfare.

The Preamble is brief but carries a tremendous amount of cultural significance, normative gravity, and weight of authority. Its terms make clear that natural people, not politicians at any level of government, are the source of constitutional power:

> We the People of the United States, in Order to form a more perfect Union, establish Justice, insure domestic Tranquility, provide for the common defence, promote the general Welfare, and secure the Blessings of Liberty to ourselves and our Posterity, do ordain and establish this Constitution for the United States of America.

The Preamble's value was not lost on one of the earliest and most influential expositors of the Constitution: Alexander Hamilton made clear in a tract supporting ratification that the terms of the Constitution trump statutes. Ordinary laws and regulations are the products of the people's "agents." Political representatives must advance the interests of the American people. Rather than being dependent on some judicial, legislative, or executive beneficence, Hamilton wrote in *Federalist No. 84*, the people are empowered by fundamental law set by the Constitution: "Here, in strictness, the people surrender nothing; and as they retain every thing, they have no need of particular reservations." The Constitution opens with an anti-autocratic statement providing further details about the national ethos, first announced by the Declaration of Independence.

The Preamble establishes the character of sovereignty that informs the exercise of authority for the entire Constitution. It also describes the people's demands on the federal and state governments, which they created to safeguard their welfare and liberties.

A. From Declaration of Independence to Preamble

The Preamble begins with the assertion that the government's sovereignty comes from, "We the People." The subject of this phrase should be understood in contemporary terms rather than according to some purportedly original intent or meaning. In a case holding that a state's male-only military academy violated the Equal Protection Clause, Justice Ruth Bader Ginsburg rightly pointed out that when the Constitution was ratified "women did not count among voters composing 'We the People.'"[1] Inclusiveness should therefore inform our interpretations, not some original chauvinism. Her statement may also be extrapolated to many other outgroups, who too long experienced second-class citizenship, prohibited from participating in representative politics. Justice Thurgood Marshall said much the same, indicating of the constitutional clauses that protected slavery: "In their declaration of the principles that were to provide the cornerstone of the new Nation, therefore, the Framers made it plain that 'We the People,' for whose protection the Constitution was designed, did not include those whose skins were the wrong color."[2] Historic realities of the Constitution's details do not, however, diminish the resonance of the first three words of the Preamble. But the shortcomings of the original Constitution and its ratification do speak of the country's need to evolve through the general terms of the nation's founding documents to better achieve their universal language.

Chief Justice John Marshall drew attention to the Preamble's importance in one of the most influential cases in American history, *McCulloch v. Maryland*.[3] Quoting the Preamble, Marshall emphasized, "The government proceeds from the people; is 'ordained and established,' in the name of the people; and is declared to be ordained, 'in order to form a more perfect union, establish justice, insure domestic tranquility, and secure the blessings of liberty to themselves and to their posterity.'" In 1833, Marshall wrote with the same perspective in *Barron v. Mayor & City Council of Baltimore*: "The constitution was ordained and established by the people of the United States for themselves, for their own government, and not for the government of the individual states."[4]

The states' acceptance of the Constitution did not shake this federalist foundation because, "the people were at perfect liberty to accept or reject it."[5] It was they, not the states that ratified the document. Having accepted it, the people placed conditions on their state governments. Conceiving the people to be the source of the Constitution, rather than state or federal entities, means that they are the creators of American democracy. Any governing bodies they adopt should operate at their behest and to their benefit: This is the structure of representative democracy. Nothing in this statement eclipses the Declaration of Independence; to the contrary, there is every reason to believe that the people's interest in creating an independent nation to protect the lives, liberties, and pursuits of happiness is very much intact. Certainly a government created by the people must be self-consciously beholden to the intrinsic interests of its human-oriented basis of power.

One of the principal purposes of adopting the Constitution, as the Preamble asserts, is to establish "a more perfect Union" than existed under the Declaration and the Articles of Confederation. The latter, which had been ratified in 1781, left the central government too weak to operate. To address the earlier inefficiency, the US Constitution created three branches of government for coordinating, regulating, and nationalizing certain obligations (such as coining money, regulating copyright, leading the military, and adjudicating federal law suits). Thereby a nation was born on the fertile soil where earlier there had been an association of self-interested states under the Articles of Confederation. The people's entitlement to inalienable rights, as it was set out by the Declaration of Independence, was strengthened by a structure of government with checks and balances. The Preamble further recognizes that securing individuals' "blessings of liberty" can best be promoted with an eye to the "general welfare," whereby domestic tranquility is more likely to be preserved against the social frictions engendered by state favoritism for their own populations.

When combined, the Declaration's deontologically oriented statements and the Preamble's consequentialist statements provide the textual sources for maxim consequentialism, which I will flesh out more fully in Part II (Chapters 5–7). Together, those two legal instruments support the foundational maxim of United States republicanism: Government is obligated to protect personal liberty on an equal basis in a manner most likely to advance the common good.

B. Preamble as Constitutional Gateway

The Constitution, which Congress passed 11 years after independence, was a more pragmatic document than its 1776 progenitor, but it retained the people's will to establish a government favorable to their collective interests. With no bill of rights in the original Constitution, the Preamble supplemented the Declaration's formulation of the national norm and established a structure of government. As with the earlier document, James Wilson provided clarification about the Preamble's function in establishing a national polity: "[W]hat is the interest of the whole, must, on the great scale, be the interest of every part. It will be the duty of a State, as of an individual, to sacrifice her own convenience to the general good of the Union."[6] According to two constitutional luminaries of the 19th century, Justice Joseph Story and George Mellen, the Preamble establishes the primary objectives of the entire Constitution.[7] Those objectives include the authority to secure inalienable rights for the people in furtherance of the Declaration of Independence. While it did not confer specific powers, as Justice Story wrote in his much-studied commentary to the Constitution, statesmen and jurists refer to the Preamble when interpreting the Constitution.[8] In the 20th century, Professor Charles Black pointed out that the Declaration of Independence and the Preamble are "[t]he two best sources" for "striving toward rational consistency, . . . keeping the rules of legal decision in tune with the society's structures and relationships, . . . [and] reaching toward higher goals."[9] Along the same lines, Professor Mark Tushnet has stated: "The Declaration and the Preamble provide the substantive criteria for identifying the people's vital interests."[10] To elaborate on the significance of national consistency in substantive criteria, Black posited that even without a First and 14th Amendment it is not fathomable to think a law prohibiting the public from discussing political candidates for Congress could be remotely valid, given the importance of public communication to our "national government."[11] The Declaration and Preamble are at the root of the written Constitution's meaning.

Similar to my earlier examination of the Declaration's directive, a historical analysis of the Preamble to the Constitution is critical to understanding the governing principles of US constitutionalism. History, however, is the starting point. If it were the end of the analysis, Americans would benefit from the wisdom of the framers but also be burdened by their narrow-mindedness.

The Preamble states in general terms that the federal government must advance general welfare. In a society where each individual's well-being is relevant to the advancement of the common good, public conduct based on racism, ethnocentrism, and sexism is illegitimate because they controvert the equality basis of governance.

The Preamble establishes that the federal government was created to "secure the Blessings of Liberty." This is a positive injunction, not a suggestion nor merely a hopeful statement. The racialism of the founding generation is only the most glaring example of shortsightedness and outright hypocrisy in the face of the social contract into which the people entered. When coupled with the Unalienable Rights Clause of the Declaration of Independence, the scope of the General Welfare Clause must include every class of person, irrespective of race, gender, religion, or ethnicity. Even though in the aftermath of the Revolution northern states either immediately or gradually abolished slavery, on a national level the founders made no constitutional nor statutory effort to wipe the stain of slavery from the land.[12] Thus they failed to vindicate the very claim of human birthright to life, liberty, and the pursuit of happiness that they adopted as the social ethos. Indeed, many viewed the Constitution as a license for slavery because of its Three-Fifths, Fugitive Slave, and Importation Clauses. On the other hand, John Parrish, a Maryland antislavery advocate, asserted that it would be "ignoble" and "below the dignity" of politicians to define the Preamble as a license for states to persist in slavery. Parrish, a Quaker who advocated gradual abolition, believed that the Preamble should be understood within the context of the Declaration of Independence's proclamation "'that all have an unalienable right to life, liberty, and the pursuit of happiness.'"[13]

The wording of the Preamble clearly lends itself to that reading. It announces that the people at large, not the states, ordain the creation of the Constitution and, thereby, reconfirm the Declaration's directive that government's primary obligation is to natural people. Government is created to satisfy their need for a social structure with the authority to maintain safety. The populist character of the document was widely acknowledged, although not always supported. Anti-Federalists, who were opposed to ratification of the Constitution, warned that the Preamble's use of "We the People" rather than "We the States" demonstrated the plan to establish "a compact between individuals entering into society, and not between separate States."[14] For those disposed against stronger national government than existed under the Continental Congress, there was indeed much reason for concern because the Constitution eliminated the explicit language of the Articles of Confederation that had reserved state sovereign independence.[15] This omission indicated a greater centralization of governmental power and structure. Only with the later addition of the 10th Amendment would the states' retained, reserved powers be mentioned, and even then they were limited to matters not within national scope of authority.

The Anti-Federalists and Federalists agreed that the Preamble was a statement about the people's retained natural rights, but they disagreed about the locus of power and the sufficiency of the Constitution to achieve its stated aim. Opponents of ratification warned that the federal government's power to "provide for the common defence [and] promote the general Welfare," might allow it to use positive power to erode "the personal rights of the citizens of the states."[16] Naysayers were unable to prevent its ratification. In response to the Anti-Federalists, the Constitution's supporters linked the power of Congress to "promote the general Welfare" through national legislation with the enjoyment of private rights. In support of ratifying the document in New York, Hamilton wrote that the Preamble's assertion, "'We the People of the United States,'' was meant to establish a federal government "'to secure the blessings of liberty to ourselves and our posterity." ' This, he continued, was to be understood as a guaranteed "recognition of popular rights." With this assurance no "minute detail of particular rights" was needed because the people never gave up their rights through the Constitution, but only meant to "regulate the general political interests of the nation."[17] But more was necessary.

The protection of rights required not only political debate but institutional structure, one that could check the exploitation of power while exercising authority for the betterment of the whole. On its own, the Preamble's statement of purpose was insufficient for governance. If the Preamble and Declaration were the brains, the remainder of the Constitution was the skeletal structure, organs, vessels, and flesh of how the people's will should be carried out. All three branches were granted limited powers to administer a republic where citizens could pursue their vision of a happy life. The social ideal that the people adopted for themselves and for posterity mandated government to protect inalienable rights by passing and enforcing laws for the general welfare. Such a broad ideal left room for civics and individuality but also authorized certain limitations for the betterment of the whole. Specific clauses of the Constitution, the framers realized, were themselves only starting points for developing the statutes, precedents, and executive orders necessary for fleshing out the contours of federal government.

The Preamble functions as the Constitution's introduction. It states the thesis of government: its duty, purpose, and unity. What comes after that creates mechanisms for the administration of each branch of government and for their interactions. Later amendments to the Constitution provide greater specificity to the general terms of representative democracy. They limit government's reach—by protecting rights, like free speech, against intrusion—and its obligations—such as the regulation of interstate commerce. As an author wrote in 1788 during Virginia debates on ratification, the Preamble is "the key of the Constitution."[18]

The Preamble's abstract terms can be understood through contextual interpretation. As is the case with the rest of the Constitution, in Chief Justice Marshall's words, the Preamble "does not profess to enumerate the means by which the powers it confers may be executed." Courts fill in those details through precedents, building on the wisdom of generations. Writing in a similar vein as Marshall, Justice Story asserted that the Preamble does not confer explicit powers like other parts of the Constitution; lawmakers must look to it for "the nature, and extent, and application of the powers actually conferred by the constitution."[19] The Preamble is a broad statement of principle that applies to parts of the Constitution that confer specific authority over various functions of government.

The mandate that federal government "secure the blessings of liberty" is likewise connected to other aspirational statements, such as the Liberty Clause

of the 14th Amendment and the Unenumerated Rights Clause of the Ninth
Amendment. The duty to "promote the general Welfare" requires the federal
government to "secure the blessings of liberty." The welfare of the people as
a whole can be achieved only through a rights-based legal scheme. The statement of general constitutional purpose, as Justice William O. Douglas wrote in
a 20th-century concurrence, is linked to "a catalogue" of rights that include "customary, traditional, and time honored rights, amenities, privileges, and immunities."[20] The Preamble therefore supports a plethora of individual rights on a
national foundation laid by the people for their enjoyment of happiness in a safe
environment.

Innate rights can only be enjoyed in relative safety; thus, as Chief Justice
John Roberts pointed out, "The Preamble to the Constitution proclaims that
the people of the United States ordained and established that charter of government in part to 'provide for the common defence.' "[21] Justice Roberts went on
to say that government can prohibit a variety of public dangers, such as those
caused by criminals who funnel material support to terrorists. But that is a logical extrapolation; it is not a literal meaning. Safety must be understood within
the context of specific circumstances, such as the war on terror. It must also be
balanced against other rights, such as free speech, the right against unreasonable
searches and seizures, due process, and so forth.

While the Preamble should be understood to be an inspiring statement of
principle, it remains one of the Constitution's least parsed gems. Not all judges
have found interpretive value there. Justice John Marshall Harlan, for one, dis-
counted its value in a decision that upheld a mandatory vaccination law, *Jacobson
v. Massachusetts.* Justice Harlan did not even bother trying to examine its meaning
but dismissively stated that the Preamble "has never been regarded as the source
of any substantive power. . . . Such powers [*sic*] embrace only those expressly
granted in the body of the Constitution and as much may be implied from those
so granted."[22] His conclusory comment runs counter to Chief Justice Marshall's
injunction in *Marbury v. Madison*: "It cannot be presumed that any clause in the
constitution is intended to be without effect; and therefore such construction
is inadmissible, unless the words require it."[23] It is reminiscent of similarly dismissive statements of other justices about other portions of the Constitution;
in particular, Justice Oliver Wendell Homes now-dated description of the Equal
Protection Clause "is the usual last resort of constitutional arguments."[24]

Nothing in the Preamble indicates, nor even hints, that it is a nullity or empty
banter. Quite the contrary, the Preamble is the gateway for understanding federalism, the separation of powers, representative democracy, and other facets of
the Constitution.

In *Goldberg v. Kelly*, a seminal case about sufficient procedural safeguards
that states must provide welfare recipients before terminating their benefits, the

Court relied on the Preamble for the proposition that, "Public assistance . . . is not mere charity, but a means to 'promote the general Welfare, and secure the Blessings of Liberty to ourselves and our Posterity.'" This passage explicitly recognizes a positive duty to provide public assistance for the benefit of those members of the national community who lack some minimal resources. Justice William Brennan, writing for the majority, conceived of the Preamble as a guarantee of rights and a limit on government power. Public assistance is a federal objective for enabling individuals to enjoy a boon of general welfare, requiring ordered administration rather than ad hoc eligibility review. The majority did not by any means apply a purely utilitarian formula but one that was conscious also of the needs of litigants, who were entitled to enjoy "the same opportunities that are available to others to participate meaningfully in the life of the community."[25] This formula echoes the general welfare aspiration of the Preamble and the national aims of the Declaration. Put in the context of maxim constitutionalism, government is required to provide welfare recipients with procedural safeguards enabling them to pursue their happiness and enjoy freedom on an equal basis with more affluent citizens.

Perhaps the differences between Justices Harlan's and Brennan's perspectives on the Preamble are inevitable. After all, the wording of the paragraph is obscure. By simply parsing the words, one cannot divine what it means. Neither is there any central committee—some sort of bureaucratic body—assigned to its interpretation. Even the judiciary cannot claim final interpretive authority, as, at a minimum, the people should be able to override judicial interpretation by constitutional amendment or some narrowly tailored piece of legislation to address a compelling state interest. Who, then, is primarily responsible for construing its meaning? The Preamble itself provides the answer: "We the People" are the ultimate source of constitutional definition and meaning.

It is up to the people to petition their representatives to advance the general welfare and to develop programs and laws necessary to bring about the best good for the whole populous. The fact that the Preamble can be quoted by actors on differing sides of a legal divide does not gainsay its relevance. Many general clauses of the Constitution, such as the Due Process Clause on which Justice Brennan based his decision in *Goldberg*, can be used by opposing parties in litigation.

Adjudication of claims requires a look at precedents and contexts. This process does not promise the only correct answer, as Ronald Dworkin might have hoped, but a fair answer to a legal dispute with an appellate process to follow. Despite its generality, the Preamble is clearly part of a scheme of governance that secures individual rights for the common good. The range of possible interpretations of its brief statement of national principle creates constitutional stability in a world of deep ethnic, religious, political, and ideological diversity.

It establishes a federalist structure that presupposes the possibility of debate, litigation, and other ways of expressing differences while maintaining a national identity.

C. The People of the United States

"We the People," who established the government of the United States, are the collective source of federal sovereignty. The Supreme Court adopted this view of joint constitutional venture: "The people taken collectively, constitute the people of the United States. . . . [I]t is in their collective capacity, it is as the people of the United States, that they established the Constitution."[26] They are individuals, who reside in states, with unique local interests, but also members of a national community who are bound by a common mission to "establish justice, insure domestic tranquility, provide for the common defence, promote the general welfare, and secure the blessings of liberty to ourselves and our Posterity." The creation of a federal government and its raison d'etre are explicitly linked to public order, security, fairness, mutual interests, and freedom. The same year that the Bill of Rights was ratified, 1791, the Attorney General of Massachusetts acknowledged that the Preamble created a unified government whose functions affected state and federal spheres of influence. The Preamble, as he put it framed government as a creation of "a union of individuals, by which the states are deprived of the power to act as sovereign states in certain matters . . . [of like interest] to them all."[27] The Preamble announced a new direction, one that clearly broke with America's first attempt at constitutional government.

America's first constitution, the 1781 Articles of Confederation, had specified that the "states . . . entered into a firm league of friendship with each other." The current Constitution, on the other hand, begins by explicitly stating that it is the people, not the states, who are the ultimate constitutional authority. Madison links the people's prerogative of governance to the Declaration's statement of self-representation. If the people were to find their government to be "adverse or inadequate to the purposes of its institution," they retain "an indubitable, unalienable, and indefeasible right to reform or change their government." Their prerogative, he explains, was "prefixed to the Constitution," asserting "that all power is originally vested in, and consequently derived from the people."[28] These statements, which Madison made in Congress in the year of constitutional ratification, link the Constitution to the Declaration's paragraphs, which we examined in detail in the previous chapter, on "unalienable rights" and the necessity of "one people to dissolve the political bands which connected them with another" to throw off the bands of autocratic oppression.

D. Pluralistic Federalism

The Preamble's opening words graft the standards of self-government onto the rest of the Constitution. The introduction was drafted in an emerging polity of persons raised under colonial rule. They sought greater participation in governance and an end to aristocratic privileges. The people were an obvious locus of diffuse power. Participants at a Massachusetts state constitutional convention asserted that "political honesty" was more likely to be expressed by "the body of the people" rather than "a single person, or a very small number."[29] Another author of the cataclysmic period brought together this collective vision, observing that the Preamble's broadly stated principle of national government signaled that, like the Declaration of Independence, the Constitution granted the people "an ultimate right to correct or to overthrow the whole fabrick" of government.[30]

More than 200 years later the Supreme Court acknowledged the continued cultural significance of this legal landmark, asserting that the Preamble's formula, "We the People," referred to "'the People' acting collectively."[31] By laying a constitutional maxim for government, the people can judge its actions according to a central standard not simply by its administrative efficacy. Unwilling to countenance their exclusion from legislative enactment during British colonialism, the people secured their right to set national policies. State laws are also subject to federal constitutional review.[32]

Authentic self-governance empowers the people. Even before a bill becomes law, it must be transparent enough for ordinary citizens to examine whether the proposal meets short- and long-term expectations, should be remodeled, or entirely scrapped. Civic introspection is part of what the First Amendment protects, with its safeguards of free speech and free association.

The text of the Constitution speaks of the people making collective judgements for protecting privacy and liberty, as they are covered by a variety of provisions such as the First, Fourth, and Ninth Amendments along with other clauses like the Guarantee and Habeas Corpus Clauses. All of these substantive provisions—as well the procedural ones dealing with due process, juries, and so forth—fall under the Preamble's statement of purpose. These are not the only functions of the Constitution. There are plenty of others dealing with self-government and collective decision making, including clauses on elections, the separate roles of the president and Congress in war and military appropriations, and even establishing that the president's veto power is not absolute. The people retain the power to turn to Congress for an override of the will of the executive. Sharp differences of opinion are bound to animate the people in a polity as diverse in ethnicity, religion, politics, culture, and class as is the United States. The people's ability to speak for their interests, in a manner that allows each to pursue his or her happiness and equally share community goods, comes in many guises. In the United States, federalism is a means for collective decision making because it gives the people a voice at various levels of government. That is, people's ability to formulate, express, and press their arguments is not only a national endeavor. Sometimes assemblies and petitions are more effective when they press causes on the state, municipal, county, and neighborhood levels. The Preamble's statement of purpose safeguards the people's will at all of these levels of public intercourse.

The federalist scheme of dual federal and state sovereignty should not (and certainly need not) undermine the central maxim of constitutional governance; indeed, local activism can strengthen and embolden persons seeking social change by helping to identify members of their immediate community with similar views and then further amplifying their voices by linking up with like-minded, communicative associations. By joining others, such as in civil rights organizations or labor unions, parties are able to develop close links, embolden, and energize each other to collective action. Each individual's voice is more likely to be heard at this level than in much larger congressional districts.

Many programs critical to the nation are now run by state entities. There are multiple congressionally created statutes that establish state-federal partnerships. A variety of statutes directly grant states powers to exercise various federal undertakings. For instance, the Medicaid healthcare program for the indigent and some elderly patients is a federal program that state administrators operate. Each states' regulatory agency is answerable to unique constituents. States are required to maintain certain services and to provide for specific beneficiaries, but the statutory program also allows states to expand eligibility.[33] Engagement in self-government often has interlinked national and state components.

Deliberative democracy requires continuity through change; otherwise it will implode, become a Tower of Babel, or pave the way for majoritarian abuse. The maxim of equal individual rights for the general welfare remains constant as the fulcrum of procedural, structural, and substantive constitutional authority. Constitutional continuity need not mean stasis. Each generation has the power to examine and elaborate on its meaning with heightened empathy for those who have historically been excluded from the boons of self-government. This power is the collective one spoken of in the Preamble, and on the micro level it enables people to operate through coalitions, social groups, and short-term alliances by way of social media, political lobbying, or individual letter writing.

Divergent voices are welcome and inevitable in a society that respects free speech for the advancement of personal and common goods. A slew of expressive avenues at the political, social, and cultural levels are open to apply the constitutional maxim to real life dilemmas. Through representatives, elected pursuant to fair elections where each citizen's vote carries equal weight, the people can lend their voices to the evolutionary process of defining the breadth of inalienable rights. In the words of the Supreme Court, "The concept of 'We the People' under the Constitution visualizes no preferred class of voters, but equality among those who meet the basic qualifications."[34] There will of course be losers; but in an open society they will be free to lobby, engage in dialogue, provide a contrarian voice, and to run for political office (or support others with political ambitions). All facets of federalism—from the national to the local—must remain open for them to voice their unique perspectives. Hearing all angles of the debate is also in the interest of society, which is enriched by disparate views about policies.

The people can contribute to state and national dialogue. Federalism is itself beholden to the will of the people. The significance of basing the Constitution on the will of the people rather than state sovereignty cannot be overstated. The issue came up repeatedly during the Civil War in congressional debates and newspapers. As one contemporary historian put it:

> The Constitution was not drawn up by the States, it was not promulgated in the name of the States, it was not ratified by the States. The States never acceded to it, and possess no power to secede from it. It was ordained and established over the States by a power superior to the States—by the people of the whole land in their aggregate capacity, acting through conventions of delegates . . . independently of the State Governments."[35]

This 1861 perspective was based on a much older conception. The power to dissolve the government, as James Iredell explained in 1788 to the North Carolina ratifying convention, resided in the people alone who could later choose any other form of government that would "be more conducive to their welfare."[36] Because the people had agreed to the Constitution, only they could alter it. In response to Georgia's claim that during the Civil War it was not bound by the Constitution, Justice Noah Swayne wrote that the secession was impermissible because the Constitution, "as its preamble recites" was adopted by "the people of the United States." They created "not a confederacy of States, but a government of individuals."[37] The states therefore cannot deviate from any norm established by the people's act of Constitution-making.

The foundational norm of individual rights for the common good is not just a passive ideal. It is the core of legitimate public actions. By no means is it tethered to the founding generation's limited conception of deliberative democracy. When thinking how long the Constitution should remain in effect, Thomas Jefferson wrote that each generation would need to update it because legal systems as all other things on earth belong to the living.[38] Rather than taking Jefferson's recommended route of expiring after a set number of years—he recommended

19 years—the US Constitution has survived. In over 200 years, only 27 amendments have been made to it. True enough that some of those amendments are composed of several parts, such as the Eighth Amendment with its prohibition against cruel and unusual punishment as well as excessive bail, but the limited number of modifications to the original document is truly remarkable given how many changes there have been to the character of the citizens, electorate, technology, federalism, and virtually all areas of public life. Changes to the Constitution have primarily come about through alterations to Court doctrine. But the evolution of constitutional understanding has also been achieved outside of formal institutional methods by way of social advocacy, legislative lobbying, and cultural awareness. These popular approaches to interpretations of the ancient document have enabled the people to empower their representatives to pass laws to positively impact their own lives and those of their communities. Many of the changes were based on modern sensibilities about things like gay and women's rights, which would have been beyond the purposes of the founders. This raises the question of how true contemporaries should be to the framers' Constitution, and I'll return to that subject in Chapter 8.

E. General Welfare and Federal Involvement in Public Programs

The Preamble's General Welfare Clause empowers the federal government to administer programs that improve the lives of ordinary Americans by promulgating and enforcing laws for the benefit of the economy, environment, and civil rights. The easing of travel, increased commerce between states, and steady intergovernmental interactions have rendered federal involvement essential in matters previously controlled by the states.

One prominent example of this trend to a greater interlinked general welfare principle is the involvement of federal government in welfare and healthcare. In the days of the early republic, private organizations, such as churches and local committees, administered poor laws. It was only after the Civil War that a national public welfare agency, the Freedman's Bureau, began administering relief efforts, but its reach was limited. By 1872, Congress cut off its funding. Following Reconstruction, the distribution of public relief remained in the hands of charities, organized unions, and at the behest of individual states. The popularity of Social Darwinism in the late 19th century, which was a political philosophy concentrated on individual strengthens rather than alleviating social needs, drew politicians away from offering public support for the indigent. A changing vision of government obligations to provide welfare took root during what came to be known as the Progressive Era, with activists like Jane Addams and Richard

T. Ely, who called for an end to laissez-faire governance in favor of economic and political assistance for healthcare, education, and other social services. Despite their successes in expanding public schools and aiding dependent children, it was only during the New Deal Era that federal spending and commerce power became used for positive national support of social services. The Social Security Act (SSA) became law in 1935. It provided the elderly with monthly cash assistance and also included federal Aid to Dependent Children (later renamed, "Aid to Families With Dependent Children"). SSA would become the basis for Great Society programs; among them, Medicare and Medicaid. A final statute to mention in this quick rundown in history of social welfare is the 2010 Patient Protection and Affordable Care Act (ACA), which established a universal health care mandate and will be further discussed in Chapter 9.

Administering public healthcare programs can help preserve dignity and advance the common good, just as in *Goldberg* Justice Brennan recognized that public benefits for the poor were aimed at helping individuals become more engaged and productive for their own and social goods. Lobbying empowers the people to engage in policy debates, enabling them to weigh in on issues affecting rights and the public goods. The opinions of supporters and opponents of mandatory health insurance were critical to the debates in Congress, around the country, and in the media; but at some point legislators had to choose between competing views. And, if dissatisfied with that choice, the people can vote the politicians out of office or challenge the law in the courts.

This brief survey of welfare assistance is meant to demonstrate how over the decades the federal government increasingly made positive impacts on individuals and US culture. The US Supreme Court has explicitly connected public assistance programs to the Preamble's General Welfare Clause. In *Goldberg v. Kelly*, the Court asserted that public assistance was a means to fulfilling the blessings of liberty for the general welfare.[39] Operating public assistance programs, such as food stamps and medical clinics, is now regarded to be part of the federal government's responsibility. While the programs are relative newcomers to the legal realm, their roots lie in the foundation of the Constitution. Justice Brennan observed that "[f]rom its founding the Nation's basic commitment has been to foster dignity and well-being of all persons within its borders." The battle against poverty and its many handicaps is part of the broad range of public accountability. The need for due process hearings before terminating assistance, Brennan wrote, is connected to the government's duty to the people to work for the common good to enable citizens to enjoy the blessings of liberty. By meeting the needs of the poor, society empowers them with "the same opportunities that are available to others to participate meaningfully in the life of the community." This, in turn, reduces class tensions and adds to the pool of talent available for continued commercial, social, and political betterment. Welfare programs should provide the poor with the resources needed to participate meaningfully "in the life of the community" and "guard against the societal malaise that may flow from a widespread sense of unjustified frustration and insecurity." Brennan's communitarian formula is one that recognizes that individuals are more likely to enjoy dignity and contribute to the common good when secure against arbitrary confiscation of public entitlements. The mixed private/public concern is exactly in line with the maxim constitutionalism approach to constitutional interpretation that I have advanced throughout this book.

While the specific subject of *Goldberg* concerns pre-termination proceedings for welfare recipients, its constitutional relevance readily translates to other socially responsible laws. Although the Court has explicitly held that education is not a fundamental right,[40] once a community has opened a public school system due process would require a procedural fairness under the 14th Amendment before a state could remove this cultural "blessing of liberty." The overlap here with public assistance is government's obligation to help members of the community become self-sufficient. Education is essential to any deliberative democracy; without it, one would neither be on an equal footing in employment or politics.[41] Thus, the Court's rejection of indigent parties' equal protection claims against states' much lower funding of schools in indigent neighborhoods than of schools in affluent communities[42] is out of step with the Equal Protection Clause and the Preamble's General Welfare Clause. Indeed, the need for education as a tool for personal growth and social responsibility puts into strong doubt the validity of the Court's rejection of education as a substantive constitutional value.

The message of the Preamble is simple. Government is made to "promote the general welfare." That can only be achieved through regulations effectively designed to "establish justice." While "the People" who granted sovereign power to the United States are a collective who formed "a more perfect union," the only way to fulfill the mission set out is for all three branches of government to secure "the blessings of liberty" for each successive generation. The Constitution, therefore, is a document for the collective defense and tranquility, but this can only be achieved by representatives and judges who must preserve, in the words of the Declaration of Independence, "unalienable Rights," among which are "life, liberty and the pursuit of happiness."

PART II

ETHOS AND MAXIMS

|| 5 ||

Constitutional Ethos

The first part of this book sought to demonstrate that the Declaration of Independence and Preamble to the Constitution establish a constitutional ethos, concerned with individual and public good. Constitutional ethos is not, however, a textual creation. It refers, rather, to the principle of justice that the collective group, commonly referred to as "the people," recognizes to have higher normative status than any contemporary majority. While a stable ideal, its details are variously worked out through social movements, judicial opinions, codifications, popular culture, and a host of other deliberative channels. The maxim of constitutional governance is not merely advisory but binding for the establishment and administration of an impartial state. To put it into effect, the populous grants institutions enforcement powers necessary to secure citizens' equal legal status. The overarching norm also serves as a limit on government conduct. To be legitimate, public policy must be synthetically deontological and consequentialist, benefitting individuals and advancing societal interests.

Put in general terms, the constitutional ethos is a principle that empowers individuals to flourish by pursuing their unique life quests while also maintaining coercive standards for government to advance policies likely to achieve collective goods. Constitutional maxim does not envision agreement on contentious constitutional topics. To the contrary, conflicting views are not only to be expected but welcomed in a vibrant and pluralistic society. Indeed, government should encourage public debate and solicit input from people with a wide range of perspectives. A pluralistic society must explore the merits of differing rational views about how to proceed on projects but immovably determined to act against intolerance. An abstract and enforceable maxim is needed to which a community of volitional and purposeful individuals can hold government accountable. A national ethos mandates public agents to seek the public good, which in turn means the betterment of individuals living in a collective society and subject to reciprocal laws.

A. Constitution and Ethos

The normative standard must create general, reciprocal obligations and benefits for society as a whole. A free and equal community must set certain regulatory limitations for maintaining public order. Coercive restraints are logical features of constitutional communities that have empowered sovereign entities to resolve legal disputes. The possibility of groups averse to liberal equality gaining power through democratic politics (as occurred in the United States with the Jackson administration and its policy of Indian Removal or the racist Dixiecrat Party's victories in four southern states in the 1948 election) render deliberation alone an insufficient guarantor of rights and reciprocal betterment. Legal debate requires an ideological anchor. If a constitution contains portions that are overtly racist, as did the Confederate Constitution, then the derivative ethos will also be intolerant and non-inclusive. But where constitutional provisions are inclusive, they engender tolerance; although, actual public practices may be discriminatory. Adoption of constitutional maxim is not meant to produce uniform conduct nor opinion; to the contrary, nuanced thinking and debates about liberty, equality, and justice force each generation to reassess and reevaluate policies, laws, and judicial decisions.

The central ethos of a constitution informs all subordinate legal obligations. That is by no means to say that all legal questions are constitutional. Rather, any policy that directly violates the constitutional ideal is illegitimate, either on its face or in its application. The written Constitution and its interpretations play a role in determining whether ordinary legal matters—from crime, tax, property, and other topics—arbitrarily impede individuals' equal rights to enjoy the benefits of pluralistic culture. A legitimate law is one that is born of state efforts on behalf of the people.

Any ordinary law—be it derived from statute, executive order, administrative law, or judicial opinion—must have the dual justification: It must comport with constitutional norms and provide clear notice to pertinent parties about the legality of behavior. Institutional actors authorized to weigh differing interests in the effective execution of a law are authorized to place reasonable limits on the ability of individuals to exercise their wills. In turn, constitutional ethos along with structural constraints place limits on what can pass as justifiable authority. No branch of government is empowered to substitute its will for a fundamental constitutional norm.

In the United States, the courts are regarded to be the final arbiters of constitutional meaning. If I am correct, however, judicial opinions are illegitimate if they displace the social ethos guaranteed in the Declaration of Independence and Preamble to the Constitution. Hence judicial interpretation is not supreme and should not be equated with the authority of the Constitution. Where it violates the general ideal of governance, the people, who are the ultimate sovereigns of representative democracy, should be able to resort to deliberative channels for overriding the opinion by a supermajority of legislators. The precise percentage of congressmen needed to override judicial interpretation might be the same two-thirds majority it takes for Congress to override a presidential veto. Constitutional amendment is only one method for overturning Supreme Court holdings, indeed in the United States that is currently the only means,* while in parliamentary democracies like England the Supreme Court cannot overturn the constitutionality of a law passed by the legislature.

What is clear, in the words of Ernest Young, is that "[d]octrine is not the same as the Constitution."[1] To this insight we might add, constitutional ideal is of higher priority than the written Constitution, which creates structural means to carry out underlying purpose. While the notion of a guiding legal principle carries the risk of subjective error, judicial interpretation also infuses private and group political leanings into controversial cases. Republican Party-appointed judges tend to vote for less government intervention in cases involving such issues as environmental and business regulations, while Democratic Party-appointed judges tend to favor government involvement in those matters. Even decisions of judges who have lifetime appointments are often not above pitched political battles. The partisan *Bush v. Gore* opinion led many to question judicial objectivity. In that case, the US Supreme Court reversed on Equal Protection grounds a Florida Supreme Court order, even though it involved a voting matter typically left exclusively to the states.[2] Thereby the conservative majority of justices, such as William Rehnquist and Antonin Scalia—who are typically associated with a state-oriented form of federalism—effectively handed the state's electoral college votes to the Republican candidate, and decided the presidential election instead of allowing for a voting ballot recount to determine the winner. Judges' leanings are not only clear from a case deciding the outcome of a political contest but also in the development of juridical doctrine. Following the Civil War, in the *Civil Rights Cases* the Court relied on textual formalism to herald a narrow reading of the Due Process, Privileges or Immunities, and Equal Protection Clauses. Because the second sentence of the 14th Amendment begins with the words, "No state shall" the Court conceived the prohibition against discrimination to apply only to public acts.[3] While seemingly objective, the "state action" doctrine has become, as the historian Eric Foner has said, "a major barrier" in the promotion of racial equality.[4] The Court might have instead read the entire 14th Amendment to advance the constitutional ideal of liberal

---

* No clause in the Constitution grants the Supreme Court ultimate authority of interpretation. But through a series of cases, the Court has elevated its status to be the final arbiter of constitutional disputes. *See* Marbury v. Madison, 5 U.S. 137 (1803).

equality containing a specific statement against state wrongs but not precluding its application against private discriminations. The *Civil Rights Cases* reflected the late 19th-century politics of sectional reconciliation between the former northern and southern antagonists, rather than the ethos of general welfare for the entire population to enjoy the boons of freedom and equality.[5] By formalistically interpreting the 14th Amendment's State Action Clause, the Court legitimized segregation in public businesses. As might have been expected, relying on the holding of the *Civil Rights Cases*, states began to enforce separation of the races in almost all public places of accommodation, including hospitals, phone booths, and bathrooms.

The long-term tragic ramifications of the Court's meddling with congressional civil rights powers indicates that it is too precarious to leave constitutional interpretation at the sole discretion of the judiciary. Recognizing the legislative role in constitutional interpretation could facilitate debate and popular participation in deciding pressing issues. Such an approach could adopt a congressional two-thirds override—analogous to the legislative power to override presidential vetoes—of judicial opinions that undermined foremost constitutional values. Congress is coequally responsible for upholding constitutional ethos, responsible to the electorate, and should be able to pass supermajority supported laws to check the Supreme Court when its decisions are driven by ideology or politics that are incompatible with fundamental rights and equality-directed policies. The people send their representatives to Congress expecting them to exercise offices to safeguard the Constitution.

Yet mechanisms are also necessary to prevent constitutional ethos to become beholden to popular whim. Therefore, where the legislature seeks to regulate the ability of persons to enjoy judicially recognized rights (as opposed to overriding judicial decisions, such as the *Civil Rights Cases*, that trampled constitutional powers to advance a civil rights agenda) only narrowly tailored laws designed to achieve a compelling government purpose will be constitutionally adequate. Parsing the statement of national purpose should not be based on the personalities who then happen to be on the bench or in Congress, which are too malleable to afford the necessary stability for a complex society. Constitutional ethos must be more stable than ordinary law, which is subject to replacement by majority vote. The will of partisan populism, while inevitable in any democracy, should not undermine the representative nature of pluralistic society. The codification of inclusive norms, in the form of civil and political rights laws, provides a structure for redress and relief. Constitutional ethos sets the limits of legitimate activism just as it sets the limits of government offices.

As a matter of constitutional law, ethos is not identical with personal morality. Quite the contrary, public ethos is one to which persons of all tolerant moral suasions can agree. Pluralistic society accepts and respects the practice of all manners of creeds and secular persuasions. Even hateful views are protected unless they migrate from beliefs to attempt or commission of harmful conduct, in which case the state has an interest in preventing the violent sentiments from disrupting private peace and public order. This perspective implicitly recognizes the equal innate right of liberty of conscience and practice, but goes further than deontological theorists like Immanuel Kant or Robert Dworkin. The existence of innate individual rights alone does not explain why the state should exercise its power to help anyone further her sense of enjoyment. The bridge lies in the joint public commitment to a polity of equals. Arbitrary favoritism shown to any group in the enjoyment of fundamental rights or the administration of fair procedures constitutes a breach of the public ethos.

The ideal is not primarily discursive, as Jürgen Habermas claims, nor linguistic, as R. M. Hare describes, but secularly ethical. The Preamble to the Constitution and Declaration of Independence safeguard the human will to live a volitional life free of arbitrarily imposed limits. Habermas writes that the normative content of moral laws is derived from rational discourse, leading to the formulation of valid norms.[6] While dialogue is indeed indispensable to the construction of value theory, rational discourse may not always lead to the formulation of democratic norms. Even tyrannical regimes find rational argument to support their claims for aggrandizement. Dehumanization, for instance, has historically been a common rationalization for group exclusion. A normative anchor is necessary against which discourse can be tested. Discrimination and prejudice are wrong even if the general population, based on prejudices, calls for their perpetuation.[7] The self-understanding and impartiality of democracies, of which Habermas writes, is not dependent on discourse alone but the dignity of each person and the need for structuring a mutually beneficial system of laws.

The need for consistency is not merely descriptive. Thus, linguistic logic of moral thinking, which runs through Hare's writings, does not provide a comprehensive theory of ethics and morality. Hare's method can thus help identify analytical flaws (such as discrimination in a legal system committed to universal equality) and validate public decisions (such as evenhandedness in keeping with constitutional due process protections); but, without a social ethos, linguistic morality lacks a basis for asserting the rectitude of certain claims above others. His argument is descriptive, but lacks the normative component sufficient to criticize existing morality by meta-linguistics. The imperative of legislating to achieve social welfare by protecting inalienable rights through impartial laws is not just a matter of identifying the logical properties of moral reasoning, but an obligation of governance contained in the Preamble and the Declaration. According to my formulation, social ethos can be examined by logic but not exhausted by it. Constitutional ethos is not solely prescriptive and imperative, as Hare described value-judgments, but also evaluative and aspirational of how a representative society should function.[8]

The public obligation extends to all legal commitments—from federal laws to local regulations. A central ethos tethers those disparate efforts to a unifying ideal. Consequently, constitutional challenges can be brought against any level of public decision—from those made by the president, such as incarcerating enemies of war at Guantanamo Bay, Cuba, to the local decisions of school board officials not meeting the needs of special education students. Litigants and social movements can raise challenges to existing practices on the basis of constitutional clauses, but on a more fundamental level the question is whether the challenged policy violates core values and undermines the mutual commitment to a complex, pluralistic society. By this, I mean that the Constitution itself contains a positive description of a social ethos; the document does not create that ethos.

I next sketch some necessary features of a legal structure that both respects the dignity of the individual and balances the good of the community. An objective standard is needed to check the overreaching of government actors and political factions.

B. Stable Ideal of Government

The existence of a social ethos, obligating government to provide for the general welfare by protecting the intrinsic rights of the people, implies the existence of an objective standard for the resolution of disputed interests. Ethos must be a testable concept, albeit one that will be contested and whose contours will be disputed in political and social discourse. The texts of the Constitution and the Declaration of Independence provide a roadmap for the development of institutions not beholden to the political leanings and personal wishes of officeholders. For the ideal of government to remain stable through generational change, individual vantage cannot be definitive; otherwise, the justification for law would be the power to impose a particular vision onto the community without consulting its interests. Ours is not a system that calls for polling the populous on each public issue but the representation of the electorate within permitted powers of political office. Civics must remain open to the people, who, except for matters of local concern, typically exercise their will as a voting district through the auspices of political representatives. It should be added, as a matter of free speech, that each member of a community has the opportunity to participate in constitutional interpretation by lobbying legislators, litigating cases, and appealing to fellow citizens to do the same.

The central principle of governance confines the range of possible meanings, but to every social problem there can be multiple approaches. Decisions about matters like how much money to spend on particular government programs, how many years to incarcerate a felon, or how long to keep negative information on the credit report of a person in bankruptcy are all matters for debate subject to a large range of legitimate answers. Constitutional ethos does not pretend to reveal an epiphanic answer to legal dispute; instead, it contains the core maxim of normative constitutional judgments. Any arbitrarily discriminatory solution or method for addressing public controversy runs counter to the constitutional maxim of liberal equality for the common good and is therefore illegitimate.

Many decisional directions can positively impact representative democracy. The extent to which politicians should take into account particular suggestions must be judged on a case-by-case basis. But the rule of law will certainly be undermined by any approach that uses arbitrary standards, showing unjustified favoritism. Constitutional theory should provide both a stable principle of action respecting the dignity of individuals and recognize the fluidity and dynamic nature of publics in their quest for social improvement.

This notion of objectivity differs from that of legal positivists, who regard law to be only the embodiment of enacted norms rather than universal standards of conscientious governance. For positivists, like H.L.A. Hart and Joseph Raz, law is valid by virtue of social facts rather than some external moral rationale.[9] In his famous debate with Hart, Lon Fuller pointed out that the oppressive institutions of totalitarian regimes, like the Nazi government in Germany, demonstrate the need for criticisms based on values external to culturally accepted norms.[10]

Sociological reflection is important for recognizing law but is insufficient for critiquing existing institutions. There is an explanatory value in Hart's description of the rules of conduct (primary rules) and systemic modification, recognition, and adjudication (secondary rules).[11] He is surely correct that the rule of recognition identifies "settled law" and specifies "the sources of law and the relationships of superiority and subordination holding between them [that are] necessary."[12] But Hart's method is insufficient for looking outside of the status quo (evaluating norms not captured by the rule of recognition) to improve or to jettison existing legal constructs.

The relevance of constitutional norms to specific circumstances involves more than linguistic assessment or epistemic rule recognition. Objectivity requires the interpretation of relevant constitutional texts to circumstances in accordance with core standards of representative democracy. For instance, the Supreme Court's decision in *Brown v. Board of Education* that public school segregation violated the Equal Protection Clause was not based on existing social norms. At the time, segregation enjoyed widespread approval throughout the South. The Court transcended the facts on the ground and moved decisively to strike down a recognized system of racial degradation. The Court based its findings that separation of the races was inimical to students and "democratic society" on the basis of a normative interpretation, not, and indeed contrary to, the recognized Southern legal norms of the day. Just as states' laws and community customs were not determinative in the assessment of constitutional norms to the dispute in *Brown*, neither should judicial opinions be the final points of objective readings. *Dred Scott v. Sandford*, in which Chief Justice Roger Taney asserted that blacks could never enjoy the privileges of citizens to the United States, may have described the recognized rule in many states, but it undermined the mandates of the Declaration of Independence and Preamble to the Constitution for a truly national ethos. While states and the judiciary are important sources of normative discourse, they are not the exclusive loci of legitimacy and are subject to criticisms for falling short of impartial justice.

All government bodies, at the state and federal level, are bound by constitutional values and institutions grounded in personal liberties and public welfare. Institutions cannot themselves be the final arbiters of public values because their authority comes from the Constitution, which, in turn, must be contextually interpreted. The judiciary did not construct the perspective that school segregation was wrong. The Supreme Court turned to the Constitution's Equal Protection Clause to derive an objective standard based on common human dignity and participatory democracy, requiring equal access to education for each citizen.

Constitutional interpretation rests on more general provisions than ordinary legal decision making. There are, no doubt, some very specific provisions of the United States Constitution such as the minimum age requirements for holding the offices of president, senator, and representative. Abstract provisions—such as the Equal Protection Clause—and structural—like the Guarantee, Tax and Spend, or Necessary and Proper Clauses—are not so easily parsed. The latter grant elected officials a breadth of discretionary latitude.

Objectivity cannot be teased out solely from the words of the Constitution. Ascertaining their meanings and contemporary relevancy requires careful study of history, custom, tradition, doctrine, aspiration, and mandate. The indeterminacy is not a weakness but a strength of democracy, leaving ample room for policy debates about a variety of legitimate alternatives to solving social puzzles. Norms of justice, equality, liberty, and human good keep the debates tethered to a central purpose of nationhood. The lack of specificity under those circumstances empowers the citizenry to lobby for a variety of legitimate approaches for resolving social problems. To give an example, from the general principle that government is created for the health and safety of citizens come a slew of civil and criminal laws fleshing out the specifics of statutes, such as those prohibiting armed robbery, murder, and manslaughter, and common law negligence. Even more specific are elements lawyers must prove for conviction, defense, and burden of evidentiary proof. Procedural rules establish further guidelines. The general principle of health and safety is needed for any society governed by law to prevent chaos, but the details of statutes and rules governing human interactions are open to political debates and amenable to many courses of action acceptable to groups subject to them. Judges, when they are drawn into interpersonal conflicts by state or private litigation, must remain true to rational schemes adopted by legislatures and consistent with precedents which speak to long-term values. Courts have the authority to reflect and issue decisive orders on whether a law violates constitutional norms.

The indeterminacy in many clauses of the Constitution is not a license for utter breakdown of interpretive value. There are clearly wrong answers to the meaning of even the most indeterminate clauses. Take for instance the Safety and Happiness Clause of the Declaration of Independence. There is no agreement about its meaning and hashing it out is part of the function of a representative government, which is secured through the Guarantee Clause of the Constitution. But it would certainly run afoul of the Declaration, and *ad fortiorari* the constitutional scheme, for the federal government to do away with criminal and civil law altogether. That would be undermining safety, not furthering it, and lawlessness would clearly be contrary to the happiness of vulnerable people.

C. Generalities and Facts

Without determinate features of legality, the structure of government and people's rights remain at the mercy of politically powerful groups. Constitutional norms are not part of a recipe for stasis; to the contrary, general principles establish terms for holding government accountable for the protection of fundamental rights and for the advancement of social betterment.

During the early 20th century, legal realist scholars expressed skepticism about any such claim of coherent legal meaning of law. They believed abstract legal principles to be indeterminate. According to them, law is a system of social control with "gaps and contradictions," containing all manner of "exceptions for almost every legal rule or principle."[13] They drew attention to how judges' backgrounds and quirks affect the resolution of cases. But they told only part of the story of constitutional interpretation.

The long-settled view that the Constitution trumps other laws is not merely socially descriptive but also normative in its implications; it signals that there are certain principles that resonate throughout society, irrespective of what lesser laws local communities have adopted. Of even higher order of priority are the equal dignity of humanity and the establishment of institutions that benefit each member of the constitutional community. Thus, after the Civil War, reconstructionists were inspired by universal ideals to amend the Constitution and end slavery and to create birthright citizenship in order to live up to the national ethos, thereby revoking those portions of the original document that were incompatible with it.

The legal realists brought the need for empirical sources to the forefront of judicial and academic attention. Information about actual conditions, rather than abstract theory, are indispensable for deciding controversies over matters like industrial policy, poor relief, and trust busting.[14] They regarded deductive reasoning to be off the mark in a world where the legal system needed to address real human dilemmas. And yet, practice cannot determine principle, contrary to the claims of the realist Walter Wheeler Cook.[15] The maxims identified in the Declaration of Independence and the Preamble to the Constitution were not simply deductively discerned by American revolutionaries but rather the products of centuries of carefully sifted political thought. Those principles were not derived from common law precedents alone, nor should their meaning be constructed on the basis of cases in dispute, as Cook believed. Principle should rather be predicated on stable ideals whose authority comes from government's obligation to the public good and to the individuals who compose organized society.

Stable constitutional norms supersede practices. They provide the structural foundation against which judges can gauge the legitimacy of laws and their application to the resolution of disputes. This is not to say that the Realists failed to recognize the importance of ideals to law, but that they were mistaken in thinking those ideals could be discovered by sifting through facts and decisions of "specific law suits."[16] The rules of law reflect policies, they certainly are advanced by opinions in lawsuits but their ultimate source is not judicial enforcement but the will of the people as it mandates itself through constitutional norms. Ideals and policies should, therefore, direct judicial considerations. When judges overturn laws for being facially unconstitutional, the basis of their reasoning should include reflection on the social ideal embodied in the relevant clause. To illustrate the point, judges may find that voter dilution through racial gerrymandering undermines the one-person, one-vote principle, which protects the representative nature of government. Behind the doctrine used to decide apportionment cases is the ideal of equal political representation, which, in turn, is rooted in the maxim that institutions must protect individual's equal right to engage in policy making decisions affecting the general welfare.

The contextual scrutiny of facts relevant to particular legal issues helps schematize social problems and to evaluate whether they accord with principles or specific laws; however, evaluation of collected data cannot by itself prove or disprove the constitutionality of laws on matters from child labor to the distributive safety measures for selling noxious chemicals. An interpretive framework should not only evaluate social science data but also orient them in the context of systemic structure and policy. A constitutional schema created for the better-ment of the people must include internal checks, rather than allowing judges to manipulate society on a case-by-case basis.

Policy makers should reflect on how constitutional law fits, conflicts, or oth-erwise overlaps structural and normative features of the legal system. Where a statute is incompatible with constitutional principle, the latter trumps. But what if two constitutional clauses conflict? For instance, before the Civil War the Due Process Clause of the Fifth Amendment—which guarantees the rights to life, liberty, and property—was incompatible with the Three-Fifths Clause—which augmented the presence of slave states in the US House Representatives. After ratification of the Bill of Rights, both were binding, but an egalitarian thinker would have found that the protection of liberty was incompatible with chat-tel slavery. Under those circumstances, radical abolitionists of the 19th cen-tury were correct to say that judges should have acted to vindicate African Americans' right to the fair administration of justice.[17] That stance was not based on strictly deductive reasoning nor of limited inductive analysis of the case at hand. Instead, the combination of constitutional aspirations and southern state practices informed the abolitionists.

Principled exercise of justice does not simply describe social facts but parses them in the framework of a cohesive ethos of impartial legality.[18] Ideals should inform the establishment of verifiable and objective constitutional principles. On a factual level subjectivity certainly plays a role in judicial holdings, as legal realists pointed out. But judges must remain true to constitutional norms to avoid making arbitrary decisions. The evaluation of constitutional controversies requires analyses of specifics and generalities. Whether at the appellate or trial levels, judges must harmonize facts with existing mandates, aspirations, statutes, precedents, and social expectations indicated by the evolution of state and fed-eral laws. This analytical schema does not provide definitive, incontrovertible answers but the room necessary for people to make deliberative choices in litiga-tion and social policy coupled with fundamental principle.

D. Norms and Aspirations

At all levels of government, policies must stay true to constitutional principles while adjusting existing rules to address social challenges. By themselves, de-scriptive statements fail to provide the analytic hook for legal changes, ending existing wrongs or displacing archaic practices. The legitimacy of statutes, exec-utive actions, and judicial decisions, are not based on subjective beliefs but their function in a just society. Some fundamental principle should be used to explain why segregation was always wrong, not only after the Supreme Court announced its opinion in *Brown v. Board of Education* and states began to dismantle Jim Crow, but at all times in the nation's history, even when those practices were accepted norms in states and in the federal capital. The reason lies in the general purpose of free and equal representative democracy, which transcends existing practices—even those codified by laws. Norms and standards are relevant today for addressing perceived inequalities in the enjoyment of liberties, such as same-sex marriage, polygamy, polyandry, and so on. Social assessments should be based on objective standards of personal dignity and the common enjoyment of legal fairness, rather than contemporary mores. That means a state violation of human rights is not solely wrong because it violates a positive law but because it harms an individual by treating him unequally and excluding him from the benefits of community membership.

Humans are too fallible in their assessments and too often wedded to contemporary norms for constitutional interpretation to rely only on popular judgments. Neither can politicians, nor even social groups, be trusted to define objective standards for fairness; they too have interests, especially in the acquisition and retention of power and wealth. That is not to say that corruption is ubiquitous but that the constitutional norm transcends the interests of any living or deceased persons. Even the official repository of constitutional interpretation in the United States, the Supreme Court, adds only opinions with premises whose legitimacy, I believe, the public can regard with various degrees of skepticism. Justice Robert Jackson poked fun at the notion that the Supreme Court should be trusted as the bastion of ontological validity: "We are not final because we are infallible, but we are infallible only because we are final."[19] In rendering rights-protective judgments, another justice pointed out that the Court must be aware of its counter majoritarian function and the Constitution's "public nature, obligatory character, and consequentialist aspect."[20] Such a perspective is keenly alert to the deontic and consequentialist functions of the document.

The Declaration of Independence and the Preamble to the Constitution provide the broad mandates of governance. Those statements of constitutional law create a substantive obligation to safeguard unalienable rights and provide for the general welfare. Thus the process-perfecting views proffered by John Hart Ely in works like *Democracy and Distrust* and Cass Sunstein in *The Partial Constitution*, only get at part of the function of democracy. Unwritten norms dealing with privacy, rights of audiences, presumption of innocence, among many others are substantive ends for the protection of which fair procedural rules are created. The scheme is a cohesive one, requiring state actors to provide institutional means for the vindication of rights and laws created to punish their infringement. A stable system that both enables individuals to pursue their desired paths in life and provides fair conditions of social cooperation must remain true to values that transcend private moralities and changing mores.

Thus, the principle of governance must remain firm irrespective of what is actually in statute books, state constitutions, or judicial precedents. In this regard, the theory of constitutional law is not only mandatory but also aspirational. The latter perspective is valuable for both prospective and retrospective analyses. It provides a basis by which the people can, through their elected representatives, articulate their vision of democratic process to move the country in a direction more in line with the goals stated in the Declaration and Preamble. Rather than settling for separate starting points, a unified norm provides persons with disparate interests a common aim. From an agreed upon point they can proceed to deliberate about specific steps to its effectuation. Beginning with an abstraction provides a common ground for what can often become rancorous debates about the best means to proceed. General principle requires parsing out by interested parties through equal access to the channels of communication. An aspirational norm also allows for review of existing and past practices. Feminists, abolitionists, manhood suffragists, labor organizers and many others used the country's shortcomings to indict the political and social establishments and to vindicate their rights in a complex society of equals.

Thus, aspirational norms are not solely country-specific, as scholars like Mark Tushnet, Jack Balkin, and James Fleming suggest. Aspirational constitutionalism should not be wholly country-specific: American history is filled with constitutional provisions and interpretations that at times safeguarded slavery and justified racism, chauvinism, and bigotry. The aims of the Constitution should, instead, be grounded in fair governance whose ultimate purpose is to create mechanisms allowing persons to enjoy universal human rights on an equal basis.

Balkin writes compellingly about the power of constitutional persuasion but is too particularist in his attribution of its source. He asserts that the Constitution should operate based on the "shared memories, goals, aspirations, values, duties, and ambitions" of we the American people. He separates the people's aspirations from any notion of "higher law" or "basic law." His understanding of the redemptive role of constitutional aspiration is tethered to U.S. historical events and the evolution of U.S. thought.[21] In a similar vein, Tushnet recognizes that the Declaration of Independence's statements that "all men are created equal" works jointly with the Constitution to constitute a people committed "to the realization of universal human rights."[22] I share his vision, as I do Balkin's eloquent statement that "[t]he Declaration is our constitution,"[23] but I diverge from their perceptions that the aspirations that framework inspires are ones that should be understood only in the context of the US historical experience rather than as a universal and objective statement of human rights.

I come most closely to Fleming who believes that "aspiration principles" are not tied to specific historical practices, many of which are elitist, a view he shares with Balkin and Tushnet but then moves in a different direction. Aspirational principles, Fleming goes on to say, "are more akin to principles of natural law or natural rights than are our historical practices, including our statutory law, common law, and constitutional law."[24] Despite this statement, Fleming has elsewhere written that his "constitutional constructivism is not a theory of natural law or natural rights, and does not conceive the foregoing substantive liberties as prepolitical or given by a prior and independent order of moral values that is binding for all times and all places."[25] These two statements seem at odds with each other unless we are to understand that Fleming thinks the aspirational value of the Constitution is similar to but not identical with natural rights morality. Constitutional constructivism is Fleming's theory for constructing principles of justice to establish "fair terms of social cooperation on the basis of mutual respect and trust among free and equal citizens in a morally pluralistic constitutional democracy such as our own, rather than to discover principles of justice that are true for all times and places."[26] From this, I infer Fleming's point to be that the Constitution sets constitutional norms, as opposed to their being set in natural law abstractions. These norms could then be said to establish a positive duty on how government officials must carry out the powers of their office to achieve a just end.[27]

I agree that principles are set by the Constitution but think that their source is not the Constitution nor any abstract philosophical construct of natural law. Rather, fundamental rights are given entitlements of humanity, while basic rights are those granted by the state. The former are indeed pre-political, their equal protection is the ultimate function of government seeking to actualize the common good. Basic rights, on the other hand, and various legal entitlements are enacted to fulfill the fundamental principle of equality for the common good. Fundamental rights are entitlements against the state and fellow citizens, not grants of the state. Inalienable rights, whose protection the Declaration of Independence mandates, are not the constructs of civil society. To the contrary, the reason for creating a complex legal order is to guarantee equal treatment of individuals, regardless of status, race, ethnicity, sex, capabilities, talents, organizational affiliation, and other traits that are unrelated to core human dignities.

The right to pursue happiness within a society of equals is not granted through any political process but every person's entitlement by birth. At an even greater level of abstraction, a person's right to choose a path in life or to nurture a personality trait are intrinsic to his or her humanity, not politically created by constitutional, statutory, regulatory, nor common laws. Limits placed on the exercise of those rights are legitimate insofar as they are necessary for the general welfare, to protect social tranquility, and advance pluralism against discrimination, oppression, or other harms to autonomy and liberty. Interest in equal liberty is not the individual's alone but that of society, which relies on the polity to make relevant collective decisions that affect current and, often also, future generations.

The contours of these rights are not exhaustively detailed in the Constitution. The inevitability of interpretive evolution through judicial and political channels as well as unofficial discussions is presumed, but the cornerstone remains firmly set. Indeed, structural components of the Constitution—such as separation of the three branches of government, checks and balances, and regulatory administration—are also understood through the interpretation of text but require creative development commensurate with the people's interests. Representative governance enables ordinary citizens, organizations, and politicians to engage each other in debates about the uses of power necessary to meet their responsibilities to the people.

The deliberative process cannot supersede but is essential for clarifying constitutional ethos. The search for objective standards commensurate with the Declaration of Independence and the Constitution is an evolving process that enables each generation, each community within a generation, and each individual to evaluate achievements and shortcomings, to set priorities and goals, and to better order positive law to match national aspirations. Abstract generalities found in those documents are neither exhaustive statements on the protection of equal rights for the common good nor are they bereft of substantive content. Each generation must have a voice in the progress of representative democracy but not the latitude to arbitrarily breach the fundamental rights of citizens.

E. Modality and Procedure

Objective value is not only an important framework for evaluating culture but also for developing constitutional theory. The evaluative process requires unpacking text, breaking it down into explicit and implicit components, understanding its relation to society and history, drawing on values, applying federalist principles, and developing a consistent and predictable interpretation.

Legal scholar Philip Bobbitt elegantly describes six accepted grammatical modalities of US jurisprudence: the historical, textual; structural; doctrinal; ethical; and prudential. Bobbitt's approach is descriptive. He demurs from presenting any grand constitutional meanings.

Richard Fallon develops a slightly different list of formally accepted constitutional arguments that judges and lawyers use to construct the meaning of various clauses: Text, historical intent, theory, precedent, and value. Fallon and Bobbitt turn these brief theses into sophisticated explanations of judicial interpretation. Both reject an overarching constitutional value as a tool of interpretation. Fallon points out that difficult questions cannot be answered through determinate rules but should be understood through "rich, fluid, and evolving set of norms." Both of their kaleidoscopic perspectives correctly note that jurists and lawyers use a variety of models to expostulate law. They do not, however, provide adequate accounts of normative arguments that reject the status quo and radically refine or modestly reform existing legal order. What factors should lead a policy maker to adopt one mode over another or to combine several modes in his or her reasoning? Bobbitt provides no meta-mode against which the application of the others could be tested. In fact, his own definition of the ethical mode is quite narrow. He conceives "fundamental American constitutional ethos" to be "the idea of limited government." This formulation provides insufficient guidance about how to think through the legitimacy of large-scale government action, rather than inaction, such as the prohibition of slavery in the territories following the Compromise of 1820, establishment of the Social Security system, the Medicaid program, or the Affordable Care Act.

Many progressive thinkers have conceived of constitutional ethos in substantially broader terms than Bobbitt's definition. For instance, women suffragists and abolitionists expressed themselves in ways that could fit into one or another modality–often, for instance, relating narratives of the nation's founding or speaking of constitutional text supporting the institution of slavery–but, unlike Bobbitt, basing their calls for justice on an objective perspective of equal human status. Those activists did not conceive value statements to be flourishes of rhetorical rectitude. Neither was constitutional ethics a simple matter of limited government, but an assertion of rights and obligations to secure them. Their views of intrinsic human value, irrespective of race and sex, condemned arbitrary public policies. Many of their greatest advocates, like the abolitionist William Lloyd Garrison or the feminist Elizabeth Cady Stanton, relied on principles of representative governance found in the Declaration of Independence and Preamble to the Constitution, not simply legal rhetoric. Their arguments were also pragmatic because they pursued specific goals, not abstract reasoning, but at heart they acted out of moral compunction.

Even at a descriptive level, Bobbitt's list misses the possibility that ideology may itself be a legitimate modality of constitutional argument. Bobbitt's methodology leaves only decision makers' "consciences" based on the "prevailing moral sense of the day" to decide what mode to follow, and this can lead to the acceptance of contemporary prejudices.[28] Another scholar, taking this relativistic prescription to its logical conclusion, writes that the Bobbittian modalities are not based on "normative judgments about the 'rightness' or 'truth' of a particular theory," they are rather "descriptive of our actual practices."[29] That would be well and good if the system were perfect with no need for change, but systematic improvements require more conceptual grounding. Fallon is on target to say that in a pluralistic society consensus often cannot be found "to many urgent questions of substantive justice," but that only leads to greater urgency to find an objective standard of justice.

Missing from Bobbitt's and Fallon's lists is a fundamental rights framework of constitutionalism. The foundationalist perspective can be interpreted as grounded in human nature and beneficent public policy rather than the attitudes of judges or the leanings of legislatures. The United State' formative documents, the Declaration of Independence and Constitution, are clearly tied to natural rights tradition. Determining the validity of that position, however, does not rest on historical or empirical questions but analytic scrutiny, advancing context-specific rules and standards. In our times, international instruments have increasingly recognized the universality of human rights, even as narratives about God-given rights have faded.

Bobbitt's and Fallon's constitutional semantics offer a description of many of the arguments traditionally used in legal rhetoric, but they make no effort to ground them on some underlying rule(s) of legitimacy. Closely related is John Hart Ely's perspective that the Constitution is mainly about "political process" and "representative-reinforce[ment]," not "particular substantive values." Ely contends that the Constitution's emphasis on representative democracy indicates that judicial review should strengthen participatory-oriented policy. Contrary to my suggestion about the substantive value of rights statements in constitutional documents like the Declaration of Independence, Ely believes those statements are mere posturing meant to gain support for a cause rather than binding principle. That does not, however, explain how so many paragraphs of the Declaration later became prototypes for constitutional clauses; a point we covered in Section B of Chapter 3.

F. Individual and Society

Norms that are relevant for a society of equals must be both conducive to joint enterprise and for self-assertion. The people retain rights; provide authority to their leaders; and maintain the ability to influence deliberations, litigation, and regulatory policy. Individual input is a necessary component of representative societies. Political advocacy brings the community together, giving voice to its members. Inclusionary politics is more likely to achieve social harmony by balancing a plurality of voices into organized self-government. Constitutional interpretation must take into account both the individual and collective factors. This formulation has wide-ranging implications for public obligations, which I will discuss in the final chapter.

Without going into the detail here, it is important to point out that the establishment of public assistance programs should enable individuals to increase their productivity, not merely economic productivity but more general productivity as creative human beings. Community rights, therefore, are not meant to repress personal agency but to provide a safety net against unexpected barriers to the enjoyment of liberty. Sometimes the individual requires government to direct largess into the distribution of welfare benefits, which may even trump the contrary will of the majority.

‖ 6 ‖

Maxims and Government Power

The aspirational statements of the Declaration of Independence and Preamble to the Constitution establish a singular principle for the protection of individual rights while setting policies conducive to the general welfare. The normative public duty, or maxim as I call it, requires government institutions to safeguard individual liberty by fairly enacted and administered legislation. Fulfillment of this obligation requires a balance of private and public concerns.

Representative government is empowered to benefit ordinary people. Constitutional maxims provide normative standards for legitimate uses of authority. They establish criteria for officials to make legal judgments, providing the analytical framework on which elaborations of the entire legal system are constructed. Abstractions are necessary, but they leave a host of unanswered questions: What level of government—federal, state, local, or all of the above— should provide beneficial services (be it health, environment, farm relief, and any other program)? Is government's duty only negative or also positive? More specifically, is government required to create welfare programs or only guard against encroachments to legal entitlements? In what sense is "equality" to be understood: social, civil, or political? Does the Constitution protect only against public harms or does it also give government authority to pass laws against some or all private harms? What are fundamental rights and who is to identify them? My aim is to develop the baseline criteria that can direct constitutional interpretation. Discovering answers to these question is part of an ongoing process that relies on the people's input through official and unofficial channels of deliberation. All policy is subject to debate and reconsideration. An underprivileged group of the population need not put up with inadequate social services programs but can lobby for change. An inhumane criminal justice system is likewise subject to protest. And bankruptcy procedures that poorly provide debtor relief should be revamped. Though these examples are very divergent, discourse is a meta-right for achieving various ends. Lurking even further in the structural background of representative democracy is the notion of individual right and public good.

Differences of opinion on how to translate maxims into practical actions are only to be expected in a pluralistic society where freedom of thought is respected. Diverse perspectives are indeed crucial to the political process for arriving at sound policies. Deliberation on key matters must, therefore, remain open to ordinary people, community leaders, social activists, and, indeed, members of all sectors of the polity. While each person must be afforded the opportunity to express a unique point of view, there is no way to avoid policies with which some members of the public will disagree. Fairness in the deliberative process is, nevertheless, insufficient if the resulting law is oppressive or authoritarian. Both the process of developing law and the substantive result can be subjected to scrutiny.

Constitutional structure must therefore conduce both to establishing stable institutions and preserving personal autonomy. The Constitution is the foundational basis for law, but its text is subject to a general maxim about the intrinsic worth of people and government's obligations. That maxim must set a unified national purpose. This umbrella statement sets the baseline for policy justifications, government structures, and individual rights.

A. Maxims of Public Trust

Objective reasoning refers to the process of dispassionate rational deliberation about factual inputs through a theoretical matrix, directly or inferentially connected to constitutional text, that produce fair and beneficial results. There might be various possible solutions to the same policy question, but to be legitimate they must be the product of deliberative scrutiny, contextually fair, and likely to produce public goods. A maxim is subjective if it is person-specific and objective when it sets a duty of conduct for all rational beings in the same and like circumstances.

The maxim of constitutional law, as it is set out in general terms by the Declaration of Independence and Preamble to the Constitution, is not a statement of personal duty to other autonomous beings, which is the subject of ethics. It is, rather, a binding statement of the legitimate functions of government, answerable to the will of constituents, and its duty to enact and execute laws for the public good. Ethical obligation is rooted in each rational being's autonomy, while the constitutional obligation is a binding norm of governmental authority. The latter sets secular norms for elected and appointed officials, who are entrusted to fulfill duties as citizens exercising the public trust. Maxims of governmental actions are binding irrespective of any particular judge's, legislator's, or administrator's subjective preferences.

While a maxim sets objective government obligations, it operates in the context of various inputs—legal, factual, political, social, philosophical, and so on.

The Constitution fills in details about the operation of representative democracy. But the text of that document is also not detailed enough for nuanced resolution of disputes. From the higher orders of abstraction, we come to statutory details, judicial rulings, executive actions, and administrative regulations. But there is also a personal touch in every public decision. While subjective insights add to the richness of public thought, the Constitution and its objective principles limit decision makers and subject them to set higher public moral standards.

At each interpretive stage, whether at the public policy or personal advocacy levels, the public actor must abide by both general and specific terms of authority. Representative democracy puts many decisions about how to comport law to constitutional maxim in the hands of elected or, in the case of federal judges and administrative regulators, appointed officials. Persons holding public office must abide by the Constitution, but they cannot be expected to wholly discard their personal sensibilities when reasoning about official matters. Indeed, as long as their judgments are based on the merits of policy, personal depth contributes to the diversity of pluralistic decision making. Independent judgement is necessary at all stages of enactment and enforcement, in part, because no law can be wholly comprehensive. Judges, legislators, executives, and regulators must fill in the blanks with their own competence but remain bound by precedents, historical practices, and normative duties.

Abuses are inevitable in a system that must rely on human reasoning. Several mechanisms are therefore built in to minimize risks of abuse against the public. Separation between the branches of government, for instance, sets limits on political actions. Federalism likewise allocates different powers between federal and state governments to prevent autocratic rule. Judicial review allows ordinary citizens to also raise issues about the promulgation or administration of law. Discretion, however, is not license to abuse power.

Even when dealing with day-to-day operations of governance—say filing documents, fixing downed electrical wires, or organizing court records—general principles of constitutional governance remain binding, albeit they almost always linger in the background of the problem at hand. No level of government—from national to county or water reclamation agency levels—can justify arbitrary intrusions into liberty, equality, or fairness. Whether conducting foreign policy or purchasing paperclips, public servants must stay true to the public by, for instance, being frugal with government finances and efficient in their work. In his writings, James Madison combines the dual function of government to benefit the public and to safeguard individual entitlements. A national government in accord with the "devotion to true liberty, and to the constitution," he writes, should maintain "inviolably the maxims of public faith, the security of persons and property, and encourage, in every authorised mode, that general diffusion of knowledge which guarantees to public liberty its permanency, and to those who possess the blessing, the true enjoyment of it."[1] General principle describes the limits of authority and sets mandatory ideals for its beneficial exercise.

B. Living Up to Ideals

Just as the Constitution is a barrier against any contrary statutes and government actions, a higher standard of justice, as it is stated in the Declaration and Preamble, must be used to evaluate the Constitution. Hence, the immediate abolitionist William Lloyd Garrison indicted the Constitution as a "covenant with death and an agreement with hell."[2] The original Constitution's protection of slaveholders' property interests (the Three-Fifths Clause, Importation Clause, Fugitive Clause, and others),[3] undermined the very foundation of republican democracy, because it denied political representation to an entire segment of the population. Garrison contrasted the Constitution's protections of slavery with the assertion of inalienable rights found in the Declaration of Independence, which are "conferred by the Creator, and which they possessed in common on equal terms with all men."[4]

Until the Reconstruction Amendments were ratified after the Civil War, the Constitution perpetuated the injustice of slavery. Although the word slavery was nowhere used in the Constitution, Congress used its authority to pass laws protecting the institution. These included the Fugitive Slave Laws of 1793 and 1850, which were enacted pursuant to the Fugitive Clause of Article IV. Several constitutional clauses were at odds with the founding commitment of the Declaration of Independence to human equality and the Preambular non-racial, inclusive statement about the general welfare. As Frederick Douglass convincingly put it:

> Liberty and Slavery—opposite as Heaven and Hell—are both in the Constitution. . . . If we adopt the Preamble, with liberty and justice, we must repudiate the enacting clauses, with kidnapping and slaveholding.[5]

The lasting effect and influence of the Constitution, which the antislavery 13th Amendment and other changes to the original document helped to extricate from the original muck, are based not only on written provisions but also on the nation's aspirational grounding in humanistic legal mores. Its principles were not born of whole-cloth but a deliberate decision to shed the oppressiveness of autocracy in favor of pluralistic sovereignty.

The United States has been able to maintain much of its ancient Constitution while shedding many of its long-accepted customs of chauvinism, racism, xenophobia, and religious bigotry. Formal change to the document by way of amendments has only been made 27 times in almost two and a half centuries. Far more typically, changes to the judicial and cultural understandings have been the outgrowths of evolving attitudes about inequalities incompatible with the nation's core commitment to human rights and common welfare. The document has been reinterpreted to render provisions like the Jury, Spending, Equal Protection, Privileges or Immunities, Due Process, and Guarantee Clauses more true to the ideals of representative democracy. During the Civil Rights Era of the 1950s and 1960s, new layers of principled construction were added through legislative and judicial initiatives.

Neutral constitutional clauses require normative thinking to apply them contextually to specific circumstances. The tenets of sound policy are not, however, sufficient. While abstract analysis is necessary for constructing a vision of fair governance, normative statements remain unfulfilled generalities without the will to pass laws and to carry them into effect. General statements of negative and positive rights are made real through civil rights laws—such as, the Civil Rights Act of 1964, the Voting Rights Act of 1965, or the Americans with Disabilities Act of 1990—and ones for the development of infrastructure—such as, the Clean Water Act, the Federal Highway Act, and the National Park Service Act.

Statutes must conform and elaborate on clauses of the Constitution—such as the Tax and Spend or Habeas Corpus Clauses. They also detail the duties of government—such as Federal Accountability Act, the Administrative Procedure Act, or the Office of Personnel Management Act. The underlying purpose of representative democracy, which is the exercise of self-government in a community of equals, must inform policy decisions and statutory drafting.

United States constitutional discourse has unfortunately grown almost mute about the extant features of the Constitution that remain tied to the vestiges of human exploitation. Perhaps the most obvious of these is a clause of the 13th Amendment that excludes prison slave labor from the general prohibition against slavery and involuntary servitude. This vestige of a bygone era can also be said to be an agreement with hell, to borrow Garrison's phrase, because it empowers judges and prison officials to force convicts to perform uncompensated labor. The all-too-common judicial and academic oversight of principles stemming from the Declaration of Independence and Preamble to the Constitution has led to the broadly accepted premise that the text of the Constitution is only enforceable from Article I to its conclusion, while ignoring the meta-structural mandates of those two statements of overarching national purpose. The foundational value of individual rights for the common good should inform both historical and contemporary inquiries into constitutional text and doctrine.

C. Principles and Public Opinion

Stable principles provide predictability and accountability. All three branches must demonstrate commitment to central tenets of nationhood found in the Declaration and Preamble. This mandate is as applicable to substantive components of the Constitution, such as the prohibition against cruel and unusual punishment, as it is for structural ones, such as the limit on Congress's authority to suspend habeas corpus "unless when in cases of Rebellion or Invasion the public safety may require it." Institutional stability positively impacts social tranquility. Public polling demonstrates that support for government is predicated on its ability to produce positive goods and evince consistent and neutral enforcement of fair statutes.[6] Policy must be consistent with tenets of public good and personal wellness. Legislation consistent with constitutional mores is more readily recognized by the public as a legitimate exercise of authority.

Some liberal democracies, such as Great Britain and Israel, have opted for unwritten constitutions. Most countries, however, have found that written constitutions add clarity to the structure and obligations of their legal systems, making them more accountable and transparent to the will of the people. Even with a unified purpose of governance, a system requires multiple statutes and regulations to carry out its stated purpose. The bases of these statutes should be both principled and popularly supported. Being civic beings, with their own interests and social personas, people are likely to evaluate the Constitution and lesser laws on the basis of personal needs and general values about state operations. Parts of the Constitution are formulated in general terms to grant officials interpretational and experimental latitude to develop policies while simultaneously setting normative parameters that tether decision makers to norms of public conduct. The people voice their views about existing order and future direction by voting, participating in popular governance, and litigating to vindicate legal entitlements. No matter how much popular support a measure enjoys, constitutional legitimacy nevertheless depends on its compatibility with the objective standard of the civil state. The people can rely on that standard to demand public accountability that is independent of changing political rhetoric. The popular will is therefore intrinsic to government. Citizens infuse law with varying personal perceptions and priorities, but they too are limited in achieving desired ends by principles of human equality and impartial administration of justice. Constitutional maxim provides stability against the contingencies of power and prejudice.

Ordinary people are not trained in the use, memorization, and development of legal vocabulary. They are unlikely to memorize specific passages of the Constitution, much less statutes and administrative regulations. They are more likely to remember general ideological concepts of liberty, equality, and federalism and then to relate those to specific state actions affecting their lives. The public must remain vigilant against government attempts to distort the Constitution by claims that are illogical when considered in light of the structure of fair and equal democracy. To give just one example of this form of distortion, segregationists understood equality to only apply to whites rather than universally to all races. The substantive values of the Declaration's and Preamble's abstract principles must therefore inform the public's intellectual and emotive internalization of a unified constitutional maxim, offering liberty and justice for all. Objective legal mandates empower citizens to exercise self-governance by holding officials accountable—typically through elections, lobbying, political discourse, and litigation—to uphold constitutional norms of public conduct.

The legitimization of constitutional maxim is not a purely theoretical exercise but requires consistency in the administration of impartial laws (on paper and in practice). The people's ability to organize and decide elections is essential for political development and accountability. Change sometimes comes about through constitutional amendment and much more often by the passage of laws or the rendering of judicial decisions. Political self-determination, a bedrock of American politics, is given more specificity in the voter protections of the 15th, 19th, and 26th Amendments. Those portions of the Constitution advance a more ancient and rudimentary ideal of representative government, which grants Congress the necessary and proper power to carry out its mandates. The judiciary is entrusted to check legislative exercise of authority. The broad principle of the Constitution, with its mandate of running a polity committed to representative democracy, also translates to the states. Among the principles that states cannot outright reject nor subtly violate are those establishing voter equality.[7]

D. Interpreting Principles

An authoritative mechanism for resolving legal disputes provides finality and helps to prevent constitutional crises. Officials often hold divergent views about how principles apply to substantive and procedural disputes. In the United States and most democracies around the world, there is a general consensus that the judiciary must be empowered to review the constitutionality of actions undertaken by other branches of government. The two most common domestic systems either recognize a common law court's ability to review constitutional matters or empower a specialized constitutional court to render those decisions. The United States has opted for the former. A paradox for those democracies where legislators lack the authority to override a highest court's interpretations of the constitutions is that unelected judges are left to resolve some of the knottiest social problems.

Once a final judgment has been rendered, as long as it does not arise from some exclusively political question, the legal system grants the Supreme Court's definition as much deference as it would to the text of the Constitution. This, in effect, allows the Court to create rules that have the force of constitutional amendments, which neither Congress, the President, nor states can violate without running afoul of a broadly defined "Constitution." No higher government entity is then left to determine whether the Supreme Court acted outside the scope of its powers. In the United States, if the president disagrees with a statute, he can veto it. If Congress remains at odds with the president, it can override the veto by a two-thirds majority. But the only way to strike the high court's pronouncement on the Constitution is to ratify a new amendment, which in the United States is exceedingly difficult. And the litigation strategy, which seeks to overturn previous holdings, is tremendously slow given the backlog of cases. What's more, efforts of getting a case from trial court, through circuit courts, and onto the Supreme Court, much less to have the justices rule against a previous precedent, rarely succeed.

Judicially created doctrines have elaborated the meanings of both principles and specific texts. The doctrine of *stare decisis*, whereby precedent becomes governing authority for future decision making, including legislative and executive policies, implants systemic meaning to clauses and ideals that on their face are amenable to a variety of interpretations. Precedents establish analytical tools— such as balancing tests and levels of scrutiny—for constitutional construction. Some structural difficulty arises, however, when unelected justices become supreme arbiters of constitutional meaning in a representative system of government. Under that hierarchical regimen, the people can never override judicial interpretations through the ordinary political channels.

The US Supreme Court has opined that it is the final arbiter of the Constitution. One of its clearest statements on the matter appears in a case mandating that the City of Little Rock, Arkansas, abide by the Court's earlier holding that segregation violates the Equal Protection Clause. State and city officials had tried to thwart desegregation efforts, but the Court categorically asserted that "the federal judiciary is supreme in the exposition of the law of the Constitution."[8] The Court has also placed limits on Congress to make authoritative pronouncements about the meaning of the Constitution. In a significant 21st century holding, the Supreme Court denied Congress's ability to define substantive rights under the 14th Amendment.[9] The majority reasoned that only the judiciary has the authority to identify constitutional rights while Congress's power is solely remedial. This absolutist form of judicial supremacism has since severely hampered legislators' initiatives. The Court has thereby weakened popular sovereignty. In an earlier case, the Court similarly restrained the president from defining the limits of his power, even when exercising the duties of Commander in Chief of the armed forces.[10]

Some scholars—most notably Mark Tushnet and Jeremy Waldron—have advanced significant counter arguments to the Court's supremacist approach. It certainly shuts the people's representatives out of the process of identifying how to apply core principles to issues ranging from school safety to gender-motivated violence. It leaves unelected judges to be the only legitimate elaborators of constitutional principles, capable of enjoining any legislative or executive efforts to establish policies. This diminishes the input available on how to apply ancient ideals to contemporary situations, leaving analysis to the views of a few judges usually picked from elite backgrounds in terms of education, wealth, and political connections. Ordinary citizens would be better empowered to exercise their sovereign right of governance if they could engage with their elected representatives in effective deliberations about the contemporary meaning of the Constitution. The discourse would need to consider principle, history, aspiration, and foundational commitments. And nothing in the Constitution, but only judicial opinion and tradition, prevents legislative overrides of Supreme Court holdings, such as *Dred Scott* and *Plessy*, that violate the maxim of equal fairness for the common good.

This is not to say that the judiciary should have no say in constitutional interpretation, but that lawmakers should represent the people in their evolving understanding of how the bedrock maxim of the Constitution applies to manifold public challenges. The very function of representative democracy is to express the people's will in the form of enforceable laws. Each person's ability to have a meaningful say in the development of social institution is predicated on having an effective voice in formulating statutes, regulations, and advancing the aspirational features of the Constitution. Supermajority legislative process—using the two-thirds supermajority formula I suggested in Chapter 5—allows for more oversight, enabling voters to choose new representatives while federal judges enjoy lifetime appointments. Judicial independence is a positive aspect of that system, with judges less likely to engage in political rancor than might elected officials, but judges are people who, like everyone else, hold strong political views that influence decision making.

Public sovereignty has a flipside: the Court often champions human rights to rectify legislative or executive overreaching. Judicial opinions have often demonstrated a clear commitment to unwritten principles about fundamental interests and the limits of government powers. Whether or not the judiciary should be the sole interpreter of constitutional maxim, principle clearly plays a role in a variety of rulings. Many resolutions of problems are directly linked to ethical issues. For instance, a substantive definition of liberty

is unavoidable in understanding the validity of *Lawrence v. Texas*, which recognized same-sex couples' right to intimate privacy, and *Bowers v. Hardwick*,
which held that there was no such constitutional right and maligned gays and
lesbians. How we perceive the strengthening of homosexuals' right to live without the indignity of state intrusion or an official statement of disgust about their
conduct, draws from a norm of human equality. When liberty is conceived as
an inalienable attribute that everyone enjoys in a pluralistic society, criminally
punishing adults for engaging in intimate, private conduct violates core constitutional commitment to the individual pursuit of happiness in a society of
equals. This notion is not purely intuitive, but deduced from the country's
core commitments, written into its constitutional statement. In the United
States, that may be found in the Unalienable Rights Clause of the Declaration
of Independence, the Unenumerated Rights Clause of the Ninth Amendment,
and the General Welfare Clause of the Preamble. None of those three textual
sources explicitly mentions intimate privacy, so the development of the specifics is an evolving matter left to collective wisdom. According to the human
rights statements of those three constitutional provisions, public morality must
tolerate self-exploration. Hence even if intolerance is supported by a majority
of the population, it remains outside the norm of constitutionalism.

The same principled reasoning explains why the Supreme Court correctly
read the Equal Protection Clause in *Brown v. Board of Education* but was wrong
in *Plessy v. Ferguson* to hold that the Clause countenanced segregation on public
carriers like railroads. Given the growth of segregation that burgeoned after the
Plessy Court justified states' codification of exclusionary customs, strong doubt
may be cast on the notion that the Court is the best source for protecting human
rights. It was the Supreme Court, even before *Plessy*, in a different decision
known as the *Civil Rights Cases*, that overturned Congress's effort to desegregate
the entire country through the Civil Rights Act of 1875. One might argue that
these opinions should be read as the products of their times, and that the Court
decided each one according to the sensibilities of its era. But this take on judicial
review is highly problematic. Temporal relativism rationalizes injustices, if only
for a time, and attempts to absolve those leaders who pursued discriminatory
policies. I think, rather, that *Plessy* and the *Civil Rights Cases* were wrong as soon
as they were issued. The wrong done by segregation was not the product of some
affirmative creation of later law. That form of positivism would leave rights at the
behest of popular mores, not all of which are benevolent nor publically oriented.

Nor should *Plessy*, the *Civil Rights Cases*, nor *Bowers* be justified as legitimate
readings of ambiguous constitutional texts. Unlike some legal theorists, I do not
think that, at least in difficult cases, interpretation of text can nor should be done
separately of constructing its meaning.[11] Defining words and phrases without
context is meaningless. Segregation and anti-gay laws were an affront to the basic

constitutional maxim of the Declaration of Independence and Preamble to the Constitution from the country's beginnings and remained so irrespective of the justices' or public's readiness to countenance official policies of inequality in cases like *Plessy* and *Bowers*. When the Equal Protection Clause is read according to the underlying assumption jointly stated in the Declaration and the Preamble that all persons share a human dignity and are, therefore, equally entitled to participate in the general welfare. It is clear from this premise that state actions based on prejudices and stereotypes are constitutional wrongs irrespective of public opinions, semantic ambiguities of texts, or the Supreme Court's political fancies.

Despite the horribly injurious mistakes of these cases, judicial precedents more typically provide avenues for relief from injustices. Social improvements through judicial action are, however, somewhat unpredictable. Rulings that change the perception of constitutional culture typically are rendered only by the Supreme Court. There are those rare lower court judges—like Richard Posner, Frank Easterbrook, Henry Friendly, or Learned Hand—who have written similarly transformative decisions, but precedential values are jurisdictionally and geographically limited, unless later adopted into statutes or Supreme Court holdings.

The next chapter seeks to define with greater specificity the higher maxim that functions as the overarching, aspirational mandate for the people to check the actions of all three branches of government.

|| 7 ||

Maxim of Constitutional
Governance

Constitutional law consists of textual and aspirational components. As we have seen, the Declaration of Independence and the Constitution present a framework for unified national sovereignty. Jointly they establish a normative foundation and structural basis for exercising power, restraining the government and establishing a mandate for social betterment. Legitimate uses of authority must balance collective interests of the polity against those of equal individuals empowered to pursue their own interests. That synthetic model of policy making is not dependent on positive law. When actual laws violate the maxim of constitutional governance, the ideal of creating a socially conscious republic of equals nevertheless remains binding and aspirational on all facets of government.

Restraints on liberty within a community of equals must not be used to suppress individuality but to better the lot of the whole. That is not to say that all laws are or should be national in their scope or effect. To the contrary, many legal solutions on matters such as school districting or street cleaning are better handled at local levels. Ordinary people are likely to have greater access to local politicians, who work on policies with substantial effects on day-to-day community life. Lawmakers must remain in touch and address the needs of relevant communities, keeping in mind that they are not elected to amorphous conglomerations but composites of individuals.

The Declaration and Constitution establish a national maxim for policy making that sets criteria for lawmaking at federal, state, local, municipal, and county levels. The central norm of representative democracy prohibits arbitrary uses of power in violation of inalienable human dignity. This norm is general enough to allow for creative initiatives, while anchoring the country to withstand the winds of popular opinion or charismatic personalities. While principle establishes a consistent, fundamental standard for rational social advancement, the ideal is stated broadly enough to inspire activists and politicians.

Constitutional theory not only gives citizens notice of the presumptive purpose of government, but also the limits of its power. My premise is that general conformity with the Constitution's schema has a greater tendency to achieve results beneficial to the community. Arbitrary regulations are incompatible with the obligation of government to treat individuals equally. Maxim constitutionalism regards each person as one when evaluating the benefits of policies, and presumes that the cumulative happiness of each is greater than discriminatory approaches that would augment the benefits of one group to the detriment of another. Thus, even the benefit of a majority does not justify the disempowerment of a minority. Specific clauses of the Constitution and its overall structure set criteria for rebutting claims—be they racist, sexist, or otherwise exclusionary— contrary to national aspirations.

A constitutional maxim must guide the interpretation of text and explain how various clauses fit into the structure of governance. But it must also have practical significance, such that ordinary people benefit from its normative values. In this chapter, I elaborate the maxim of constitutional government to which I have made reference throughout the book. My premise is that:

Government must protect equal individual rights for the common good.

The explanatory value of such a principle is based on the criterion it sets for legitimate uses of power. Overarching aims are not, however, identical with ordinary legal rules. Objective principles are first-order generalities with the constitutional maxim as the cornerstone of the entire system. Collective wisdom, which draws from the deliberative process of democratic self-governance, focuses and clarifies the meaning of principles. Progress is often not linear, with many unsound steps making up a nation's unsteady progress, but the foundation remains firm, untainted by sexism, racism, xenophobia, bigotry, and all of the other injustices incommensurate with the central purpose of liberal equality for the common good. General welfare is defined not by the greatest good for the greatest number, as act utilitarians would frame it, but by the fair administration of laws and regulations that are beneficial for a community of equals to pursue personal visions of happiness. Collective reasoning should be channeled through representative institutions, facilitating dialogue between citizens and office holders. The process relies on the ideal of fair play and social justice to craft laws and institutions conducive to self-determination and social welfare among equals. Abstract principles create a broadly stated obligation of governance, not a recitation of minutia necessary to resolve some focused issue of policy. A universal maxim of constitutional governance provides the background authority for consistent, coherent, predictable, and procedurally even-handed governance.

Normative constitutional statements establish legal commitments to justice, equality, legal restraint, and impartiality. Those norms should be grounded in the premise that dignity is a universal human attribute,* which formal laws codify into government duties. These become enforceable through the promulgation of laws addressing social issues. The instantiation of maxim into law is as relevant to structural portions of the Constitution, such as those establishing separation of powers between the branches of government, as it is for substantive ones, such as the Bill of Rights. The structure of government is not only meant to be efficient but especially to guarantee rights to people of diverse backgrounds and interests and conduce to their welfare.

A. Interpretive Construction

The previous chapter described the need for general principles to ground constitutional democracy. The manifold exercises of public functions—from mail delivery to the administration of public welfare—must adhere to the abstract purpose of constitutional government: the protection of equal rights for the common good. Government agencies create and enforce laws, while social groups and individuals informally help in their formation. Clauses of the Constitution are for the most part general, requiring official and unofficial explication. The specific ones—such as those dealing with the minimum age requirements for presidents, senators, and representatives—are few. Most clauses—such as the Necessary and Proper, Commander in Chief, and the Judicial Power Clauses— require much interpretation. Abstractions create possibilities and uncertainties. Without acknowledged ideals, power is easily abused. Norms carrying the weight of constitutional authority are necessary to set limits and obligations on persons holding political and judicial offices.

Those norms should be based on more than human inclinations, which are too capricious to direct governance. Desires are malleable in time and space, and each person will have a different perspective on what constitutes right behavior. In disputed cases, some commonly recognized instrument of authority and norm is necessary for reaching agreement or allowing for third-party resolution. On the other hand, exclusively relying on legal texts often involves the parsing of abstract wording, which can lead to differing, often contradictory, interpretations.

Wording of the Constitution should be understood contextually. Most of its provisions are meant to create broad principles and powers of government. The

---

* I do not mean to imply that dignity is an exclusively human attribute, but in this book will not parse a theory of environmental rights and the law.

text sets general mandates, but all public officials must apply its significance to unique sets of domestic and international circumstances. Judges are additionally empowered to safeguard the system from legislative or executive misinterpretations. In reality, though, judges are also prone to error and sometimes act out of political leaning rather than from principle. Moreover, their authority is limited by various rules about the proper standing of parties to sue and the ripeness of cases and controversies. Thus, the people retain the power to check the judiciary and to demand that it abides by core values. The general idea is that like any other branch of government, the people retain their sovereign authority over every part of the government, even the judiciary. Court interpretations that run counter to the Constitution, I believe, should be subject to supermajority overrides by the people's representatives in Congress. While that is not the current rule, which gives judges the final say on constitutional interpretations, the amendment process allows citizens to overturn Supreme Court holdings. This makes for a complicated, much politicized process, with different state factions trying to achieve separate agendas, which would be more efficiently achieved through supermajorities in Congress.

Comprehension of the wording and construction of the Constitution's meaning are interwoven into the resolution of real disputes. Understanding the precise definitions of a word or phrase, such as "liberty" or "due process," which are found in the Fifth and 14th Amendments, does not resolve specific conflicts. Neither do solely empirical assessments of private or public disputes provide decision makers with sure footing. Rather than trying to semantically parse all the possible meanings of words such as "free" and "speech" or the phrase "free speech," it is more meaningful to ask what ideals of personhood and society they are meant to protect. A steadfast principle must be used to test linguistic understandings and their relevance to specific disputes. The same is true of any other abstractly worded portion of the Constitution, such as the Search and Seizure Clause and its meaning to specific police frisks or property impoundments. Defining the clause's words alone does not provide police with enough guidance about whether a warrant is needed before undertaking modern monitoring techniques, such as the thermal testing of a house's interior to determine whether heat lamps are being used to grow marijuana.[1]

In a series of articles, Lawrence Solum points out the distinction between interpretation and construction of constitutional texts.[2] His account is quite helpful for understanding how normative methods elucidate ambiguous linguistic phrasing. However, he does not recognize any central premise on which constitutional understanding should be based; rather, he believes construction to be the province of judges who can choose various methodologies of normativity (such as the principle of deference to the legislature or H.L.A. Hart's rule of construction discussed in Chapter 5) for constitutional construction.[3] However, it strikes me that without a determinative principle, one premised on fairness and likely to achieve the common good, relying too strongly on judges or the political branches risks mistaking subjective, political leanings for constitutional norms.

Solum defines "construction" as: "[T]he activity that determines the content of constitutional doctrine and the legal effect of the constitutional text." "Interpretation" he defines as: "[T]he activity that discerns the communicative content (linguistic meaning) of the constitutional text."[4] This presumes that where the text is clear, it has some intrinsic meaning that can be arrived at simply by looking at the wording of a passage. This dichotomy strikes me as true of some constitutional clauses—such as those dealing with minimum ages for presidents, representatives, and senators—but the vast majority of constitutional controversies are likely to fall under the construction rubric. Matters on gay marriage, labor organization in the public sector, abortion, the use of force during interrogations, the definition of "religion," poor relief, religious symbols on public property, and so forth are decided by analyzing the text, history, and structure of a specific clause and the Constitution more generally. Thus judges consistently construct meaning, but the determinative factor should not be precedent, methodology, nor some philosophical notion of virtue but whether prior cases create laws in keeping with the country's commitment to social and individual well-being.

Resolution of heated debates about constitutional meaning and application need not be exclusively left in the hands of unelected judges. Construction is the province of all three branches of government.[5] Jack Balkin has likewise pointed out that other public institutions along with the judiciary should be involved in construction.[6] The deliberative loop between people and government creates a living constitutional interpretation predicated on principles, but also informed by various historical, sociological, and other information allowing for analogical thinking capable of extending reasoning to new cases. Understanding the Constitution in the context of contemporary issues requires filtering policies and specific legal disputes through the principled maxim that takes into account any relevant rights of parties involved in disputes and social purposes of legal actions. This method of construction places textual and analytical demands on all three branches of government to fulfill the mission statements of the Declaration of Independence and the Preamble to the Constitution. The process is not static but dynamic, building on legal culture through a consciousness of past legal error and achievements as well as aspirations for the future. A balance must be struck between constitutional rights and community interests. It is a process that does not yield predetermined answers, is prone to error, and is correctable through elections, lobbying, litigating, and debates.

The Constitution's abstract wording is bundled with its practical relevance to ordinary people. Substantive values are critical to the workings of government, but so too are its administrative practices. Procedural regularity and regulatory rules are modes of legal justice. This is true, for instance, of the constitutional value of the "beyond a reasonable doubt" burden of proof in criminal trial, which Supreme Court precedent links to the Due Process Clause.[7] The phrase "Due Process" raises a litany of concerns for criminal justice: Who should determine what legal process will suffice, legislators or courts? What amount of state resources should go into proving a charge? How soon after an arrest must the accused be put on trial? How shall a hearing be conducted to provide the accused with the opportunity to rebut evidence of culpability? What is the function of punishment (as opposed to deterrence) in diminishing public dangers? The text of the 14th Amendment provides no answers. It must rather be understood through a normative prism, reflecting the human and social costs of evidentiary rules, procedural rules, and penalties. At its most fundamental level, society's obligation is to provide safeguards against the arbitrary deprivation of liberty while advancing public security. This duality reflects the premise that governments, at the state and federal levels, must provide the defendant with procedures for a fair hearing while also establishing mechanisms for punishing the harms of extreme, anti-social conduct: This constitutes a synthesis of deontological and consequentialist reasoning.

Policy makers interpreting text to address real world problems must be conscious of how their choices are likely to affect individuals and communities. Cognizance of these two constitutional concerns requires officials to demonstrate flexibility in the construction of constitutional meaning. For instance, states can use a variety of regulations that for fiscal reasons benefit only some businesses, such as those in defense or automotive industries. Tax revenues raised thereby can go into public programs that must operate according to the norm of universal human dignity. However, no fiscal utility justifies unequal treatment because of race, color, or national origin. These and other prejudicial motives are beyond the pale of the Declaration's Unalieable Rights and the Preamble's General Welfare Clauses. Each policy must reflect situational and empirical factors, but certain values are so core to the functioning of representative democracy that they cannot be set aside for pragmatic reasons. Norms inform the resolution of conflicts, and empower the people to hold accountable those in power.

B. Collective Cooperation

The foundational constitutional maxim creates a dual obligation to exercise individual and collective justice. It empowers representative institutions to pass, enforce, and adjudicate general laws for the needs of a pluralistic culture. It establishes an analytical anchor for decision makers and empowers the people, separately and as members of various social groups, to hold officials accountable for public actions. Lesser principles of governance establish duties and limits on the uses of authority and also render institutions and their administrators accountable, not only to abide by the letter of the law but also its underlying value. Thus, while the Equal Protection Clause is so neutral that in 1896 the Supreme Court held it gave states the prerogative to segregate public transportation,[8] the commitment to equal inalienable rights in the Declaration and common welfare in the Preamble later led the justices to reverse that holding and declare Jim Crow to be an injustice.[9] In the intervening years, advocacy groups like the National Association for the Advancement of Colored People, the Urban League, and the American Jewish Congress successfully challenged racist policies, condemning the failure to abide by collective expectations established by the nation's founding documents.

Construction of the maxim of constitutional accountability should not be predicated on who holds the reins of leadership. Of course, the personal views of presidents, congressional representatives, and judges factor into prioritizing specific policies. But as an independent standard for government legitimacy, the constitutional maxim of protecting individual rights for the common good sets a limit on the uses of power. The Constitution provides the point of convergence for people with different subjective goals. High order of normative generalization is needed to anchor pluralistic society to a collective aspiration.

Statutory, judicial, and regulatory laws create enforceable means of resolution, superseding local customs but not constitutional norms. The function of most federal and state statutes and regulations is to establish instruments for collective problem solving. Creating socially beneficial policies for the enjoyment of individual, autonomous rights necessarily entails a balancing of private and public interests.

An overarching constitutional norm sets the standard by which ordinary laws must be judged. In the recent past, the federal government began addressing the problems many individuals faced paying high-cost premiums for health insurance or having no access to coverage. Congress passed the 2010 Affordable Care Act (ACA) to help make available coverage for those for whom it had been practically unattainable. The statute demonstrates a large-scale national consensus that federal regulation was needed to provide broader access to medical services and treatments. The statute signaled the negative and positive aspects of constitutional power. The commitment to private and public rights means that the state is obligated to refrain from acting in ways that harm people's health, but it is also under an affirmative obligation to create a state-administered regulatory system to advance the wellness of the public.

The ACA generally attempted to address the needs of individuals, but it was also designed to deal with big picture social problems. Its aims were far more ambitious than any state could have dealt with on its own. The ACA, for instance, mandates that insurance plans cover preventative healthcare services to decrease disease treatment costs and prohibits insurance companies from denying coverage or charging higher premiums for persons with preexisting conditions.[10] The statute requires all individuals, except those for whom the cost of coverage would exceed eight percent of the household income, to obtain health insurance or pay a tax for their non-participation.[11] It is an example of a regulation meant to fulfill the Preamble's mandate for government to advance the general welfare. Whether justified on the basis of Congress's authority over taxation, spending, or interstate commerce, matters that would be too great an aside to resolve here, lawmakers passed the ACA to address a matter of private and public urgency. Justice Ruth Bader Ginsburg pointed out in a concurrence that "Congress' intervention was needed to overcome th[e] collective-action impasse" in rising health insurance and emergency room costs that "individual States are unlikely to take the initiative in addressing."[12]

Another law addressing a collective problem, widespread racism, is the Civil Rights Act of 1964. It included provisions prohibiting segregation in public service businesses, such as hotels and restaurants[13] and conditioned school receipt of federal funding on compliance with anti-discrimination obligations.[14] The statute was part of a national effort to combat widespread inequities. Decades of addressing the segregation on state-by-state and city-by-city levels left a patchwork of inequalities, with each locality choosing its level of racial tolerance. The Civil Rights Act was a national law for putting an end to racial exclusion and separation.

Collective actions, whether undertaken at the federal or state levels, empower individuals to expand the reach of their political voice. Human will has singular and joint aspects. Each of us has unique interests, proclivities, and desires. Those do not dissipate even when we modify behaviors to meet sensibilities and be conscious of sensitivities while in the company of others. Considerations that lead an individual to behave differently in various circumstances—outdoors, at work, at home, and so forth—do not compromise autonomy.

As members of the polity, individuals make significantly greater accommodations to others than they do in more intimate settings. Attaining goals may sometime require concessions to increase the likelihood of successful enterprise. This is especially true of civic life. "Peace" in Hobbesian terms requires some order, albeit in a representative democracy that order is not at the sole discretion of a single nor yet a coterie of leaders.[15] Unless ordinary people can participate in the deliberative process of governance, many of them will emerge empty-handed, especially those in meager socio-economic circumstances and without political connections. Citizens are like participants at an improvisation theater who throw out suggestions to their representatives, who must in turn apply those ideas to the unpredictable skit of civic content. If citizens or theater-goers do not like how their suggestions have been translated into actions, at the expiration of the established period they can either vote for a new representative or demand a new actor.

Cooperation with others will often increase a person's likelihood for achiev-ing positive outcomes. This is not always the case, as when a person is picking clothes to a performance, at which point the decision making is not at all col-lective. Legal societies, however, are a different story. They are a collection of persons, each of whom has a legitimate claim to liberty and equality. Donald Regan has rightly argued in *Utilitarianism and Cooperation* that each agent must "cooperate, with whoever else is cooperating, in the production of the best con-sequences possible given the behavior of non-cooperators."[16] The Declaration even anticipates the possible need for revolutionary overthrow to end extreme forms of tyranny. But one must remain leery of calls for revolution given the hei-nous slaughter initiated by powerful leaders in the French Reign of Terror, the Soviet Bolshevik murders and oppressions, or the Khmer Rouge's killing fields. In the vast majority of cases persons can achieve desired ends by mutual cooper-ation and civil disobedience.

Often, coordinated action can better be achieved at state and local levels, where the people have greater access to elected and appointed officials than they do at the federal level. Much as many examples can be given to demonstrate the benefits of local cooperation, it must be born in mind that state agreements and joint actions are legitimate only so long as they do not overstep exclusive functions of the federal government—such as regulation of bankruptcy and in-terstate commerce—nor violate the maxim of legal rights for the common good.

Commonly shared ends can unify a disparate group of people into a cohesive community, increasing the likelihood of success for addressing complex social problems through collective actions. Cooperation in mutual endeavors need not require the sacrifice of personal ambitions. Rational actors can reason that by participating in joint civic efforts, through representative government, they can achieve something on personal and collective levels.

Sometimes pressing policy concerns prevent the state from accommodating the desire of a private party, requiring even the unwilling to pay taxes, vaccinate their children, and the like. When faced with legitimate public safety concerns, criminal law can punish anti-social behaviors, even when that means suppress-ing aspects of personality—such as violent sexual urges or even religious rituals like those involving practices of animal cruelty. In circumstances where personal decisions are likely to significantly diminish others' options to pursue happi-ness, custom or law can threaten to limit liberties through injunctions, monetary fines, or incarcerations. In those cases, concern for the common good trumps autonomy interests.

To decide between personal and collective claims in the constitutional realm, a decision maker must determine whether a specific clause of the Constitution provides an answer to the controversy at play. If not, the decision maker must turn for construction to more abstract clauses of the Constitution, such as the Equal Protection, Due Process, or Privileges or Immunities Clauses; to the various statements in the Declaration of Independence about equality, representative government, inalienable rights, or authoritarian overreaching; to the Preamble's statements about the sovereignty of the people and general welfare; and to the Ninth Amendment's Rights Retained by the People Clause. These provisions need not be read in isolation. Where several of them apply, lawmakers should consider them separately or in concert and in keeping with the general maxim of constitutional government. In many cases much more specific laws will apply that codify norms, such as fair treatment, into applicable tests tailored for specific situations. For example, a case of discrimination, such as one targeting the handicapped, might implicate local discrimination laws, the Americans with Disabilities Act, the substantive due process to liberty, inalienable right to dignity, and the right to be treated as an equal. A balancing inquiry must also be conducted to determine whether co-operative reasons can justify providing some with affirmative action, or, in the reverse, not providing some citizens with the means of enjoying opportunities available to others. Such balancing may be relevant, for example, when taking into account costs for building wheelchair-accessible courtrooms. Relevant to what courtroom access government must ensure the handicapped is the Seventh Amendment guarantee that criminal defendants can choose to be present at their trials, despite the extra public expenses needed to make hearings open to all. Building disabled-accessible courtrooms is not only good for those defendants who are currently handicapped but for society at large because any of us might become wheelchair bound and in need of affirmative state assistance. Thus, courtroom access is a personal right and of public interest. It is, therefore, cooperatively advantageous and conducive to the disabled individuals.

Social cooperation is, indeed, necessary for resolving all manner of complex problems. The reliability of government in the administration of law is necessary for stability. Human relations—from contracting to the acquisition of wealth—rely on laws governing specific interactions. On an even more fundamental level, humans expect justice—born of their own senses of dignity and empathy and the function of a representative polity—which requires public institutions to treat them fairly in the milieu of pluralistic egalitarianism.

Well-functioning society addresses the reasonable demands of the people without making arbitrary distinctions among them. Otherwise the will of a few

would thwart the reasonable expectations of targeted members of the population. Laws and norms that facilitate interactions are most likely to be effective
when they appeal to rational faculty or self-interest. Divergence of views about
what counts as rational public policy requires some established baseline for the
legitimate exercise of state power, not mere access to power: The Declaration
and Constitution set the cornerstone of maxim constitutionalism—requiring
equal treatment for the betterment of the whole—against which all lesser
laws can be tested. Empirical studies demonstrate that when laws are fairly
administered the government is more likely to achieve widespread compliance.[17] Collective expectations are more likely to be internalized when regulations contain provisions that respect dignity and seek to achieve evenhanded
goals. By working together, in a community where the common dignity of all
is respected (put another way a community where prejudice and stereotype
do not determine public policy), the likelihood of mutual success increases.
When agreement becomes impossible, law becomes a vehicle for resolution
and punishment.

Ordinary interactions do not typically involve the principle of representative
democracy, to which parties only draw attention in difficult, partisan disputes.
Otherwise, government's day-to-day operations are more concerned with concrete problems. However, an abiding maxim provides a stable reference point of
legitimate government.

C. Rights and General Welfare

Collective flourishing, then, has two components: The first is the acceptance of
rights as a natural facet of all persons, irrespective of their backgrounds, talents,
physical attributes, or preferences. This perspective is quite different from an
empirical method, such as the one undertaken by H.L.A. Hart to describe social
rules without seeking to link them to any normative foundation.[18] The aim of
maxim constitutionalism is to describe constitutional entitlements on the basis
of a foundational ideal. The second component of community prosperity is at the
organizational level. It concerns methods for developing, applying, enforcing,
and changing binding rules. The common good is ascertained through a holistic,
contextual analysis of quantifiable data, such as the gross domestic product, and
inchoate factors, such as domestic tranquility. This dual-layered framework of
protecting the individual while striving for the general welfare is explicitly set
by the Constitution's and the Declaration of Independence's statements of sovereign purpose. Those documents institutionalize individual entitlements, representational democracy, and a government of the people designed to exercise
power for their betterment.

Primacy is given to individuals, who precede and empower state institutions to formulate policy for the common good. All levels of government have an obligation of fair dealing to persons as rational, equal agents. This public duty is not the product of the state. Laws are not the sources of dignity but the means of protecting it. Rational faculty, a characteristic that exists to a lesser or greater degree in all conscious persons, confers value on thoughts and actions irrespective of the law.

Responsible public action should administer civic programs formulated to advance the people's deliberative choices about substantive, procedural, and institutional rules as well as flexible standards. Public entities should develop and run programs that are likely to guarantee human entitlements, known as rights, while also securing channels for social betterment.[19] With all of them, effective positive uses of authority are linked to negative analogues that prohibit, deter, and punish anti-social behaviors. The variety of human behaviors implicated by these two Janus faces of government power can be dizzying; the legitimacy of all of them, however, can be judged by the constitutional maxim that the underlying function of government is the advancement of equal rights for the common good.

The positive and negative uses of power should reflect government's obligation to personal development in an environment also conducive to social growth through the just exercise of power. All of us share the desire to choose independent courses of action that seem best to us under the circumstances. Ordinarily, as Amartya Sen has pointed out, it is better for society to leave individuals alone to follow inclinations rather than trying to stifle personalities.[20] However, society is not obligated to allow anyone to act on desire when an action is likely to bring about significant harm to others. When the rights of others are at stake, a community need not defer to personal proclivity or even wisdom; instead, law sets enforceable criteria for community concord. A person might covet the property of another but must follow laws preventing trespass and theft because the protection of personal and real possessions is necessary for social peace, stability, and predictability. This is to say that rights often conflict and must be balanced against social interests. Government can set enforceable terms for the resolution of conflicting personal interests in a manner that meets criteria of neutral statutory law and does not violate the norms set by the nation's constitutional documents. This provides individuals the space to explore their own sense of life's purposes while setting limits necessary for preserving public order.

There are at least as many conceptions of the good life as there are people; government has no authority to show preference for one vision or another unless it seeks to achieve some community benefit through a legitimate (and, when constitutional rights are involved, narrowly tailored) means. That does not diminish the authenticity of desires but requires them to be tempered by public concerns. Some of these concerns are directly raised by written portions of the Constitution—in the General Welfare, Guarantee, and Common Defense Clauses and elsewhere; while others are driven by contemporary debates about how an ancient document can address modern concerns, such as the reduction of pollution, the regulation of securities transactions, minimum wages, and so forth. A weighing of interests is meant to identify when the public good outweighs conflicting personal liberty interests. Policy makers should not be driven by personal preferences but by tools of construction such as textual, historical, precedential, structural, prudential, and moral analyses.

Criminal law is one obvious example of a social mandate that supersedes the human desire for liberty. Limits on wanton behavior are meant to promote conditions necessary for persons to pursue varying conceptions of what is good, irrespective of their social standings. By limiting the liberty of anti-social members of the population and punishing them for violating social norms, those who live unobtrusively can better pursue their goals. Equal treatment implies the fair administration of law, not a lack of differentiation between human conduct.

The constitutional maxim of liberal equality for the common good generates normative standards for government conduct respecting personal entitlements to liberty and security. Safeguarding these requires prescriptive rules against their arbitrary deprivation. But, more controversially, a person's ability to enjoy his or her happiness requires positive government action in matters of subsistence, health, education, police protection, and other boons of positive government programs. Without effective basic services (fire, police, medical, etc.), an individual would be unable to realize their reasonable expectations. Society must therefore promote welfare through evenhanded policies designed to promote human flourishing.

Conflicts are of course unavoidable in the private and public spheres. Contacts with other people do not always go smoothly and government programs are bound to be met with some (sometimes significant) pushback. Often people want to exploit public resources for their own interests and to exclude others from enjoying them. Public programs must steer clear of favoritism, unless it is warranted by special circumstances, such as to provide specific programs tailored for persons who are handicapped or members of a group that has historically suffered identifiable discrimination. Policies should reflect a balancing of interests and a clear understanding of how best to achieve legitimate goals. Law places restraints on conduct and limits access to common resources. Quite often laws reflect a consensus position. Sometimes no middle ground can be found on disputatious matters like death penalty punishments or punitive damage tort reform, but officials must seek middle ground; in my example that means taking seriously the claims of groups calling for harsher or more proportionate punitive punishments and civil damages, engaging with the perspectives of different segments of the population, and enacting laws that reflect the best wisdom under the circumstances.

Claims pitting persons against each other must be resolved on the basis of fair laws that treat people as rational equals. Under certain circumstances, a select group of persons will enjoy special privileges based on objective achievements, such as passing exams and receiving licenses. But the state must equitably regulate everyone who possesses those special qualifications. Assumed in this is the government's obligation to create conditions—or breathing spaces—for persons to enjoy their liberties as equals in a stable community where laws are administered through predictable institutions. Even the allocation of special privileges must be based on some legitimate social outcome. For instance, in providing physicians and attorneys a monopoly to practice their professions, the state benefits license holders and the public by confining the administration of services to a knowledge-based community. The same is true about empowering only trained police officers exclusively to carry out certain public safety functions, such as incarceration, allowing only qualified individuals employment and the public to benefit from their expertise. In some cases, privileges—such as affirmative action programs—are predicated on particularly important or compelling public reasons, such as rectification of historic forms of discrimination.

Rights are not absolutes even though they impose duties on public entities to create conditions for their flourishing. Freedom to exercise them must be respected, however, absent some conflicting interests of equal or greater importance. Subjective perception about the hierarchy of public duties is of minor relevance here; what is important is that each individual has the opportunity to constructively voice opinions about matters affecting the community of equals. Various institutions, through deliberative processes that represent the will of the people, should weigh calls for action or inaction—many of them contradictory—while remaining cognizant of history, culture, tradition, judicial precedents, expressive associations, and the other important factors having a nexus to the constitutional question. The Constitution is negative, because it places certain limitations, and positive, because it establishes powers for acting to achieve maxim constitutionalism by welfare maximization.

Flexibility, a willingness to experiment with various laws conforming to the maxim of constitutional governance, is essential for change, improvement, and modification of existing order. But the principle of human dignity and public welfare provides the crucial framework against which all laws can be tested to prevent arbitrary abuses of power.

Policy makers should aim to benefit individuals and the community of equals. The devil is in the detail, but the general principles check the possible dimensions of authority. Contract law, for example, offers relief for a party who suffers loss as a result of a breached agreement, but it is also subtly advantageous for others not privy to the terms of the agreement. Legal rules for contracts provide defined boundaries for productivity, reliability, joint ventures, gain, and confidence in formal agreements. Individually this means people can turn to legal relief to remedy breaches. Without rules requiring parties to fulfill terms to which they agree, people would be unwilling to risk making arrangements; this, in turn, would negatively impact the economy, creating all manner of financial and fiscal instability. Laws against discrimination in contracts, such as the Civil Rights Act of 1866,[21] are both negative, because they prohibit biased business dealings, and positive, because they expand the opportunities of persons who might otherwise be excluded from commercial and even private dealings. Cumulatively this amounts to a free market that protects individual liberty and conduces to economic welfare.

Other constitutional provisions are likewise collectively and privately meaningful. Freedom of speech, for example, is clearly of collective benefit for deliberative democracy and essential to personal fulfillment. Freedom of the press, which, like speech, is guaranteed by the First Amendment of the US Constitution, serves the informative function of disseminating knowledge to the community. A free press allows journalists to follow their career ambitions, spread ideas of self-governance, explore their individual creativities, and enables the audience to expand its cognitive horizons. As a Supreme Court Justice elegantly put it in a dissent: "An informed public depends on accurate and effective reporting by the news media."[22] Likewise, the ability to spread one's views through the press opens avenues for individuals to voice concerns and opinions; blow off steam; spread elation, agony, affinity, and rejection. This is especially the case in the age of the Internet, where the average person can report to persons across the globe on local or even international events. Individuals benefit from living in a society in which ideas are exchanged freely and the expression of their convictions are not stifled. This allows each person to develop informed opinions and to participate in debates about issues both big and small. Open channels of communications pave the way for catharsis, politicking, and personal fulfilment. Because we are a society "of the people, by the people, for the people," these private benefits help the community thrive in the aggregate by introducing a plurality of voices to resolve a plethora of concerns. Speech and press freedoms, just like contractual ones, are personal and collective goods of liberal democracy.

Statutes that on their face prohibit the perpetration of acts against specific classes of people, like racial and gender groups, serve the common good. The Civil Rights of Act of 1866 allows parties to contract without racial restrictions, thereby expanding the pool of available commercial partners for purchasing goods and services, buying and selling real estate, and the manifold other transactions that take place in a capitalist society. Likewise, Title VII of the Civil Rights Act of 1964, which prohibits employment discrimination based on race, religion, sex, color, and national origin, expands the talent pool of avail-able workers. Title VI (also part of the Civil Rights Act of 1964) bars public schools receiving federal funding from discriminating on the basis of race, color, or national origin. The latter law enables students to advance their potentials and raises an informed citizenry. The Matthew Shepard Act and James Byrd, Jr., Hate Crimes Prevention Act of 2009 ("the Matthew Shepard Act) contains criminal penalties for violence committed because of the victim's perceived race, color, religion, national origin, gender, sexual orientation, gender identity, or disabil-ity. Besides its retributive components, Congress found the Matthew Shepard Act was needed to deter the substantial negative impact on interstate commerce resulting from the targeted groups' diminished ability to freely travel to other states, purchase goods, and obtain employment. While these are examples of statutory protections, they each advance the core maxim of constitutional gov-ernance: the ability to pursue happiness as a member of a legal community whose aim is to act on a common interest in normative and efficient civil society.

Constitutional provisions recognizing these rights interlace individuals' interests with the well-being of the nation as a whole. Equality requires govern-ment exercise of powers for the universal enjoyment of fundamental freedoms. This is not to underplay local ties; these, no doubt, are vital for people's sense of being and joys in life. But in this book, I'm concentrating on the collective maxim of national governance.

That maxim is embodied in the Declaration of Independence and the Preamble to the Constitution. But neither of those documents generates rights, which are intrinsic to human beings rather than created by law nor social prac-tices. In a state that regards rights to be grants, the citizenry cannot be certain that those entitlements will not be taken away by bureaucrats. The written Constitution protects against fiat. The text does not, however, cover all circum-stances. Moreover, the Three-Fifths and Slave Importation Clauses demonstrate that even the Constitution should be subjected to some more abstract principle. Even a general clause, such as the Due Process Clauses of the 14th Amendment, can be abused, as it was with the *Lochner* line of cases, without the interpretive key to identify individual and social factors relevant to the resolution of cases or the development of policy. General values, such as the Declaration's Inalienable Rights and Born Equal Clauses, and the Preamble's General Welfare Clause, are more encompassing. Constructing their meaning should include identification of public servants' positive and negative duties to citizens.

The maxim of sovereign purpose to safeguard personal dignity and advance common goods is part and parcel of the nation's social contract. Each person living in a representative democracy of equals implicitly agrees to abide by laws consistent with the betterment of society as a whole. For the minimal condi-tions to be met, and for the assumption of popular consent to hold true, the

Constitution and the institutions enforcing it must demonstrate the systematic respect for civil liberties, allowing parties to express themselves, call for change, associate with others, and protest to effectuate the political process. The consent at stake is not a matter of an oath of allegiance but the hypothetical acceptance of laws that any rational person would understand are binding as a benefit of living in a jurisdiction that respects equals and enables them to thrive through their unique notions of what constitutes a good life.

D. Personal Interests and Social Ends

People expect government to comply with explicit provisions of the Constitution, such as those setting terms of office, administering consistent and predicable rules, and not creating retroactive criminal laws; with implicit guarantees, such as the obligation to diligently administer the public trust; and with the protection of rights. While officials must answer to the public, representative governance does not require them to pursue constituents' every whim; instead, they must develop policies cognizant of the personal stakes involved and likely to achieve good consequences for the public. This is not to say that politicians can simply disregard the people's will; to the contrary, they are entrusted to meet the needs of constituents.

Elections appoint leaders with fresh ideas, sometimes gleaned at speaking events and rallies, during the course of campaigning, or while otherwise stumping in the representative's district. Communication with constituents is intrinsic to representation but cannot be the sole source of policies. Constitutional aspirations are relevant to stasis and change.

Even radical change is legitimate so long as it is accomplished in accordance with constitutional aspiration. For example, the Reconstruction Amendments fundamentally modified the Constitution—putting an end to slavery, securing birthright citizenship, prohibiting racist voting limitations, vastly expanding federal power, and so on—by bringing it in line with the essential commitment of the Declaration and Preamble. The framers had contradicted the general principle adopted into those instruments—equal human rights and common welfare—when, for the sake of state unity, the original Constitution included portions like the Three-Fifths Clause. There are also many examples of principled innovations that advanced the fundamental purpose of government without constitutional amendment. The US commitment to universal human rights was, for instance, the legal fulcrum in both the decision to pass 1952 immigration legislation removing the privilege of white race, which had been part of US naturalization laws since 1790, and in 1964 to create a federal cause of action against gender employment discrimination, which had for generations been accepted and justified on the basis of sex stereotypes. A traditionalist approach, such as the one Justice Antonin Scalia held,[23] is overly reliant on actual, historical practices, many of which are contrary to constitutional principle. Norms are not derived from practices, not even those that have long been accepted; instead, custom should be tested by explicit and implicit constitutional norms, political deliberation, and judicial interpretation.

That is not to say that specifics are irrelevant. To the contrary, policy and adjudication should not be formalistic. Practical solutions should address the context of the controversy.

In a society of equals, officials in all three branches of government often grapple with how to resolve competing claims and sometimes outright impasses result. From the lobbying stage, through enactment, enforcement, and adjudication, persons and special interest groups contend for officials' attention. Some claims can be reconciled to the satisfaction of all parties. More commonly, however, lawmakers must examine the specifics of disputed facts, principles, and pragmatics to mold a policy or to resolve a conflict.

Inevitably not all parties will be satisfied with the outcomes of legislative or regulatory debates. Those who are not can litigate, press for new laws, or elect different representatives whose views are more in keeping with their moral sensibilities. Facts matter, as does a qualified approach to the application of principles. To illustrate this point, take a law prohibiting all manner of yelling in theaters. Such a law would be overbroad and void for vagueness. It would fail constitutional muster because it would bar so much speech protected by the First Amendment; for instance, anyone crying out for help at a theater because of chest pain would be liable. On the other hand, a law that prohibits yelling "Fire!" in a movie theater could be legitimately enforced.[24] In both cases, parties are yelling in a theater, but from the statutory and constitutional standpoint nuances make all the difference. Only the latter has a nexus to the First Amendment. An ambiguous law would have a chilling effect on protected communications, not only dealing with fire but political and artistic expressions as well. A law against falsely shouting about fire, on the other hand, would be advanced for the socially compelling purpose of preventing stampedes and maintaining public safety. In both examples, the individual is exercising the liberty of speech but only in the second is the public interest significant enough to justify the restraint on expression.[25]

Ordinary situations will require no reflection on constitutional proportionality because public policy will simply not be relevant to countless mundane decisions about family, friends, theaters, work, shopping, and so on. In the vast majority of circumstances, government has no place intruding into private decisions and coercing personal dispositions. A person's hobbies, theatrical tastes, shopping habits, reading lists, and other forms of self-expression are spheres where government cannot legitimately use its coercive powers. They are matters that each person can choose based on preferences, religion, and sense of priority. But expressions that are likely to have a significant negative impact on society, such as the incitement of riots, are outweighed by other social values, such as peace and tranquility.[26]

All laws must stay true to constitutional ideal in the enforcement of regulations likely to achieve positive results in areas as divergent as campaign financing and clean water regulation. Purely pragmatic deliberations risk underenforcing commitments, such as contracts or government oversight of financial markets, for the sake of some presentist calculus. To stay true to the foundational maxim of constitutionalism, a balance must be struck between normative factors and practical considerations: Well-balanced public policy takes into account the repercussions of various decisions and the private interests they are likely to affect. No matter the political rewards, trampling on rights—such as by implementing racially based voting restrictions (through methods like gerrymandering) —is unjust toward targeted individuals, groups, and society at large.

Constitutional law must recognize the subjective and objective nature of human liberty. Put another way, the Constitution protects personal freedoms and legally recognized fundamental rights. Subjective will is a construct of personality. At the level of inclinations—say how many naps a person takes in a day or how many snacks one eats–everyone's likes and dislikes are unique: no matter how nutty the state might think me for enjoying sandwiches with tomatoes, garlic, peanut butter, and honey, it has no sovereign mandate to stop me from eating them. Besides the subjective there is also an objective element here: The freedom to eat cannot be abridged because nothing in the Constitution permits officials to intrude on a person's preferences; indeed, the Declaration of Independence's Pursuit of Happiness Clause indicates that the people did not grant to government any power over unorthodox, personal choices. That framework helps explain why rights are not merely positive grants of the state. To the contrary they are facets of human nature whose limits cannot be prescribed under the founding grant of popular authority to representative government. For instance, at a time of food shortage brought on by war some government-imposed food rationing of scarce products might be narrowly tailored to guard against starvation. However, entirely prohibiting prisoners from eating as a form of punishment when there is no such shortage would be a cruel deprivation of objective liberty implicitly violative of the Eighth Amendment and, more generally, the 14th Amendment's guarantee of life and dignity of the convict and people's trust in level-headed administration of criminal justice.

On the one hand are subjective preferences, desires, proclivities, and orientations: what persons enjoy, what inspires them, how they spend leisure time, and so on. These are all dispositions for which there is no unified valuation and no constitutional markers; each person is his or her own judge of what "pursuit of happiness" is worthwhile. People create constitutional society to safeguard personal life paths against state overreaching to prevent having their wills ruled by bureaucrats. Objective norms, on the other hand, are incorporated into constitutional law. Their value supersedes ordinary laws. All of the nation's laws with any constitutional nexus cannot violate the basic maxim of government. While based on objective human dignity and common equality, the values are amenable to consistent reinterpretation through open debate and then drafted into new statutes. Food rationing at time of an emergency would typically require public deliberations, but deciding what to order at a lunch counter or at a cafeteria in a public building surely would not.

A slightly different case involves circumstances where government is drawn into interpersonal conflicts. In a society of equals, where each person is the judge of his or her subjective preference, conflicting liberty claims are unavoidable. In those circumstances, some weighing of private and public concerns becomes necessary. Representative governance requires deliberation on the interests of each relevant party or constituency. In many circumstances, the number of interested parties will be far too large to include data of every individual who stands to gain or lose by the operation of any particular law, so lawmakers typically group interests by common characteristics. Most judicial deliberations, on the other hand, are individuated, except in cases of class and joint litigation. This layered approach facilitates governance at macro and micro levels. For the sake of staying true to rule of legal principles, to eschew arbitrary favoritism, and pursue broadly beneficial solutions in resolving disputes of constitutional importance—such as the political participation, fundamental rights, or procedural justice—policy makers must abide by core principles. Consistency requires principled decision making but also readiness to abandon incompatible past practices. As the issues and sensibilities change—and they must change with evolving technology, political preferences, regulatory demands, heightened sensibilities, and innumerable other factors—solutions require reflection on whether tradition comports with governance responsive to the will of the people.

The Declaration of Independence and Preamble to the Constitution set the textual tenets of public accountability. All three branches of government must advance their synthetic ideal of individuated and public good concerns. Without this joint framework, simple utilitarian calculations are likely to discount legitimate claims of interested parties or, from the reverse perspective, formalistic rules threaten to be acontextual. With all their eclectic personality traits, people are members of a national community where others have correlative rights. Legal rules provide enforceable grounds for the uses of power. By themselves, many rules are insufficiently determinative to arrive at undisputed solutions; maxim is needed as a bedrock for constitutional construction. This is especially the case when legislators use general language to draft laws that must be parsed in the context of specific disputes. Rules governing interpersonal relations should therefore be applied in light of specific circumstances and the potential results of various courses of action. This means that principle and rules are important but so too is nuanced evaluation of the outcomes of public policies.

Thus, constitutional interpretation should be a conscious effort to create conditions for principled exercises of authority for the betterment of the community. Granted, purposeful uses of authority may be inconsistent, and specific rules and standards must be adopted as checks on power. Rules and standards establish concrete obligations, but they must be drafted and understood in accordance with maxim consequentialism. The generality with which the Declaration and Preamble set the public duty to protect individual rights for the common good facilitates debate about hot button issues from topics like fiscal policy, to school prayer, executive privilege, habeas corpus, and anything else related to the Constitution.

Outside the realm of lawmaking, a maxim-based approach can also weed out arbitrariness and favoritism. Like everyone else, officials have special relations with family, benefactors, and friends whom they can prefer in the private but not public sphere. A general goal of good for the community sets a more objective standard but one that is open to lobbying, which will inevitably include issues favored by various special interest groups. Legal recognition of equal liberty is needed to check the use of power on behalf of favored individuals and to channel its use for the benefit of the whole. Approaching constitutionally ambiguous issues with an eye to personal autonomy and general welfare is meant to prevent the abuse of power and to direct its use for the betterment of society. The question of balance requires each person to be treated as an intrinsically dignified, equal member of the community, no matter his or her connection or lack thereof, lawmakers must take seriously concerns of individuals for the creation of public policy.

E. Progressive Constitutionalism

Reflections on how state commitments affect real people and their communities are essential to legitimate exercises of authority. Wedding the deontological and consequentialist in matters of policy is not simply a deductive exercise, but one that is consciously pragmatic in its search for better outcomes. Affected individuals must be taken into account but so too the welfare of the whole affected population. Private concerns are not absolutes, but neither are pragmatic ones. Since the New Deal Era, the Supreme Court has aided the country to make significant strides in defining rights enumerated and implied by the Constitution.

The Court has increasingly understood these provisions' abstract statements to be protective of entitlements against government encroachments. The entitlements are unalienable, in the words of the Declaration of Independence, and intrinsic to our humanity. This perspective has provided guidance for the country's efforts to overcome the ghouls of its founding, when slavery was tolerated and voting rights were enjoyed only by a select, propertied segment of the population.

From its inception, the United States has grappled with civil rights issues. The interpretive process requires institutions to evolve in their understandings about how the objective standard of equal rights for the common good applies to issues like affirmative action and gay marriage. Pluralism and representative democracy encourage a feedback loop between the people and their governments through litigation, regulatory notice, and voter petitions about how the ancient Constitution is relevant to contemporary debates.

It will be useful to examine how the Supreme Court developed privacy rights doctrine because it is a valuable example of evolutionary constitutionalism, simultaneously advancing private and public interests. The Court has identified the right to privacy most commonly with the substantive due process right of liberty, but also with the Ninth Amendment and penumbral statement of various other provisions of the Bill of Rights, such as the Fourth Amendment's Search and Seizure Clause.[27] Over time, constitutional text has diffused into judicial holdings with profound cultural implications. The Unalienable Rights and Pursuit of Happiness Clauses of the Declaration of Independence are two of the more obvious recognitions of a right to privacy, which the Court has neglected. Privacy is connected to personal, innate rights, as well as to social welfare.

On a personal level, privacy is of obvious concern because it is tied to dignity considerations, such as those related to sexual and reproductive choices. Matters of privacy are related to the people's equal entitlement to autonomy against intrusions. The constitutional entitlement to self-directedness prohibits government from engaging in draconian intrusions, such as unreasonable searches and seizures and billeting soldiers in private houses during times of peace. Privacy related concerns are likewise interlinked with social issues. Publically held values are reflected in the measures society takes to guard persons against police power abuses, trespasses to homes, breaches of parental rights, intrusions into marital life, and harms to reputation. A balance must be struck between conflicting liberty interests and legitimate state concerns.

One of the best known cases of privacy, concerns the right to marry. Marital privacy is now resolutely regarded to be a liberty guaranteed by the Due Process and Equal Protection Clauses of the 14th Amendment.[28] The right to marriage, however, is nowhere mentioned in the Constitution. The Court recently held that for homosexual and heterosexual couples the right to marry confers a dig-nity status of tremendous personal and social importance.[29] Marriage is a private agreement between two people and a unique contract creating public obliga-tions in matters like intestate succession and evidentiary privileges. Equality in marriage is also important because it prevents discrimination against members of communities whose members have historically suffered from exclusionary discriminations. At first, in cases dealing with completely different issues like the parental right to teach children foreign languages, Supreme Court justices recognized its existence in passing, simply naming marriage as one among other constitutional liberties, which included the rights to contract and seek the occu-pation of one's choice.[30] With time the Court gave more flesh to its definition, identifying privacy to include the right of married people to use contraceptives without state interference.[31] The evolutionary role of privacy has also balanced the rights of people interested in marriage against community prejudices. In the latter cases, the Court has found that the right of individuals to wed the partner of their choosing trumps popular biases against interracial unions.[32] The next logical step, which turned concerted social activism into constitutional doctrine, was for the Court in *United States v. Windsor* to hold unconstitutional a law that prohibited the federal government from recognizing valid same-sex marriages. Finally, in *Obergefell v. Hodges*, the Court held that overlapping principles of the 14th Amendment's Due Process and Equal Protection Clauses prohibit state infringement on the privacy and dignity right to marry without being subject to sexual-orientation discrimination.

Legislatures, just as courts, should reflect on private and public consequences of their actions. One of the most recent positive statutory advancements in this direction is the Matthew Shepard Act.[33] As we saw earlier, this federal statute prohibits and punishes crimes committed because of victims' "color . . . reli-gion, national origin, gender, sexual orientation, gender identity, or disability." Congress acted out of a national obligation to protect individual victims. The statute's introductory paragraphs assert that a "prominent characteristic of a vi-olent crime motivated by bias is that it devastates not just the actual victim and the family and friends of the victim, but frequently savages the community shar-ing the traits that caused the victim to be selected." State involvement is thus triggered by both private and public interests that trump the liberty interests of perpetrators of violence.

Evolution in these privacy and hate crime aspects of constitutional law dem-onstrates how a balance of core liberties along with community needs is essen-tial to progressive public policy. Whether advancing people's liberty to marry or prosecuting hateful crimes against vulnerable groups, the state must demon-strate concern for people's dignity while maintaining order. This dualistic inter-pretive method is based on the maxim of national purpose as it is set out in the

Declaration of Independence and Preamble to the Constitution. These founding statements assert the people's authority to create a representative polity where each can pursue a unique path in life, with government working for the augmentation of goods—be they health, infrastructure, national parks, food and flood relief, etc.—for the betterment of the national community as a whole.

PART III

INTERPRETIVE CONTEXTS AND APPLICATION

8

Theoretical Alternatives

The Declaration of Independence and the Preamble to the Constitution declared the people to be sovereign and set normative limits on the administration of government. The central purpose of governance, to safeguard the people's rights on an equal basis for the betterment of society, is the duty of all three branches of government. Each branch of government must be governed by constitutional norms. Over the years legal research has paid inadequate attention to the underlying function of representative independence.

Most theories of constitutional interpretation focus almost exclusively on various methodologies of judicial interpretation. This chapter analyzes several prominent theories: originalism, living constitutionalism, and proceduralism. I make no effort to provide an exhaustive analysis of any of these three schools of thought. The discussion of maxim constitutionalism in the context of other methods is rather meant to examine whether there is any interpretive advantage to relying on a central constitutional ethos of national purpose. The chapter concludes with an analysis of process-based understanding of the Constitution, arguing that it is insufficiently robust for synthetic construction.

A. Originalism

In the last four decades, originalism has left a significant mark on academic and judicial writings. The stated aim of its supporters is for judges to interpret the Constitution according to the framers' initial intent or to the document's meaning to ordinary people living in 1789, the year of ratification. This method is meant to prevent judges from rendering decisions on the basis of political predispositions, grounding them instead in historical significance.

Early originalists like Judge Robert Bork argued that judicial restraint required judges to "stick close to the text and the history, and their fair implications."[1] "[T]he only legitimate basis for constitutional decisionmaking," Bork wrote, is "original intent."[2] For Bork and other early expositors of this schema, much of the Warren Court's legacy was based on faulty reasoning rather than verifiable "meaning attached by the framers to the words they employed in the Constitution."[3] Reagan Administration Attorney General Edwin Meese III took this line of thought into the public sphere. Meese advocated a "jurisprudence of original intention" requiring judges to consult "the original intent of the Framers."[4] Scholars, judges, and politicians who promoted the intentionalist branch of originalism believed that the framers established interpretive standards that they intended to be binding on their own and future generations.

While their efforts to prevent judicial overreaching were commendable, Intentionalists' historical claims came under fire for being inferential, driven by legal and political agendas, and often historically inaccurate. The record of ratification conventions, Madison's notes of the Constitutional Convention, and political pamphlets of the day are too inconsistent, incomplete, and partisan to make incontrovertible or decisive conclusions about their contribution to contemporary debates. Furthermore, the framers were not intellectually unified. Simply put, it is disingenuous to ascribe a collective conscience to individuals as disparate in their views as Alexander Hamilton and Thomas Jefferson. While at the time of ratification, the Early Republic only had one political party, the acrimonious disputes between Federalists supporting the Constitution and Anti-Federalists opposing it without changes to the Philadelphia Convention's formulae were anything but unified. Sometimes there was overlap even among rivals, which allowed Hamilton and Jefferson to work in the Washington administration and Federalists to acquiesce to Anti-Federalists' demands for a written bill of rights, but there were also profound differences of opinion, such as Hamilton's preference for strong national government and Jefferson's advocacy for local, agronomic self-government, or the Federalists' willingness to ratify the original Constitution with only implicit protections of rights and the Anti-Federalists' condemnation of the omission of those written guarantees. Some of the most influential Framers' views evolved, indeed morphed, after ratification. Jefferson, for instance, clearly changed his view about the capacity of the United States to expand territorially without constitutional amendment after France agreed to sell the Louisiana Territory. James Madison initially argued against inclusion of a bill of rights in the Constitution, fearing that it would be construed to only protect enumerated rights and thereby leave other natural rights unprotected against government intrusion. But he later served as the floor leader in the House of Representatives on behalf of adopting the Bill of Rights. This fluctuating political landscape did not alter the nation's permanent commitment to the maxim of individual rights for the common good.

What is important for contemporary interpretation is to vigilantly hold government accountable for maintaining the aspirational principles of the Constitution and Declaration of Independence, not the founding era's racism, chauvinism, and classism, which were regarded as legitimate standards for political and social exclusion. The failures of the founding generation did not gainsay the nation's obligation to abide by the constitutional directive of socially responsible governance. In the post-Reconstruction and post-Civil Rights Eras, a vastly more inclusive comprehension of fundamental rights and the common good has become part of federal law through statutes like the Civil Rights Act of 1964, the Voting Rights Act of 1965, the Age Discrimination in Employment Act, and the Americans with Disabilities Act. The Declaration of Independence, Bill of Rights, and the northern manumission acts of the post-Revolutionary Era are just some examples of accomplishments of the framing generation from which we stand to learn. But they also pursued inimical policies, like passage of the Fugitive Slave Act of 1793 and ratification of the Importation Clause and the Three-Fifths Clause, which raise some serious doubts about their judgments and motivations. History is a tool for understanding various advancements of and failures to live up to the core commitment of US constitutionalism, but no generation is required to adopt the complete will of its predecessors, warts and all.

Moreover, given that the Declaration of Independence and the Preamble attribute sovereignty to the people rather than the framers of the Constitution—as might have been the case had the country become a plutocracy or aristocracy—it is unclear why the views of prominent men of the day should be more determinative than those of ordinary persons living during that period. Presumably the preferences of persons engaged in drafting, writing, and ratifying the Constitution through state ratifying conventions should receive great weight with respect to the document's meaning to the founding generation. But if the Declaration and the Preamble are to be taken at their word, then a much greater number of people's views should be taken into account for determining constitutional intentions and meanings. Professors Keith Whittington and Michael McConnell have gone further, arguing that originalist judges must give effect to the will of the people living at the time of ratification.[5] But even if that were normatively correct, the ideas, opinions, and leanings of such a diffuse group cannot be ascertained with certainty, neither from our vantage point, almost two-and-a-half centuries after ratification, nor was there consensus at the time.

"The People" is, instead, a dynamic constitutional concept embracing the idea that each generation is obligated to identify rights intrinsic to the pursuit of happiness and to demand that government provide the legal means of achieving the general welfare. The structural parts of the Constitution provide the means for the three branches of government to pursue those ends. The people have exercised their sovereignty not only at the constitutional ratifying convention: their will is a continuously evolving force that is exercised through elective politics, representative governance, social organizing, communicative associations, labor unions, lobbying groups, and so on. Understanding statements about unalienable rights, found in the Declaration, or general welfare, found in the Preamble, certainly requires retrospection. They are clauses that owe their existence to a specific colonial conflict with Britain. But like the abstract statements of the Bill of Rights and Reconstruction Amendments, such as those found in the Unenumerated Rights Clause of the Ninth Amendment and the Equal Protection Clause of the Fourteenth Amendment, our constitutional tradition is a steady stream of concretizing through Article V amendments and, to a less binding degree, precedent, legislation, and regulation. The broadly stated directives for government to protect rights (in the form of life, liberty, and the pursuit of happiness) and advance the general welfare (through substantive and procedural due process) invite debate and resolution, not stasis. The concrete provisions of the Constitution, such as the age at which a person can become president or the number of senators who represent each state in Congress, are there to provide a functional framework for achieving the underlying purpose of representative governance.

Finding themselves in the crosshairs of historical and analytical criticism, originalists shifted their attention from intentionalism to structural originalism, the focus of which was on the text and design of the Constitution; to consequentialism, with an emphasis on beneficial results; and to "popular-sovereignty" originalism.[6] The most prominent, and currently most influential, branch draws its inspiration from the presumed original public meaning. That shift did not obviate the problem of identifying an unambiguous source and understanding of the founding generation. An advocate for classic originalism critically pointed out that "public meaning originalism will generate more cases of constitutional indeterminacy than will the originalism of original intentions."[7] There is, furthermore, disagreement among public-meaning originalists. As Thomas Colby and Peter Smith have pointed out, original-meaning scholars are split between those that credit original understanding to ratifiers, the public, drafters, or hypothetically reasonable persons at the time of ratification.[8] There is little in common among these disparate camps of originalism except, as Lawrence Solum has synthetically stated, that they all maintain there is a fixed-in-time constitutional meaning that constrains modern interpretation,[9] but they vociferously differ about the details. Andrew Koppelman has stated that, ironically, while "[o]riginalists do not think that their field is in crisis[, t]hey should," because their approaches are so methodologically fragmented.[10] The different meanings of the "originalism" label renders untenable the central claim of the movement that it provides certainty in adjudication. The reality, to the contrary, is that, as with all other approaches, judges who adhere to originalism must make normative decisions where constitutional clauses are not fully explained by the historical record, which often yields ambiguous results.

The ideology most originalists espouse is too closely related to the conservative political agenda to ignore the overlap between it and party partisanship.

An originalist judge, whether relying on intentionalism or public meaning, cannot avoid exercising discretion when deciding facial or as-applied challenges. Conservatives tend to think that the federal government has overextended its regulatory reach into areas that the Constitution has left to state decision makers. Hence an 18th- and 19th-century mentality, which idealized a period of balanced federalist powers, goes hand-in-hand with a nostalgic, albeit unworkable, method for understanding the Constitution. That notion of the past is more ideological than it is historical. For instance, as Reva Siegel and Jamal Greene have pointed out, Justice Antonin Scalia's originalist proclamation in *District of Columbia v. Heller* that the Second Amendment protects the right to private gun ownership is rejected by almost all 18th-century historians.[11] For originalists, then, the ideological value of labeling something as historical can be of greater value than of analyzing the matter according to the historical record.

History is of vital importance to the interpretation of the Constitution. However, sifting through precedents, social developments, statutory emendations, social and political advocacy, and other relevant data of legal culture does not call for blind adoration of the past. The framers' wise counsel does not mandate contemporary results, nor does it preclude interpretive advancement based on normative sensibility. Previous generations' legal conclusions, insights into human behaviors, legislative enactments, constitutional adjudications, administrative changes, and the plethora of other achievements best make sense within a unified framework of national ethos. That framework is neither beholden to the intent of the founding generation nor any supposed public meaning of the Constitution's wording. Originalism requires inferences outside its stated purpose when addressing questions far beyond what the framers could fathom, such as the Fourth Amendment's application to searches and seizures using global positioning systems (GPS),[12] thermal imaging devices,[13] and telephone booths.[14] Sometimes resorting to the historic record by both the majority and dissent amounts to two reasonable interpretations of the extant sources that arrive at opposite conclusions. This was the case in *U.S. Term Limits, Inc. v. Thornton*,[15] which held unconstitutional a state's limitations on the number of terms representatives and senators could serve in the US Congress.[16] Legitimacy of constitutional determinations is, rather, based on whether government action or inaction is made in accordance with the underlying directive of representative democracy, established in the Declaration of Independence and the Preamble, to protect individual rights for the common good. And that judgment is a contested one. The details must be hashed out in legislative debates, judicial conferences, and presidential cabinet meetings. If the people dislike the conclusions reached by powerful actors, they can vote them out of office and start afresh in the next election cycle or they can join with like-minded people to continue working for change. Elected officials are responsible to the people to appoint judicial candidates who are committed to the maxim of representative governance and the precedents and traditions it has engendered.

Jack Balkin has recently proposed a "living originalism" approach, which frames the Constitution in general terms, based on original "semantic content."[17] He bases the approach on neither the original intent nor the original expected application of the founding fathers. Living originalism, instead, requires fidelity to the content of provisions like the Equal Protection Clause, but recognizes that "changing social demands and changing social mores" should influence constitutional construction.[18] This is a welcome understanding that mores play a central role in decision making. Balkin writes that future generations must abide by the Constitution's original framework. This "framework consists of the original semantic meanings of the words in the text (including any generally recognized terms of art) and the adopters' choice of rules, standards, and principles to limit, guide, and channel future constitutional construction."[19]

This approach provides Balkin with a method of explaining the legitimacy of modern precedents like *Roe v. Wade*,[20] despite the dearth of grounding that opinion has in any original semantic meaning of the 14th Amendment's Privileges or Immunities Clause. Social mobilization is crucial to his model "in building the Constitution" and shaping constitutional construction.[21] Balkin does not, however, adopt a central principle for judicial review and all other functions of governance to help explain, justify, or condemn any given trajectory of US social, political, and constitutional change. A unified principle of governance provides a grounding on which social groups can demand change. Its simple ideals do not require advocates for change to be specialists in constitutional law, they need only seek the protection of individual rights in order to further the general welfare, where everyone is treated as an equally valuable member of society regardless of ethnic background, affluence, or political clout. I agree with Balkin's model of social advocacy but believe that maxim constitutionalism adds a necessary grounding for aspirational construction left out of his formulation of constitutional advancement.

In the previous chapter, I suggested that the central purpose of government is contained in the maxim that the people have created a representative polity whose raison d'être is the use of constitutional powers to safeguard inalienable rights to further public good. This is a normative matter, not merely a semantic one. That norm is stable and provides the initial constitutional content to publicly eschew intolerance and group animus. Under my maxim-constitutional approach, the protection of rights is regarded to be essential for pluralism because it requires the executive, legislative, and judicial branches to respect individual difference while administering just laws for the betterment of the whole. While Balkin is erudite in his explication of how the Constitution provides the aspiration for "higher law,"[22] it is not the document itself but the human aspiration to live in a society obligated to protect the individual's unobtrusive pursuit for the good life that is at the core of legitimate state power. That will to power is best exercised through a representative government, responsive to the will of constituents but not beholden to the discrimination of the majority. Freedom of human sexuality, which the Court recognized under the term "privacy" in *Griswold v. Connecticut* and *Lawrence v. Texas*,[23] is an example of one constitutional right that is based on innate human aspirations instead of textual semantics, original intents, or original meanings. More recently in *Obergefell v. Hodges*, finding restriction on same-sex marriages to be unconstitutional, the Court went even further in its expostulation of universal human qualities protected by the Constitution. In that case, the majority acknowledged that concerns for human "liberty," "identity," "dignity," as well as "profound hopes and aspirations" are relevant to constitutional adjudication.

Maxim constitutionalism regards key constitutional provisions, foremost the second paragraph of the Declaration of Independence and the Preamble to the Constitution, to be defined by ontological human rights, not determinative of them. The maxim of individual rights for the common good is that principle upon which all other constitutional principles must be justified, and it owes its authoritative place to neither historic semantics nor extant text but to the rational worth of people establishing a government capable of protecting their essential interests as the best means of enjoying well-being. Put another way, the rights protected by the Constitution are preconstitutional.

B. Living Constitutionalism

In response to Balkin's living originalism, a proponent of a rival school of interpretation asserted that any form of originalism that calls for "constitutional construction . . . is not originalist; it is living constitutionalist."[24] Some supporters of the living constitutionalism, most prominently David Strauss, contend that judicial precedent is the primary means for evolving and adapting the Constitution to social progress without needing to formally amend its antedated provisions.[25] Balkin, in response, suggested that judges should be unwilling to defend decisions that are not faithful to the Constitution's original framework.[26] Original intent and original meaning proponents would be even more averse than Balkin to following precedents that deviated from the will of the founding fathers, the framing generation, and the meaning they breathed into the Constitution.

Living constitutionalism is often associated with judicial decisions that redefine the meaning of the Constitution. Scholars and judges in this school of thought argue that constitutional meaning resides not in the text nor can it be construed through any form of originalism; rather, they seek to demonstrate how precedents define and alter the significance of various clauses. The Supreme Court is regarded as the locus of constitutional change, redefining the Constitution through major precedents during the New Deal, the Civil Rights Era, and throughout the course of US history. The Judiciary is therefore responsible for updating constitutional principles. Justice William Brennan cautioned that when judges rely on judicial review to guide constitutional meaning they should act "with full consciousness that it is . . . the community's interpretation that is sought."[27] Brennan recognized the value of reviewing the history of the framing, but wrote that the "ultimate question" is what the words of the Constitution mean today.

Brennan's approach left undefined how a justice should pick among contradictory community opinions to decide which is worthy of her or his attention. The maxim of constitutional interpretation I have developed in this book might help to fill that gap and prevent exclusionary members of the community from having too much influence on the Court's reasoning. The maxim of liberal equality for the common good can provide structure, requiring the president and Congress to likewise be aware and direct their public conduct in a manner likely to protect fundamental interests for the general welfare. Living constitutionalism can also be associated with the other branches of government guiding constitutional development. Professor Bruce Ackerman, for example, praised the common law approach to adaptation but criticized the judge-centered approach for slighting "the central importance of popular sovereignty."[28]

Balkin's and Ackerman's criticisms about placing too much trust in judges to guide constitutional evolution reject Strauss's vigorous defense of common law constitutionalism. Strauss believes that in the United States "precedent and past practices are, in their own way, as important as the written U.S. Constitution."[29] He further argues that Supreme Court decisions should be at the forefront, or, as he puts it, should be the "all-but-exclusive" means, of constitutional change, even when the precedents are not clearly based on the text of the Constitution. This precedent-centered model emphasizes the importance of building on past understandings and altering them in light of new sensibilities. It takes for granted the progressive nature of *stare decisis* and puts resolution of political disagreement into the hands of unelected judges. One weakness with such an approach is that it overlooks analytically faulty precedents and the judiciary's periodic regressive decision making. The resolution of disputes between different democratic factions are typically thought to be in the realm of bicameral conferences and congressional-executive deal making, not judicial oversight. Strauss's defense of the gradual common law process of precedents does not gainsay the fault of a system that would have to rely on judges almost exclusively for progress.

Supreme Court precedents have well-known high and low points. Some of the most obvious examples of judicial manipulation of the Constitution to suit justices' political and economic world views were *Dred Scott v. Sandford*[30] and *Lochner v. New York*.[31] In both cases, the Court construed substantive due process to impede legislators from safeguarding the rights of vulnerable groups and to address a public crisis—the crisis of slavery in the first and public health in the second. In the case of slavery, it was Article V of the Constitution that eventually facilitated change, through passage of the Reconstruction Amendments. Even after the ratification of the Amendments, the Court denied the constitutionality of a federal statute that prohibited the segregation of public places of accommodation, like inns and theaters,[32] and in another case turned back a private claimant's assertion that women have the same privilege and immunity as men to pursue careers, over the lone dissent of Chief Justice Salmon Chase.[33] With *Lochner*, the abandonment of judicial manipulation came through presidentially initiated programs during the New Deal. At first, the Court refused to go along with the increased nationalization of economic regulations and only conceded the validity of federal economic stimulus after striking several pieces of legislation that had been aimed at ending the Great Depression. The interpretational finality that the Court has bestowed upon itself has sometimes led to social uplift but at other times hung like a millstone around the necks of progressive social movements. One of the Constitution's structural complications is the difficulty of ratifying amendments under Article V—an even greater complication when the Court prevents the advancement of civil rights and by its narrow interpretation harms classes of people seeking to pursue their equal right to happiness.

That said, the Court has certainly played a visible role in advancing general welfare and the equal protection of fundamental rights. But in contrast to Strauss's model, progress has often occurred through cases that broke with past precedents rather than through gradual, inevitable change. *Brown v. Board of Education* was one of the decisions in which the Court overtly helped end a social evil by relying on the public value of democracy and the individual value of equal treatment.[34] In that case, the Court cited previous decisions that required limited desegregation, like *McLaurin v. Oklahoma State Regents* and *Sweatt v. Painter*, but those two cases were still rooted in the *Plessy v. Ferguson* regressive doctrine of separate but equal accommodations.[35] The moral clarity of *Brown* came from its deviation from precedent to protect the right of each student to an equal education and the common value of informed politics. The unanimous majority recognized that a pluralistic society's obligation to secure the common good of educated, political participation required the equal protection of minorities. When Herbert Wechsler criticized *Brown* for not being based on a neutral principle,[36] he was descriptively accurate, but his criticism of the Court's value-rich approach was off target. *Brown* was in keeping with the dual constitutional aim of protecting individuals for the mutual good of the population as a whole. The Declaration of Independence was first to place civic morality into political discourse. The Constitution later openly recognized the public's interest in federal enforcement of individual rights through a variety of amendments, beginning with the Bill of Rights. What the Bill of Rights failed to require of the states was supplied by incorporation through the 14th Amendment, with its grant of congressional authority to enforce national, constitutional norms and judicial authority to apply them to the states. The philosopher John Rawls explained the intertwining of personal and civic interests in education, stressing the "important . . . role of education in enabling a person to enjoy the culture of his society and to take part in its affairs, and in this way to provide for each individual a secure sense of his own worth."[37] Similarly, Justice Brennan, writing in a concurrence, explained that "Americans regard the public schools as a most vital civic institution for the preservation of a democratic system of government."[38]

Just as *Brown* was a definitive break, so too the abandonment of *Lochner* made a sharp turn away from previous common law constitutionalism. In *West Coast Hotel Co. v. Parrish*, the Court belatedly acknowledged that legislators can pass minimum wage laws for the sake of "public interest with respect to contracts between employer and employee."[39] In short order, the Court followed up in *United States v. Darby*, upholding the Fair Labor Standards Act of 1938.[40] This new line of cases, then, carved a legislative path for Congress to use its Commerce Clause power to set policies for the general welfare that could better the conditions of individual workers. The Court recognized the constitutionality of protecting workers by enforcing statutes that were rationally designed to expand ordinary people's ability to participate in a national economy. Some judicial opinions, congressional statements, and academic publications in the late 1930s and early 1940s claimed a connection between increasing the wages of economically disempowered individuals and the improvement of living conditions in the United States as a whole. This too was the connection between individual rights and the general welfare that I argue is at the forefront of legitimate-exercise governmental authority.

The possibility of change through the constitutional maxim interlinking the constitutional values of rights and general welfare, which are set down in the Declaration of Independence and the Preamble to the Constitution, is even more readily visible in the gender equality cases. That is, underlying common law constitutionalism is a maxim that creates the reaches of legitimacy for the exercise of federal power. The Court only began to adequately address the endemic harms of gender stereotypes in 1971, with its decision in *Reed v. Reed*.[41] Decisions that followed discarded the Court's previous tolerance for chauvinistic policies, such as it had upheld in *Bradwell v. Illinois* and *Minor v. Happersett*.[42] Without overturning either decision, since the 1970s the Court has swept away its previous rationalizations for stereotypical treatment of women in professional and political life. The change was not based on the text of the Constitution, nor can the advancement of women's rights be readily explained as judicially spearheaded progress. In fact, it was the outcome of advocacy that had begun with first- and second-wave feminists, not judicial leadership. In cases like *Nevada Department of Human Resources v. Hibbs*, which held that states were not immune from the Family and Medical Leave Act, the Court followed the evolution of more even-handed norms of family, profession, and politics;[43] the justices did not set them. To put it another way, the correctness of the Court's belated recognition of women's equality is not based on the justices' discursive reliance on past precedents but on the constitutional value of laws safeguarding intrinsic human equality to enjoy the benefits of living in a representative republic. If the Court had remained recalcitrant in upholding states' uses of gender stereotypes, its decision making would have been better adjudged by the maxim of constitutional governance, which sets the ethos of national constitutionalism, rather than past precedents, which have sometimes been mired in longstanding prejudices.

Strauss's common law living constitutionalism is significant because it draws attention to the role that precedents play in constitutional change. But to his account should be added a stable principle against which developing doctrine must be tested. The principle cannot come solely from historical judicial sources, many of which are tainted with discriminatory intents and meanings of the past. Even the text of the Declaration of Independence and the Preamble to the Constitution are not transparent.

C. Neutral Principles

An evaluation of whether public policies and judicial opinions protect the people's pursuit of happiness and provide for the general welfare can be either normative or procedural. This section analyzes a number of neutral standards of interpretation and evaluates them in light of the substantive maxim constitutionalism.

Philip Bobbitt developed a highly influential discursive analysis for judicial reasoning. His six modalities of legitimate legal analysis—historical, textual, structural, doctrinal, ethical, and prudential—provide no normative foundation for interpretation. Bobbitt articulated the rationales judges provide for their holdings, but he recognized no value to a meta-theory. The modalities are descriptive, but Bobbitt's methodology contained no underlying constitutional purpose for determining whether a judge's reliance on them is purely formalistic or substantively valid.[44]

The inquiry that I have suggested is at the root of maxim constitutionalism—of whether policy protects individual rights for the common good—plays no explicit role in his modalism. Even if it falls under Bobbitt's "ethical" mode, it would be one value among others rather than, as I suggest, the core value of the Constitution and therefore relevant to all rights and institutions covered by it. On his account, a judge applying any or several of the six accepted rationales need not reflect on whether a law infringes on fundamental rights and excludes a group from the enjoyment of mutual benefits of representative democracy. The modes do not discriminate between their proper use by proslavery antebellum judges, by judges in Jim Crow courtrooms, or by judges in post-Civil Rights Era settings. The ethical semantic in his system lacks an objective component that could be used to test a judge's use of normative language.

The modal approach only allows for neutral rather than normative criticism of judicial opinions. Bobbitt's discussion of Chief Justice Roger Taney's opinion in the *Dred Scott* case, for instance, does not criticize the Court for the faulty holding that free and enslaved blacks were an "inferior class of beings" who could not hold citizenship in the United States.[45] Bobbitt only drew attention to the textual implications of Justice Taney's reasoning:

> A textual modality may be attributed to arguments that the text of the Constitution would, to the average person, appear to declare, or deny, or be too vague to say whether, a suit between a black American citizen resident in a state and a white American citizen resident in another state, is a "controversy between citizens of different states." I would imagine that the contemporary meaning of these words is rather different than that which Taney found them to mean to the framers and ratifiers of 1789.[46]

This retrospective statement left unexamined whether Justice Taney's assertion that the Constitution precluded blacks from being citizens violated their inalienable and political rights and, thereby, diminished their opportunity to enjoy the common good.

Contemporary critics of *Dred Scott*, like abolitionists and the then newly formed Republican Party, certainly thought Justice Taney to be acting against the nation's normative standards. A Milwaukee newspaper summed up a Republican Convention that had convened in Madison, Wisconsin, at the end of summer 1857:

> Our Platform, too, is as good as our ticket. It reaffirms the principles upon which the original organization of our party was based; renews the pledges of opposition to the extension of slavery, to the Fugitive Slave Act, and to the admission of any more slave States into the Union; denounces all proscription on account of birth, creed, or color: declares for equal rights to all citizens of the Republic, native, or foreign-born;

takes high and impregnable grounds against the *Dred Scott* decision, and on that issue appeals from the dicta of partizan Judges to the great tribunal of The People. We stand, therefore, in this canvass as the advocates of Free Soil and Free Labor, of Equal Rights and Civil and Religious Liberty, of State Sovereignty and the true Interpretation of the Federal Constitution; and as the opponents of slavery aggression and slavery extension, of political proscription, and of judicial miscon- structions of the great charter, ordained and established by the fathers and founders of our Republic "to form a more perfect Union, establish justice, insure domestic tranquility, provide for the common defence, promote the general welfare and secure the blessings of Liberty to our- selves and our posterity."

A meeting of "colored" citizens in New Bedford, Massachusetts, determined that *Dred Scott* was not merely a wrong statement as a matter of interpretation but substantively flawed. Their meeting convened with a statement that "colored people of this country have ever prove[n] . . . their loyalty to its interests and general welfare." Participants resolved that "the infamous '*Dred Scott*' decision is a palpably vain, arrogant assumption, unsustained by history, justice, reason[,] or common sense."[47] The New Hampshire Senate and House of Representatives jointly issued a statement that the people of that state confirmed their "devoted attachment to the principles embodied in the Declaration of Independence" and in the Preamble to the Constitution and, therefore, rejected the *Dred Scott* deci- sion as "subversive."[48]

Merely looking at the text, without reflecting on national ideals, Bobbitt's de- scription of the case leaves the impression that it is contemporary linguistic usage that should be determinative of constitutional meaning rather than some central purpose of representative constitutionalism or intrinsic dignity of humanity, ir- respective of race. A normative approach to interpretation makes clear that *Dred Scott* is not only a textual misreading of the Declaration of Independence, but the nation's history, and judicial authority. Justice Taney's principal flaw was norma- tive: His opinion denied that the "general welfare" of the nation must apply to all persons in the United States, not merely those of European descent.

On the ethical side, Bobbitt recognized that the Declaration of Independence provides the "political basis for the idea of the constitution." To him, the Declaration's guarantee of "[u]nalienable rights" means that the people have not, and indeed cannot, renounce their sovereignty over state power.[49] Bobbitt is certainly basing this point on the people's retention of sovereignty. He did not, however, take the Declaration to be an overarching statement of national purpose to protect intrinsic human rights and thus did not couple it with the Preamble's mandate that government "promote the general Welfare[] and secure the Blessings of Liberty." But for Bobbitt, "American constitutional ethos" is of a more limited nature, "confined to the reservation of powers not delegated to a limited government."[50] His ethical modality refers to the "characterization of American institutions and the role within them of the American people."[51] But Bobbitt provided no meta-method for identifying whether, at any given point in history, American institutions and the people involved in them aimed to protect fundamental rights for the general welfare or were energized into rely- ing on a modal judgment by prejudice and exclusion. Without acknowledging an underlying purpose, Bobbitt's modes of legal practice provide no means of deciding whether judicial holdings and explanations are formalistically logical but unfaithful to the nation's core commitment to sustaining equal liberty for the common good. The modalities, then, are not means of determining whether a judicial rationale is true to an underlying constitutional purpose but "no more than instrumental, rhetorical devices to be deployed in behalf of various political ideologies."[52]

Bobbitt is, of course, not the first to defend neutral principles. Wechsler's ex- position of neutral principles was not only descriptive but also required a court to parse the meaning of the Constitution and apply it to specific cases without being influenced by the judge's personal and political convictions. In his best known exposition of this reasoning, Wechsler critiqued the Court's principled holding against school segregation in *Brown v. Board of Education*. Legitimacy lies in a judge's following precedents announced in previous decisions, apply- ing the doctrine of *stare decisis*, without deviating from them to achieve desired ends. And with the *Brown* decision, Wechsler wrote that, as much as he sup- ported the sentiment for desegregating schools, he could find no neutral consti- tutional principle for the decision.[53]

Wechsler's reasoning was suspect for a number of reasons. For one, certain portions of the Constitution—like the Equal Protection Clause, the Eighth Amendment prohibition against cruel and unusual punishment, and the First Amendment protections for speech and religion—appear to be value rich, in need of interpretation, and not neutral in value. Their evaluation and the reevaluation of past interpretations of them—like *Plessy v. Ferguson*, which *Brown* functionally overturned—are based on a deep understanding of the entire structure of popular governance, with a concomitant respect for inalien- able rights and equal legal status. The Equal Protection Clause was one of the great culminations of the Union victory over the Confederacy and, even under the most minimal reading, it secured equality of citizenship for blacks and per- sons of all races. Although not explicitly mentioned in *Brown*, the right to civic participation also played a role in the Court's reasoning. The First Amendment secured political speech, and its safeguards were incorporated through the 14th Amendment. And the *Brown* Court found that integrated education was essential for equality and civic dialogue. Where a new case before the Court concerns a moral dilemma for society, the Supreme Court must stay true to *stare decisis* but also choose whether to overrule its past error or to broadly interpret its previous decisions.

Furthermore, where previous decisions have misguided constitutional law—as was the case with *Plessy v. Ferguson*—a new course must be steered, one that deviates from past precedents but is true to constitutional principle. This position bears some overlap with Ronald Dworkin's assertion that the Supreme Court should make decisions on the basis of the principle "that government must treat people as equals."[54] The equality principle, first stated in the Declaration of Independence and then adopted into the Constitution, is by no means neutral but instead maxim-oriented.

I disagree with Dworkin, however, that reflection "about how the general welfare is best promoted" should play no role in constitutional interpretation.[55] To the contrary, the Preamble mandates policy reflections on the general welfare, and such reflection allows for the differentiation between the exclusionary reading of equality in *Plessy* and the inclusionary version in *Brown*. It was only in the latter that the Court formally recognized that equality must include the ranks of all Americans, joined together in the pluralistic efforts of representative governance. The task of identifying how the maxim of equal liberty for the common good applies to specific social dilemmas requires a balance of authority between the President, Congress, and the Supreme Court. It is for all of us as a people to determine, reconsider, and hone the meaning of representative democracy. The balance of rights and public needs remains a policy-by-policy, case-by-case, law-by-law, and regulation-by-regulation determination. All of these avenues of lawmaking must be undertaken without offending the central maxim of constitutionalism. There will inevitably be conflicts between the three branches of government. As I have explained elsewhere, in these inter-branch policy disputes, legislative expansion of equal rights to discrete and insular minorities should take precedence over constitutional common law that constricts national authority.[56] Congress as well as the Court can identify groups that have historically been persecuted and are covered by 13th and 14th Amendment enforcement clauses.

D. Living Up to Constitutional Ideals

Constitutional maxim creates a normative baseline for the use of authority, requiring officials to formulate and enforce policies that respect individual dignities and aim to achieve the common good, thereby balancing personal and community rights and obligations. This is a model that, like the Declaration of

Independence and Preamble to the Constitution, requires decision makers to synthesize deontological and consequentialist considerations.

In most cases—from taxing to the running of water purification plants—no constitutional issue will be involved and a court will simply defer to reasonably formulated regulations that do not aim to prejudice any particular person or group. That is not the case, however, where some constitutional issue is at stake. United States precedents require courts to use heightened scrutiny to analyze laws on constitutional rights, electoral politics, or insular groups.[57] The power of the judiciary to review policies of the other two branches of government must not be exercised willy-nilly, given that the judges, like all other officials of government, are bound by the Constitution and its underlying maxim.

Many constitutional advances are made by normative criteria rather than strict compliance with text. Louis Michael Seidman has pointed out numerous instances in which the US Supreme Court decided cases whose outcomes were not determined by any literal construction of the Constitution.[58] The Court has indeed recognized unwritten rights, such as privacy, travel, and parental autonomy, that are not explicitly mentioned in any clauses of the Constitution nor in the Declaration of Independence.[59]

Seidman argued that "all-things-considered judgments," by which I understand him to mean contextual interpretations, will often lead to more just results than ones fixated on categorical analyses.[60] He is surely correct that contextual balancing is more likely to achieve fair results than formalistic interpretation of text. But he does not believe that a set constitutional norms is necessary to achieve fair results. His notion of construction includes no unambiguous principle that judges must include in their "all-things-considered judgments." Seidman concedes that "foundational principles" should be permitted to play a role in legal discourse but only "when they preserve the possibility of legitimate contestation."[61] He further asserts that, "there is no moral duty to obey our foundational law—the Constitution of the United States."[62] This provides too limited a guidance to decision makers who seek to prevent or redress injustices. Without some foundational principle, albeit one that is not strictly limited by the text of the Constitution, there exists a risk that the strongest forces in a democracy will dominate and oppress weaker groups. Without constitutionally recognized principle, the powerful are likely to have disproportionate access to legal power and connections for carrying out their aims. Seidman would certainly oppose unjust behaviors, yet his system leaves the people with no certainty that government will avoid them.

The foundation of the Constitution, I believe, is predicated on the maxim of equal liberty for the common good as a check against the abuses of public office. It is codified in the nation's founding documents, the Declaration of Independence and Constitution, but empowers the people, as sovereigns of their country's destiny, to shape self-governance. Defining the synthetic principle of private and public goods will not yield one correct answer to social dilemmas, but it will create systematic stability for rendering judgments commensurate with both interests. I therefore agree with Seidman that constitutional interpretation should not be a semantic or syntactical exercise, but I would go further than he to argue that contextual analysis must include reflections (by way of precedents, historical documents, best practices, traditions, etc.) of the highest aspiration of national unity.

All three branches of government should derive the ultimate sense of purpose from the maxim of constitutional rights and general welfare. Analysis of whether a state's policies, regulations, and statutes positively impact society must be tempered by concerns for inalienable rights of the people. Not all efficient nor prudential policies are, therefore, constitutional, especially those that contain arbitrary limitations on autonomy and impacts on equality. A society that balances individual and common goods is equipped with the necessary theoretical foundation for tolerance and pluralism.

It requires a combined private and public mindedness to meet the basic structures of the Declaration of Independence and Preamble. The rights that these documents protect belong to everyone equally by virtue of their humanity ("unalienable rights" in the words of Declaration or rights "retained by the people" against government intrusion in the formulation of the Ninth Amendment). The philosopher Alan Gewirth explained these in more modern terms as "generic rights" of the recipient of the action "as well as of yourself." As Gewirth explains, this norm requires "action in accord with the recipients' generic rights of freedom and of well-being."[63] Government obligation is tied to social morality that places restraints on the use of power and requires the creation of social programs that positively affect the population without compromising essential freedoms. Government's obligation in such a social environment is to account for and respond to the interests of everyone as they are expressed through constitutionally predictable structures for assimilating collective wisdom into nondiscriminatory laws. The representative process is meant to give practical effect to the people's will.

The Constitution is both an expression of popular will and a restraint upon it. On the one hand, it creates institutional powers for the betterment of the people's welfare. This is evident in provisions found in Articles I, II, and III, dealing respectively with legislative, executive, and judicial prerogatives. On the other hand, the personal guarantees of the document, found in the Bill of Rights and scattered in other provisions like the Reconstruction Amendments, limit representatives' abilities to respond to constituents' demands. For instance, the Guarantee and Equal Protection Clauses are meant to restrain even the will of the majority from depriving some other class of rights otherwise shared by the general population.

When coupled with the Declaration's statement of innate human rights, the functions of government created by the Constitution must be carried out in accordance with America's founding principles. My perspective differs from that of another champion of the Declaration of Independence and Preamble to the Constitution. Mark Tushnet asserts that, "The Declaration and the Preamble provide the substantive criteria for identifying the people's vital interests. They show why we are dealing with a populist constitutional law rather than simply disagreements about the everyday stuff of political life."[64] The ideals of the "thin Constitution," as Tushnet calls it, derive from the Declaration and Preamble.[65] The generality of these documents can facilitate a broad variety of constitutional interpretations and political lobbying. The ideals they state continue to inspire a diverse society.

I regard these ideals to be grounded in objective rights that are not born of those documents but identified by them. On the other hand, by "the people's vital interests" Tushnet is specifically referring to Americans' preferences. His popular constitutionalism is positivist insofar as it is based on unique historical experiences in the United States. His interpretive approach offers important understanding of the powerful formula of those documents but does not fully account for their use of general, indeed universal, language. I believe that those rights that both documents secure (and which the president, Congress, and Supreme Court are organized to preserve) are intrinsic and inborn. While my perspective is similar to natural rights theory because it recognizes constitutional grounding in moral obligations, I think that an added layer of sociological thought is essential to regularly update laws to meet contemporary needs.

The Declaration of Independence and the Constitution were adopted in response to historical events. However, the rights they protect were not those solely of value at that time nor yet of the people then alive in the United States. Those entitlements, which government cannot divest any individual of without some compelling reasons, are instead derived from our coequal liberties. This was the shared belief of many contemporaries of the American Revolution. Celebrating independence in 1791, an orator excitedly proclaimed to a crowd of Bostonians that Americans sought not violence "but to preserve those unalienable rights, which belong to man in all ages."[66]

The Free Speech Clause of the First Amendment is one example of a constitutional guarantee rooted in innate liberties. That provision's function is not solely a signal of cultural preference; rather, it is predicated on the interest of everyone. Interpretation of the amendment has indisputably evolved from one commonly understood in the 18th century to only restrict state imposed prior restraints to the robust guarantee of speech and assembly that it is today.[67] The expansion of protections for expressive statements and symbolic behaviors has been based on an expanding jurisprudential and cultural respect for self-expression and the need for open dialogue to the success of representative democracy. These long-accepted principles of government have no real value unless they inform the creation of laws that better achieve the mandate of liberal equality for the common good.

To remain relevant, constitutional principles must be informative to practical legal questions. The original maxim remains binding because it is predicated on human nature and the structure of representative government. But judicial, legislative, and executive interpretation should not be stagnant. All three branches must be informed and responsive to current needs, the lessons of history, the developments of culture, and the will of the people. I am, therefore, proposing a system maintaining stability while providing the space needed for social change.

‖ 9 ‖

Maxim Constitutionalism Today

The Preamble to the Constitution and the Declaration of Independence jointly define the national ethos of US constitutionalism. The Constitution empowers the three branches of government to safeguard representative democracy and to devise social policies. The constitutional maxim to protect liberal equality for the benefit of the common good is the overarching purpose of governance. The Preamble's and Declaration's dictates are the animating features of the Constitution. They collectively set a duty of public responsibility to pursue policies conducive to individual and public welfare.

To this point of the book, I have sought to understand the sources, structure, and ethos of constitutional interpretation and governance to balance private and public interests. The normative purpose of representative governance in the United States is to safeguard inalienable rights and provide social and civic goods. If I am correct, then this foundational feature should play a central role in the resolution of any legal issue with a nexus to constitutional law. Having worked out the theory in the previous chapters, I conclude with an analysis of its application to several structural issues.

A. Political Community

The United States is composed of a plurality of peoples. It teems with devotees of different religions, immigrants from disparate (and often dissonant) cultures, and supporters of acrimonious political parties. To facilitate, optimize, and conciliate the legal interaction of so many diverse peoples, common sources of norms are essential for domestic tranquility. The Declaration and the Preamble provide the maxim for the use of national authority, respect of rights, and civic obligations. They set the underlying value of representative democracy. The principle that government must protect rights whenever possible, except when overriding public risks to public health, welfare, or safety are at stake, requires contextual balancing of multiple relevant factors. Without a foundational, normative fulcrum that places a universal limit on the use of authority, a majoritarian democracy is likely to pose a threat to the civil and political rights of less powerful individuals. The framers incorporated anti-majoritarian sentiment into the Constitution through a variety of structures such as the Electoral College, six-year terms for senators, and a judiciary with lifetime appointment.

The commitment to separation of powers and self-government is meant to empower each voter with meaningful opportunities to participate in formulating public policy. The ideal of participatory democracy is partly predicated on the notion that each person is endowed with the inborn traits of liberty, personality, desire, contentment, ambition, aspiration, self-directedness, and so forth. Several recent doctrinal developments have tended to undermine this system of equal representation and strengthened the hand of oligarchical forces. A series of Supreme Court cases have diminished congressional and state authority to promulgate and enforce laws against massive corporate spending on political campaigns.

The Court in *Citizens United v. Federal Election Commission* (2010) began unraveling some legal barriers against political corruption when it found unconstitutional a key limitation of the Bipartisan Campaign Reform Act of 2002 (BCRA). The law was passed with the support of both political parties. The relevant portion of the statute limited corporate campaign expenditures.

The case arose when a nonprofit corporation, Citizens United, sought to disseminate a movie that negatively depicted then Democratic presidential primary candidate, Senator Hillary Clinton. Citizens United's legal bone of contention was that a section of the BCRA (Section 203) unconstitutionally interfered with its free speech rights by preventing the airing of a commercially financed, political spot within a statutorily proscribed period of time. The Court decided that the corporation had the same free speech rights as natural persons, and, therefore, the federal law subjecting corporations to special restrictions on their efforts to influence political campaigns violated Citizens United's First Amendment right to fund campaign speech.[1]

That holding is inconsistent with the maxim that representative government is created for the benefit of natural individuals. The statute protected personal and communal political rights. It created a synthetic scheme consistent with what I have sought to show is foundational to the legitimate uses of constitutional authority. The Court's holding in *Citizens United* was formalistic. Rather than balancing personal and public interests, the holding was predicated on the notion that Congress could not discriminate based on the corporate identity of the speaker.

Lost in the Court's seemingly hard rejection to differentiating corporate speech for stricter regulation is any meaningful consideration about the contrasting roles played by artificial, for-profit persons (businesses), natural persons (ordinary citizens), or organizations voicing the collective views of natural persons. As members of a political community, natural people participate in politics to fulfill their own vision of democracy and to advance the common good by choosing whomever they perceive to be the best officials for elective office. Corporations, on the other hand, cannot participate in elections and are therefore meaningfully on a different political par than ordinary citizens. This is especially true of for-profit corporations, as opposed to those created for the express purpose of advocacy. Moreover, the amount of money a citizen has to spend on political campaigns is minuscule relative to what is available to corporations, especially publicly traded corporations, therefore making it far easier for incorporated businesses to get out their messages than almost all but the most affluent or famous private citizens. Lack of regulatory control of corporate expenditures on campaigns, therefore, marginalizes the voices of individual citizens and negatively impacts their access to civic audiences. Without engaging in the balanced analysis this book has propounded, the Court's holding did not consider whether Congress might have important, and perhaps even compelling, civic reasons to overlook the "unfair advantage" corporations gain from using "amassed" resources.[2]

The majority in *Citizens United* rightly asserted that the "First Amendment stands against attempts to disfavor certain subjects or viewpoints." But its categorical rejection of "restrictions distinguishing among different speakers, allowing speech by some but not others" overlooked a large number of identity-based categories whose regulations have not been thought to cause any free speech difficulties. For instance, it has long been recognized that people cannot practice medicine or law without licenses. Nor is anyone permitted to impersonate police officers. Such restrictions single out individuals based on categories. Just to name one of an almost infinite number of examples of professions not subject to the same limits on free expression, waitressing requires neither license nor claims special privileges against false representation. Yet the distinctions made in the regulation of those professions has never been thought to cause any First Amendment problems. On a political scale it was logical for Congress to distinguish between the speech of potential voters or associations composed of people advocating specific political agendas and of businesses running for-profit operations and unable to participate in the franchise.

Free speech is nuanced, requiring judicial review of a wide variety of relevant personal and public factors. The Court in *Citizens United* oversimplified First Amendment precedents. The commercial speech doctrine provides one obvious example of the majority's failure to reflect existing doctrine. Past decisions have typically treated commercial speech differently than purely political speech, demonstrating a distinct hierarchy of communications. The Court did not apply the commercial speech line of precedent to the Citizens United non-profit organization because it presumed that financing campaign speech was not only of economic interest. But that should not be presumed but an issue determined through the record built in the course of litigation. Political speech can be exploited to sell products. Putting an American flag in a commercial logo or even selling the American flag might be motivated by no patriotic sentiments but only a desire to profit financially. So, too, in supporting one political candidate over another, a corporation might be solely motivated by its economic interests. The Court should have closely probed this issue in *Citizens United*. Even if it found that the Citizens United organization was indeed an advocacy company protected by the First Amendment, despite partly being funded by for-profit corporations, that should not lead to the conclusion that corporations as a whole have an equal share of constitutionally protected speech rights.

The Court instead analyzed the corporate campaign financing regulation through the lens of the strict scrutiny doctrine that would have been more logically reserved for the speech of persons eligible to participate in elective franchise or of lobbying organizations. That interpretive approach was arguably appropriate for a political advocacy group like Citizens United, whose primary aim was to disseminate the views of its members, but the Supreme Court set a rule for using compelling scrutiny for all corporations, whether their aims are increasing profit margins or advocating on behalf of a constitutional association of like-minded people.

Speech related with general corporate expenditures typically concerns copyright protections, trademark laws, restrictions on insider trading, misrepresentations in the course of contractual negotiations, and advertisements. None of these categories of expression are directly connected to the First Amendment but are instead related to proprietary and economic rights. The campaign finance area, to the contrary, concerns the ability to freely disseminate, engage, and receive politically consequential information. Courts should review laws restricting corporate political expenditures through a matrix of deeply balanced analysis that allows Congress to protect individual rights—here special rights to electioneer—and the general welfare, such as the social benefits of representative governance.

After *Citizens United* some commentators understood the ruling to be based on federalist principles, increasing the latitude of states to regulate corporate electoral spending. But two years after that decision the Court quashed that notion, finding unconstitutional a state campaign financing law. In *American Tradition Partnership, Inc. v. Bullock*, a case decided in 2012, the Court struck down a state regulation prohibiting any corporation from making "an expenditure in connection with a candidate or a political committee that supports or opposes a candidate or a political party."[3] The Court found that the statute violated a corporation's First Amendment right by enforcing the law for which the state lacked a compelling state reason. The majority clearly regarded corporations to be about as invaluable to electoral politics as real people. At oral argument, Justice Sonia Sotomayor, who later was one of four justices in the dissent, pointed out that in its opinion "the Court imbued a creature of state law with human characteristics."[4]

In 2011, the Roberts Court had placed an additional obstacle, impeding state efforts to equalize access to political speech. Writing for the majority, Chief Justice Roberts held that Arizona lacked a compelling interest to administer a campaign finance system that had granted qualified state office candidates public funding to equalize privately financed candidates' expenditures.[5]

These Supreme Court decisions limit government's ability to pass legislation to increase natural persons' involvement in political campaigns. It provides special opportunities for the rich, including corporations, and dilutes political access for middle class and, especially, indigent citizens. The Court's most recent categorical opinion on electioneering speech found unconstitutional a federal aggregation limit on contributing to the campaigns of multiple candidates. In that opinion, *McCutcheon v. Federal Election Commission*, the Court likewise reacted regressively to limitations placed on affluent persons that restricted their ability to influence politics without giving adequate deference to progressive legal approaches of ending disproportionate, corrupting political influence of wealthy contributors. While campaign finance laws limit affluent individuals and corporations, they also empower most of us, who are not so wealthy as to pay for commercials, films, mass mailings, and other means that curry favor with politicians. Beyond empowering ordinary persons, campaign finance laws can equalize the playing field for all citizens to engage in the political process: They provide for the civic good by enabling all citizens to be part of the deliberative process.

These critiques of recent developments in campaign financing doctrine are not meant to deny that corporations have a stake in what candidates win elective offices. The ability of corporations to flourish contributes to the common good, especially in a 21st century world where they play such an important part in the economy through manufacture, distribution, and retail. For this reason, the BCRA had a provision exempting corporate political action committees (PACs) from restrictions on for-profit entities. Corporate participants can thereby play a meaningful role in development of laws and institutions.

The right to vote is both individual and associational. That is, an individual's ability to influence and participate in the electoral process can be enhanced by engaging with associations like the National Association for the Advancement of Colored People or the National Rifle Association, which are constituted in part to advocate the interests of like-minded individuals. When people join these organizations, they expect to ally in cooperative efforts to influence public policy. The same is true when a person contributes to a PAC. But people give money to for-profit enterprises to acquire goods and services or to invest in publicly traded companies. The ability of individuals and communicative associates to meaningfully participate in elections and thereby, in the words of the Declaration of Independence, "to effect their safety and happiness," is tied to the Preamble's guarantee of general welfare. Executives of for-profit corporations, on the other hand, bear a responsibility to shareholders to maximize profits without even being required to take public welfare or even the views of shareholders into account. The role of for-profit contributions in elections is meaningfully different in how it aims to affect individual rights and the common good.

B. Personal Heath and Public Welfare

Public health is a field in which the Court has recognized the Constitution's grant of general welfare authority. This speaks to the positive aspect of constitutionalism, which authorizes the use of government programs for the betterment of people's lives. Given the costs of healthcare, illness is an evil that can often only be relieved by public subsidies through programs like Medicaid and Medicare. Much of the American public has considered "the right to adequate medical care and the opportunity to achieve and enjoy good health" to be essential to national "equality in the pursuit of happiness," at least since President Franklin Roosevelt gave eloquent voice to that national aspiration in the 1944 State of the Union Address.[6] The source of the concept is much older than that, as the Declaration of Independence's guarantee of "life, liberty, and the pursuit of happiness" is closely related to philosopher John Locke's formulation: "life, health, liberty or possessions."[7] Authors of the founding generation often conceived representative government to be tied to the enjoyment of health, life, liberty, and happiness.[8]

Despite this early recognition, it was not until the 20th century that the federal government began to administer health programs to a significant segment of society either too handicapped, elderly, or indigent to afford adequate treatments. The provision of health has since been regarded both as a private and public matter, being linked to longevity as it is to the prevention of epidemics. One of the most important currently operating healthcare laws is the Medicaid Act of 1965. The source of congressional authority to enforce it is the Spending Clause of the Constitution's mandate to "provide for the general welfare."[9] The act subsidizes a variety of low-income beneficiaries, including children under

19 years of age; pregnant women; the elderly; and adults and children with certain disabilities, such as blindness. Another of the general welfare benefits of federal government is the Medicare program, which covers all persons 65 years of age or older, persons who have been disabled for at least two years, and those in end-stage renal failure. Both programs help individuals and provide uniform normative obligations to care for the infirm and the poor. Congress is empowered to pass necessary and proper legislation funding and regulating the administering of these and other healthcare programs for the benefit of society at large and for the good of individual patients. Both entitlement programs provide payments for physicians' services from general federal revenues derived through tax payments. Private health providers administer medical treatments, thereby, to some degree, shielding their treatment decisions from government interference. The system is imperfect because the government now dictates fee payment schedules based on specific diagnoses and treatments with inadequate particularization of treatment plans. The centralized bureaucratic scheme puts too much weight on prudential concerns stemming from the limited available funds, and thereby influences physicians' treatment plans that impact patient care and systemic administration. However, both are positive examples of society providing much-needed safety nets for the elderly and indigent throughout the United States.

The most recent development in public health is the Patient Protection and Affordable Care Act of 2010 (ACA). The statute aims to solve the collective action problem of inadequate state and private healthcare coverage for uninsured persons, especially those who do not qualify for Medicaid and Medicare. The ACA prohibits private insurers from denying coverage to any person because of his or her prior medical condition(s), canceling insurance policies except in cases of fraud, capping lifetime insurance coverage, and increasing premium payments because of medical histories.[10] These and other patient safeguards were passed in an effort to advance the national good by aiding individuals who lacked insurance coverage, combining the deontic duty to provide medical coverage to persons and the consequentialist benefits of joint congressional efforts surpassing the capacity, efficiency, and resources of any state. The ACA remains controversial in part because it paternalistically required individuals and families to acquire health insurance by a set date as a means of driving down collective costs for insurance coverage. Yet, this limitation of personal autonomy was a salubrious effort, of limited success, to drive down the cost of insurance for the population as a whole.

One of the ACA's most controversial provisions expanded Medicaid coverage in an effort to make healthcare universally available. Beside the individual mandate, the law sought to expand Medicaid coverage to more people, specifically adults under 65 years of age whose income was below 133 percent of the federal poverty level. The government committed to paying all the costs of the federal program from 2014 to 2016, reducing expenditures on a sliding scale until the lowest point of 90 percent of costs for any newly eligible beneficiaries after 2020.[11]

A variety of lawsuits challenged the constitutionality of the ACA. In *National Federation of Independent Business (NFIB) v. Sebelius*, the Supreme Court upheld the individual mandate as a proper exercise of Congress's taxing power. However, the Court found that the Medicaid expansion program violated Congress's Spending Clause authority because it threatened to withhold all Medicaid funding from states that refused to comply with the provision. States expected a significant increase in expenditures because the ACA provided coverage for many childless adults who had not previously been covered by the program. The ACA's expansion of Medicaid to persons below 133 percent of the poverty level would have also augmented the states' welfare rolls. Before its enactment most states did not include adults without children in their Medicaid programs and the average unemployed parents covered by state programs made "less than 37 percent of the federal poverty level" and employed parents covered by states' Medicaid programs "made 63 percent of the poverty line."[12] Rather than treating the expansion as an amendment to the existing Medicaid program, the Supreme Court required the Department of Health and Human Services to treat each part of the program separately, allowing states to choose between them. States would therefore only be obligated to comply with the terms of the programs to which they had agreed, rather than to the whole Medicaid mandate. Congress could not, therefore, withhold all Medicaid funds because a state refused to participate in any particular portion of the program. This was an odd holding on a Spending Clause provision.

The Court favored state rights over Congress's power to advance the general welfare by providing for medical needs of low-income individuals. The majority in *NFIB* opined that the ACA's Medicaid expansion was coercive, and therefore violated state autonomy. Prior to that holding, the appellate court from which the case was appealed had found that the expansion was constitutional.[13] Congress had modified Medicaid many times prior to the passage of the ACA. From the maxim constitutionalism standpoint, the 2010 expansion of programs was in accordance with the Preamble to the Constitution's mandate that the federal government act for the general welfare, rather than in the interest of any particular or group of states, and the language of the Spending Clause made the modification clearly within the necessary and proper powers of Congress. Personal health is a critical ingredient to the Declaration of Independence's guarantee of national policies beneficial to citizens' equal pursuits of happiness.

Rather than considering the dual constitutional principle I have advocated throughout this book—that interpretation should take into account the effect of law on individuals and the public good—the Court refused to defer to Congress's judgment. Instead, it used an undue influence rationale to abrogate the exercise of national authority, conditioning the use of federal grants. The 10th Amendment, which provides a general statement on the limits of federal authority, became a tool for hampering Congress from using largesse for the general welfare. This bodes ill for the many conditional grants of revenue associated with spending programs. The *NFIB* decision created the possibility of states raising the defense of federal coercion power to an almost limitless number of spending programs, such as Title IX or Title VI of the Civil Rights Act of 1964, which have respectively been instrumental in combating state discrimination in sports and education. Focusing more specifically on Medicaid, states retained flexibility under the expansion to increase the class of covered people, but not to diminish it. While that is good, it is not enough. Congress should be free to serve as the people's representative in advancing programs that comport with national interests, like healthcare, without judicial interference on behalf of state rights.

In a different portion of *NFIB*, the Court upheld the ACA's individual mandate that required persons to either obtain health insurance or pay a tax penalty. The law was upheld as a legitimate exercise of Congress's taxing power. But the Court rejected the claim that Congress could exercise this authority pursuant to its Commerce Clause authority. This was a somewhat surprising assertion of judicial constitutional oversight because the purchase and administration of health insurance are economic activities with a substantial effect on persons and the public.

Chief Justice Roberts's limited view of the Commerce Clause differs from the post-New Deal deferential understanding. From 1937 until the late-1990s, the Court had consistently upheld statutes necessary and proper to regulate interstate commerce. Accordingly, the Court deferred to Congress's social recognition that minimum wage, maximum hour,[14] and economic production quota legislation[15] were needed to resolve pressing social problems. In these opinions, the Court rejected the use of labels—like "direct" and "indirect," or "marketing," "production," and "consumption" —to avoid thwarting congressional Commerce Clause initiatives. In *NFIB*, the Court returned to labels—adding "inactivity" to the formalistic catalogue of legislative restraints—to thwart national purpose.

By relying on the Taxing Clause, Justice Roberts not only expanded the policies Congress can seek to achieve by taxing, but also contracted Congress's ability to find creative solutions on the basis of its authority over interstate commerce. This weighted approach, favoring judicial finality (some would say judicial fiat) to representative democracy, constrained Congress's role in identifying pressing social needs and allocating funds for broadly applicable legislation to safeguard individuals and the public as a whole. More disappointing, in the healthcare context, as in several other areas of legislation, the Court continues to ignore the

Declaration's promise of inalienable rights and the Preamble's General Welfare Clause, both of which lend themselves to empowering representative democracy to provide for the people's interest in an economically sound healthcare system for themselves, their loved ones, and their neighbors.

C. State Sovereign Immunity

Diminishing Congress's authority to use Spending Clause authority to administer programs for the general welfare, like Medicaid expansion, and increasing judicial oversight of laws passed pursuant to the Commerce Clause are part of a broader pattern of judicial buttressing of state prerogatives. The Court's heavy-handed interpretation of federal statutes affecting state sovereignty has reduced the American public's ability to challenge states' actions pursuant to federal civil rights statutes. In some circumstances, the sovereign immunity doctrine has left states with too much discretion about the treatment of vulnerable segments of the population.

From a textual perspective, the state sovereign immunity doctrine is suspect because the framers seem to have purposefully left it out of the Constitution. The silence was particularly conspicuous because America's first constitution, The Articles of Confederation, stated: "Each state retains its sovereignty, freedom, and independence, and every power, jurisdiction, and right, which is not by this Confederation expressly delegated to the United States, in Congress assembled."[16] The framers' decision to exclude that clause and even any intimation to it signals a more national reach for the federal government under the Constitution. The Court has construed that state sovereign immunity doctrine from an unlikely source: the 11th Amendment. The language lends itself to no such reading:

> The Judicial power of the United States shall not be construed to extend to any suit in law or equity, commenced or prosecuted against one of the United States by Citizens of another State, or by Citizens or Subjects of any Foreign State,

Finding this language to imply general sovereign immunity is a bit like putting a square peg into a round hole: It can't be done without some concerted manicuring. The wording of the 11th Amendment is clear; it prohibits citizens of another state or foreign citizens from filing federal lawsuits against a state where they are not domiciled. It limits federal court jurisdiction by repealing a clause from Article III of the original Constitution. The Supreme Court has modified this simple, clear text beyond recognition, holding it to be a guarantee of immunity to states against being sued for certain remedies without their consent.

The contemporary sovereign immunity doctrine began with a relatively be-nign ruling, *College Savings Bank v. Florida Prepaid*. The Court held that sov-ereign immunity shielded a state from being sued by an out-of-state plaintiff seeking redress pursuant to the Lanham Act's prohibition against false commer-cial representations under the Trademark Remedy Clarification Act's abrogation of 11th Amendment Immunity, which Congress had passed to authorize private patent suits against states.[17] The case arose when College Savings Bank, a bank chartered and located in New Jersey, brought a lawsuit against a Florida adminis-trative agency for breach of a patent that the bank owned on a method for depos-iting money in a manner later to be used for financing college education. The bank claimed that a Florida agency had misappropriated a patented financing system into a program for tuition prepayment that state residents could use to pay for college expenses. The Court held the state to be immune under the 11th Amendment from defending itself against a private party suit for patent infringe-ments. The state could only be found to have waived its sovereign immunity by expressing a clear intent to submit to federal jurisdiction as a defendant or by it-self filing a lawsuit pursuant to the Lanham Act, not by Congress forcing it to do so. This ruling arguably had negative impact on private creative endeavors that the state misappropriated in violation of federal law. Moreover, the public benefit of patent law, which is meant to incentivize innovation, also suffers from an ina-bility of the intellectual property owner to enforce claims against states. Despite these theoretical drawbacks, *College Savings Bank* seems to have fit squarely with the language of the 11th Amendment. The ruling thwarted Congress's effort to expand the federal courts' authority to hear patent suits brought by out-of-state plaintiffs against states where they had no domicile, but the opinion was well grounded in the terms of the 11th Amendment.

The direction that the doctrine went afterwards is, however, suspect. The Court followed up *College Savings* with a case that found states to be immune from private lawsuits, unless they first waive that immunity, brought by their own citizens for money damages in claims under the Age Discrimination and Employment Act (ADEA). In *Kimel v. Florida Board of Regents*, the Court found that state sovereign immunity sheltered the states from congressional expan-sion of antidiscrimination laws even though the Court had earlier found that the ADEA was a valid exercise of Congress's Commerce Clause power.[18] The creation of a federal cause of action against states, however, fell under Section 5 of the 14th Amendment. The Court decided that the ADEA was not congruent and proportional because Congress had insufficient evidence of states commit-ting age discrimination to impose federal liability. The *Kimel* majority required Congress to provide the Court with evidence of a "pattern of constitutional vio-lations" by the states. This limited elected representatives' ability to pass robust remedies to only cases of the most widespread abuses.

Relying on the 11th Amendment, the *Kimel* majority closed the federal court door to persons seeking monetary redress against state agencies committing age discrimination. This effectively empowered states to avoid federal liability for violations of a law that has effectively punished and deterred private employer misconduct. Instead, an aggrieved older worker is left with federal injunctive relief and state monetary remedies. But that precludes plaintiffs from choosing a single forum for complete redress against a state violation of civil rights law, rendering litigation more costly and time-consuming. The Court's holding in *Kimel* perfunctorily rejected congressional assessment of policy. The Court intruded into a province of Congress by claiming that it was dealing with a constitutional issue—the relationship between state and federal powers—rather than simply interpreting a statute in the context of facts involved in that lawsuit. Put into more general terms, the Court's principal failure in *Kimel* was to weaken Congress as a coequal player for the expostulation of the constitutional maxim for protecting liberal equality for the common good. It left a norm, protective of elderly individuals to allow them to enjoy the general benefits of federal civil rights, at the discretion of the states.

Similar judicial reliance on the state sovereignty doctrine diminished handicapped citizens' ability to sue states for violating the Americans with Disabilities Act (ADA). That statute, like the ADEA, is a national initiative meant to provide a class of vulnerable individuals with redress against discrimination. Relying on its *Kimel* rationale, in *Board of Trustees of the University of Alabama v. Garrett*, the Supreme Court found that state employers are also immune from private monetary damage claims under the ADA, unless the state voluntarily waves that immunity.[19] Patricia Garrett, one of the plaintiffs, had been a nursing director of the University of Alabama Hospital. After taking a leave of absence for oncological treatment, Garrett was demoted and not allowed to return to her previous job responsibilities.

As in *Kimel*, the Court asserted that the 11th Amendment is applicable "to suits by citizens against their own state." This contrived judicial doctrine is diametrically contrary to the actual wording of the amendment. The majority in *Garrett* relied on an artificially created bar to reject Congress's effort to require state entities to abide by a national standard for the treatment of disabled employees. This was despite an extensive legislative record detailing a history of states engaging in disabilities discriminations, which Congress had amassed through various committee hearings. The Court denied that Congress was competent to identify a vulnerable group whose special needs required a legislative initiative creating uniform, nationwide monetary remedies. Weakening an elected branch's ability to pass general legislation to address a collective problem was contrary to a representative system of government. At the very least, reasonable people can differ on whether federal legislative authority extends to the protection of certain civil rights; rather than exercising a presumptive authority over Congress, the Court should have deferred to lawmakers' initiative to exercise a public duty to safeguard the right of vulnerable persons to obtain remedies for violating a civil rights law. The Court's intervention on behalf of state sovereignty has come at the expense of congressional authority to pass necessary and proper legislation for the implementation of the maxim of constitutional governance.

D. Congressional Authority and Judicial Barriers to Its Exercise

As with the immunity doctrine, the Supreme Court has also limited the people's sovereignty through the state action doctrine. The Court derived the latter from the 14th Amendment's injunction that no state "shall abridge the privileges or immunities of citizens of the United States; nor shall any state deprive any person of life, liberty, or property, without due process of law; nor deny any person within its jurisdiction the equal protection of the laws." It dates back to 1883, with the *Civil Rights Cases* decision,[20] when the Court was dismantling the victories of Reconstruction by diminishing Congress's power to pass civil rights legislation. The state action doctrine is premised on the notion that the 14th Amendment does not enable Congress to pass laws against private forms of discrimination but only those responsive to "state" (more broadly including the state and local levels) misconduct. While several narrow exceptions exist—such as when a private entity, like a company town, engages in public functions[21] or when state entanglement with a private party renders the state complicit in discriminatory conduct[22]—the focus on state action has too often been a thinly veiled judicial scepter for striking civil rights legislation. Several historians, including Eric Foner, have criticized the judicial reliance of the doctrine to impede legislative antidiscrimination initiatives.[23] Michael Klarman similarly asserted that the state action requirement is "among the most formidable barriers to securing racial justice."[24] Some scholars—including Robert Glennon, John Nowak, Charles Black, William Van Alstyne, Ken Karst, and Harold Horowitz[25]—have suggested descriptive ways for courts to surmount that barrier by conceiving certain forms of private discrimination to be closely tied with state involvement, such as a court's enforcement of racist real estate covenants.[26] These scholars have offered analytically sound arguments that acknowledge the ambiguity of many public-private dichotomies. Licensing, for instance, is required of most business activities, from running a hot dog stand to trading secured instruments. The very act of granting a license can communicate the government's sanction of an entity's private conduct.

In the *Civil Rights Cases*, the Court rejected broad use of Section 5 congressional power to regulate the conduct of licensed entities, holding that the 14th Amendment protects citizens only against direct state infringements and stating that "individual invasion of individual rights is not the subject matter of the amendment." This was an unhappy result because it ruptured Congress's effort to achieve universal fundamental rights when it passed the Civil Rights Act of 1875.

Congress had enacted the statute after years of drawn-out debates. The law prohibited racial segregation at public places. Had the Court ruled in favor of a national right to enjoy public spaces, it could have provided relief for litigants and signaled a willingness to defer to the popular will—as it manifested itself through congressional enactment of the Act—to end centuries of forced racial separation. Segregation was oppressive to individuals and cleaved society into black and white communities. In its *Civil Rights Cases* decision, the Court rejected Congress's claim of authority to pass "general legislation upon the rights of the citizen," recognizing the constitutionality only of "corrective legislation that is, such as may be necessary and proper for counteracting such laws as the States may adopt or enforce." The Court refused to recognize that Congress can rely on its power under the 14th Amendment to put an end to racial segregation in licensed business establishments. Likewise, the majority of justices did not consider the exclusion of blacks from companies otherwise open to the public, such as theaters, to be a badge and incident of slavery or involuntary servitude. The holding rejected Congress's unambiguously beneficent effort to live up to the ideals established in the Declaration of Independence and Preamble.

The holding of the *Civil Rights Cases* cut the feet out from under Congress's ability to deal with the national problem of racism. By limiting the 14th Amendment to a grant of power that extended only to state offenses, the Court erected an enormous barrier in the way of the enforcement of national norms meant to empower blacks to be able to enjoy the equality promised by the Declaration of Independence, one hundred years prior to the passage of the Civil Rights Act, and to be coequal actors in developing and enjoying the general welfare. As Justice John Harlan wrote in his lone dissent, the majority's perspective severely crippled legislators who sought to use Section 5 discretion to establish a republican form of government where no individual or corporation could deny persons the privileges or immunities of equal rights. The 1875 act was tailored to deal with some of the worst abuses of licensed companies, holding them to a national commitment to personal dignity and general welfare. The *Civil Rights Cases* held the government back away from enforcing the normative scheme of constitutional governance. By ratifying the Reconstruction Amendments, the people did not entirely relinquish state power over ordinary civil rights in matters like marriage, contract formation, property ownership, and so on; rather, the federal government received authority to protect people deprived of free-men's civil rights because of their race. The Court had undermined the legal supremacy of the 13th and 14th Amendments, and, even more, the underlying purpose of equal representative governance as a whole: The maintenance of lib-eral equality for the common good.

To this day, the state action requirement obstructs federal civil rights initia-tives. The test from the *Civil Rights Cases* was never overruled. At best the di-chotomy between private business and public entanglement has become more ambiguous because of the many connections between them. For instance, op-erating a public business like a store, movie theater, or any other facility open to the public will typically require a license. By issuing a license to a business entity that refuses service to persons because of some identifiable group char-acteristics, the state becomes entangled in the wrong. Any court rendering judgment on behalf of a racist business practice and giving a free pass to it also entangles the judicial department in the unequal treatment of citizens.[27] The state action requirement interferes with congressional regulations of commerce and historic injustices that undermine the constitutional values established in the Declaration of Independence and Preamble to the Constitution. The Reconstruction Amendments made even clearer that states no longer enjoy a free hand in matters affecting civil rights, as they had prior to the Civil War. The original constitutional scheme had left too much discretion to state officials over the mandate of constitutional justice. The Reconstruction Amendments were a radical departure from the original federalism scheme. They granted the federal government supremacy to create regulations against discriminatory conduct, which would, in turn, provide vulnerable groups the breathing space to pursue happiness, requiring public entities to include them in the development of ge-neral welfare policies. The Supreme Court, however, continues to hamper such an expansive understanding of federal power. Its sovereign immunity jurispru-dence is often a barrier to the enforcement of federal legislation designed to ad-vance public safety by providing remedies to harmed individuals.

This strong-handed use of judicial power is evident in a 2000 case, *United States v. Morrison*, in which the Supreme Court reviewed Congress's reliance on the 14th Amendment's Section 5 enforcement authority and the Commerce Clause power to pass a provision of the Violence Against Women Act (VAWA), which allowed victims of sexual violence to file private lawsuits against alleged assailants.[28] A formal Senate report, compiled prior to the VAWA's passage, found a huge national expenditure for the many harms of gender-motivated crimes. Violence against women has a significant impact on the national economy: The Senate report found that the yearly costs for criminal justice and healthcare linked to gender-motivated violence were between $3 and $10 billion.[29] In the aggregate, the harm to individuals was causing a massive economic problem. But the Court's majority simply dismissed the evidence of aggregate economic effect as insufficient basis for Congress to enact civil relief for persons injured by gender hate crimes.

Congress had created a federal civil remedy after finding "that bias in state justice systems had deprived victims of equal protection of the laws."[30] Thus, by keeping these cases local, the effect of the *Morrison* holding perpetuated an existing legal problem. Furthermore, legislative history indicated that state resources were often inadequate to address the serious gender-motivated crimes and that state legal rules and practices too often attacked the victim's credibility.[31]

VAWA's substantive and procedural provisions were in keeping with the maxim of liberal equality for the common good. The law addressed intertwined private and public needs. The statute afforded victims of gender-motivated crimes with enforcement mechanisms and remedies. The private damages caused an aggregate social evil of widespread economic, physical, psychological, and emotional harms. The Supreme Court struck the law's civil action provision, finding that gender-motivated violence did not have a substantial effect on interstate commerce, and therefore Congress had lacked Commerce Clause power to pass it. The majority also rejected Congress's Section 5 14th Amendment justification for enacting the statute, holding the civil remedy to be unrelated to any state actor's conduct.

Continued reliance on the state action doctrine imposes difficulties for reformers. During the Warren Court, it appeared that several members of the Court might abandon the state action doctrine,[32] but that leaning had changed by the last two-and-a-half decades of the 20th century.

VAWA was a direct congressional response to a historical harm the Court itself identified as falling under the 14th Amendment.[33] Gender-motivated discrimination is predicated on stereotypes of inequality that are not grounded in fact and have resulted in the unequal treatment of women in areas like employment and citizenship.[34] VAWA was passed because of well-documented breakdowns in state criminal prosecutions of persons charged with committing gender-motivated crimes.

Even if we were to accept the Court's state action limit on 14th Amendment authority, poorly functioning prosecutorial and court systems, which indisputably are the components of state government, require federal engagement. Vindicating victims' abilities to pursue their sense of a happy life required national, legal intervention. To the contrary, in *Morrison*, a 5–4 majority, divided along political lines, ignored evidence that ineffective state institutions have a clear nexus to the administration of government.

The Court found that Section 5 of the 14th Amendment is not a grant for Congress to create civil causes of action against private party infractions. The majority's narrow construction of federal legislative authority stymied a policy initiative that was closely related to the country's moral ethos of equal access to courts. The civil litigation provision of VAWA was a remedial law designed to provide an alternative avenue of redress after Congress had amassed an immense record of state prosecutorial and judicial shortcomings in cases involving gender-motivated crimes. Under those circumstances, when many victims were unable to gain full access and vindication through state criminal justice systems, VAWA's federal remedy system was a legitimate national response meant to benefit public safety by deterring crime and providing for the common welfare. A case decided just three years prior to *Morrison, City of Boerne v. Flores*, signaled that Congress could rely on its Section 5 power to pass antidiscrimination laws to rectify past wrongs. In *Boerne*, the Court had asserted: "Legislation which deters or remedies constitutional violations can fall within the sweep of Congress' enforcement power even if in the process it prohibits conduct which is not itself unconstitutional and intrudes into 'legislative spheres of autonomy previously reserved to the States.'"[35] Put another way, where states violate some constitutionally protected interest, historical prerogatives do not bar the enforcement of federal law. This does not mean that Congress is at liberty to pass laws addressing all social wrongs, no matter how minor; rather, a statute must be congruent and proportional to the legislative objective. And VAWA involved the widespread interstate problem of gender discrimination, which since the early 1970s the Court has often recognized to be a violation of the 14th Amendment Equal Protection Clause. The statute was congruent and proportional given the enormous magnitude of the problem identified in evidence gathered during the course of four years from 21 state task forces on gender bias and through nine congressional hearings.[36]

As if the state action requirement was not enough of a barrier, the Court also found VAWA to be disproportionately harsh on states because the congressional record lacked evidence that the law addressed a problem which "exist[s] in all States, or even most States." Thereby, the Court constricted Congress's Commerce Clause authority to pass moral legislation that was so widespread that it caused billions of dollars of economic loss. Contrary to my assessment, therefore, the majority regarded the law to be neither congruent nor proportional to the harm Congress sought to remedy because: "Congress' findings indicate that the problem of discrimination against the victims of gender-motivated crimes does not exist in all States, or even most States."

Requiring Congress to demonstrate widespread violations among states to justify its use of legislative power read constraint into the open-ended language of Section 5 of the 14th Amendment. Professors Reva Siegel and Robert Post have pointed out that *Morrison* is in tension with an earlier deferential decision, *Oregon v. Mitchell*, in which the Court had upheld a national prohibition against voting literacy tests.[37] A concurrence to *Mitchell* drew attention to the conclusion that "Congress was not required to make state-by-state findings." Although the issues in the two cases differed, the Court in *Morrison* should have likewise found that Congress did not need to make state-by-state findings because it had constructed a record replete with evidence of a problem requiring a federal solution. Prior to Congress's passage of VAWA, in addition to state task forces, 38 state attorney generals had signed a letter calling for a federal response. Moreover, in a dissent to *Morrison,* Justice Stephen Breyer pointed out that the legislative record nowhere indicated that the procedural problems the law addressed were not found throughout the United States. To the contrary, Breyer asserted, Congress had accumulated ample documentation and oral testimony "as evidence of a national problem."[38]

In *Morrison*, the state action doctrine provided the Court with a hook for ratcheting up adjudicative authority to disrupt legislative policymaking: The Court simply denied Congress's inductions from extensive investigatory findings without any countervailing evidence. State interests became trump cards against a legitimate governmental effort to safeguard individuals' rights through a federal cause of action designed to upend states recalcitrance.

As we have seen, one alternative source of congressional authority, appearing in the text of the statute, was the Commerce Clause. The Court has often recognized that Congress can rely on it to pass necessary and proper laws to regulate private conduct, such as employment discrimination, that has a substantial effect on the national economy. But the Court's Commerce Clause interpretations have of late, in *Morrison* and other cases, become narrower, diminishing Congress's ability to address collective problems through national legislation. State sovereign immunity has thus become a foil to cut down civil rights legislation designed to create legislation meant to address states' insufficient personal liberties protections for the victims of sexual violence. The Supreme Court has thus created barriers that stymy congressional civil rights initiatives. The sovereign immunity cases, therefore, signal a step away from the underlying principle of constitutional governance: that the national government must act to protect the rights of individuals in a manner that is fair and designed to improve social welfare. Prior to the holding in *Morrison*, some of the most important cases expansively interpreting Congress's Commerce Clause power—*Heart of Atlanta Motel v. United States* and *Katzenbach v. McClung* to name just two[39]—relied on deferential rational basis authority to uphold critical portions of civil rights laws, such as the Civil Rights Act of 1964. In fact, from 1937 to 1995 the Court had not overturned a single federal statute passed pursuant to the Commerce Clause. The Rehnquist Court broke from that, formerly stable aspect of *stare decisis*.[40]

In light of the Court's recent inroads into congressional Commerce Clause and 14th Amendment powers, an important alternative for civil rights reform remains the 13th Amendment's Enforcement Clause. While Congress has rarely used that power, it continues to be a powerful constitutional tool for achieving the mandate that government safeguard individual rights for the common good.

Congressional debates on the 13th and 14th Amendments referred often to the Declaration of Independence and Preamble to the Constitution. Leaders of the Reconstruction expected that after the amendment's ratification Congress would use its new powers to advance the nation's founding ethic. In 1864, the year before the 13th Amendment was ratified, Senator John P. Hale of New Hampshire called on his fellow citizens to "wake up to the meaning of the sublime truths" that the nation's "fathers uttered years ago and which have slumbered dead letters upon the pages of our Constitution, of our Declaration of Independence, and of our history."[41]

Participants in the debates on the 13th Amendment made it abundantly clear that the modification to the Constitution would grant Congress the power to pass civil rights legislation in keeping with the principles of the Declaration of Independence. The head of the House Judiciary Committee, James Wilson, believed that the 13th Amendment created power in the federal government that would be inspired by the revolutionary proclamation of "human equality" drawn from the "sublime creed" of the Declaration of Independence.[42] In the reformed nation, "*equality before the law* is to be the great corner-stone" that the states and the judiciary would be unable to undermine.[43] Awakening to "true and real life the moral sense of the nation," the people would undo those sections of the Constitution that were "anti-republican."[44]

Given the limitations that the Supreme Court has now placed on congressional 14th Amendment and Commerce Clause powers, Congress might try pursuing a legislative policy relying in greater degree than before on its Section 2, 13th Amendment enforcement authority. In *Morrison*, the Court asserted that "[d]ue respect for the decisions of a coordinate branch of Government demands that we invalidate a congressional enactment only upon a plain showing that Congress has exceeded its constitutional bounds." The Supreme Court identified the appropriate level of review comprising "constitutional bounds" of the 13th Amendment in a case dealing with real estate discrimination, *Jones v. Alfred H. Mayer*.[45]

The majority in *Jones* determined that: "Congress has the power under the 13th Amendment rationally to determine what are the badges and the incidents of slavery, and the authority to translate that determination into effective legislation." That formulation is more deferential than the current tests for 14th Amendment and Commerce Clause authority, and it can serve as a basis for re-passing the civil remedy of VAWA if Congress finds it reasonable that the sexual violence victims' civil rights are so impaired that they cannot pursue happiness as full citizens.

The majority in *Jones* made a point of quoting *McCulloch v. Maryland* to define the term "appropriate legislation" in Section 2 of the 13th Amendment. Just as with Congress's authority to enact statutes pursuant to the Necessary and Proper Clause, judges should defer to the use of Section 2 authority. A law is "proper" and "appropriate" when it regulates activities, including private and state conduct, that hinders victims from enjoying the equal liberties secured by the Declaration and Constitution. The Court in *Jones* was clear that Congress can pass any law whose "end [is] legitimate, . . . [and] within the scope of the constitution," and which is "plainly adapted to that end" and "not prohibited, but consistent with the letter and spirit of the constitution." The Court explained that "[a]t the very least, the freedom that Congress is empowered to secure under the 13th Amendment includes the freedom" to engage in commercial intercourse without discrimination. The opinion is written in racial terms, but should be read broadly to understand the 13th Amendment as a statement about Americans' freedom and equality and Congress's authority to guarantee them.

Such a sweeping power, as Professor Laurence Tribe has pointed out, grants Congress "nearly plenary authority . . . to protect all but the most trivial individual rights from both governmental and private invasion."[46] Under that standard, if Congress were to reasonably find that some forms of gender discrimination, such as discrimination in the workplace or sexual assault, are rationally related to the badges and incidents of slavery and involuntary servitude, the Court might uphold them against facial challenges.

Unlike legislation passed under the 14th Amendment, legislation authorized by Section 2 of the 13th Amendment need not be limited to state infringements. The scope of the latter, therefore, extends to offenses beyond Congress's current 14th Amendment authority. The real hurdle of re-enacting VAWA's civil remedy pursuant to the 13th Amendment is the common belief, among jurists and scholars, that it pertains only to racial discrimination. Of late, however, a broadening of congressional enforcement authority has taken place.

In the most recent use of its 13th Amendment power, Congress passed the Matthew Shepard and James Byrd, Jr., Hate Crimes Prevention Act of 2009, punishing crimes "motivated by prejudice based on the actual or perceived race, color, religion, national origin, gender, sexual orientation, gender identity, or disability of the victim."[47] The statute additionally relies on Commerce Clause authority to preserve the hard-won achievement, on which I advised Senator Edward Kennedy, who was then on the Senate Judiciary Committee.

Cases examining the act have only recently begun to make their way through the courts. Early results have been promising with two circuit courts upholding congressional power under the 13th Amendment. Those two cases dealt with racial hate crimes.[48] Whether federal courts will find that 13th Amendment authority was sufficient to pass the portions of the act protecting against crimes motivated by gender, sexual orientation, and gender identity is still unknown. But in light of the limitations the Court has placed on 14th Amendment authority and the erosion of judicial deference in Commerce Clause matters, one can hope that Congress will be able to rely on the 13th Amendment to secure freedom and general welfare, both of which are essential to safeguarding individual and community rights to safety and happiness guaranteed in the Declaration of Independence and Preamble to the Constitution.

E. Conflicting Religious Liberties and Civil Rights

The 13th Amendment is not the end-all. Maxim constitutionalism contains the kernels of principle that run through the entire Constitution. Its mandate for lawmakers to create policies that balance relevant interests of personal liberty and the equal enjoyment of general welfare provides context for the resolution of competing interests. In a pluralistic society, conflicts are inevitable. This is especially poignant when differences involve fundamental rights.

The ACA's requirement that businesses of 50 or more full-time employees provide group healthcare plans that include contraceptive coverage has elicited religious objects. Years before the law passed, the Supreme Court had recognized both the privacy right to contraceptives and the exercise of religion to be fundamental. The law aimed to address an individual and social issue by requiring employers to provide preventative services to make contraceptives affordable for workers without having to pay out-of-pocket or turn to public insurances—such as Federal Employees Health Benefits Plan (FEHBP), Medicaid, and military family coverage under TRICARE. In a further intersection of personal and social interests, the contraceptive mandate was meant to address the disparity in out-of-pocket costs for healthcare, which disproportionately fall on women because of contraceptive and reproductive health services.[49] The statutory aims were, therefore, antidiscriminatory, aimed at alleviating the social evil of gender inequality by meaningfully reducing the higher insurance costs for women. This cost-free access triggered opposition from a closely held company, Hobby Lobby Stores, Incorporated, whose small group of owners held strong opposing religious convictions that some included methods of contraception (such as the "morning after" pill) were forms of abortion. Their case was particularly difficult because the for-profit business did not fall under the ACA's exemption for religious organizations—such as wanting to opt out of the contraceptive mandate.

In the Supreme Court case arising from these differing interests, *Burwell v. Hobby Lobby Stores, Inc.*, the majority preferred the free exercise rights of the corporation, secured by the Religious Freedom Restoration Act (RFRA), to the sex equality intent and healthcare function of the ACA.[50] The Court sided with a for-profit business that claimed it would be immoral for it to follow the law's mandate to provide women health plans with certain contraceptive coverage. Earlier, the court of appeal deciding the same case had explicitly denied the equality basis for making contraceptives free, downplaying the legislative purpose by off-handedly asserting that the action of the religious employer did not prevent women from "using their own money to purchase the . . . contraceptives at issue."[51] This perfunctory statement lacked any substantive examination of the proportionate benefits and detriments to the religious employer, women, and healthcare in general throughout the country.

Hobby Lobby set a precedent that appears to allow for-profit businesses to deny all manner of public services they sincerely regard to be immoral. A further danger is the extrapolation of the holding to businesses in general refusing to follow other civil rights laws they deem to violate religious creeds. Taken to its extreme, as was the case in a different state appellate court decision, the *Hobby Lobby* statement might imply to judges that businesses headed by religious directors can exclude people from enjoying public services such as printing t-shirts with a gay pride message, so long as the same services can be obtained elsewhere:[52] This method of judicial reasoning would gravely undermine all manner of antidiscrimination protections; including the Civil Rights Act of 1964, which prohibits public places of accommodation from denying service to persons on the basis of race, color, religion, or national origin. This exclusion from equal access to public services deprived a class of women employed by for-profit employers and gays seeking services to express a message of the personal dignity enjoyed by others throughout the country.[53]

Regulation of markets where inequality is systemic would seem rather to be at the discretion of legislators rectifying nationwide failures. Indeed, the decision favoring the supposed for-profit corporation's religious interests—based on its owners' religious claims—deviated from Supreme Court precedents that had favored social legislation, such as a minimum wage law, over the assertions of religious objectors.[54] The *Hobby Lobby* decision might have been more convincing, and perhaps come out differently, had the Court carefully analyzed whether the ACA facilitated the pursuit of happiness, and finding a conflict with RFRA then moved on to determine whether Congress had sought to achieve an end and had the power to create conditions conducive to the general welfare or whether the ACA arbitrarily discriminated against religious institutions. This sort of decision would have needed to be more contextual than the Court's simply accepting that religious convictions of business owners trumped the healthcare entitlements of women. Given that the ACA exempted purely religious institutions, while not recognizing the same exception for for-profit businesses, it is unlikely that any such animus was at play in the law's passage. The appellate and Supreme Court simply preferred the rights of the for-profit employers without deferring to

Congress's power to regulate a healthcare market that historically costs women about 70 percent more in out-of-pocket expenses than men.[55]

Insofar as the Court did consider social costs, it off-handedly proposed that government could itself cover the four contraceptives, blithely calling the $1.3 trillion extra costs "through the next decade" to be a "minor" cost "when compared with the overall cost of ACA."[56] This statement costs the majority little political capital given that the justices would not need to stand for reelection before voters whose choice of candidates would likely be informed by such an increase to the national budget. The Court's suggestion is not only notable because it oversteps its judicial boundary into legislative budgetary deliberations, but there is also an absence of empathy to the needs of women if the government were not to adopt the majority's intervention.

The *Hobby Lobby* holding opened the door for more religious exemptions without adequate weight to welfare aims of public policies. Similar to the previous example of the anti-gay printer, several vendors specializing in wedding services, such as those providing flower arrangements and bakery services, have claimed that for religious reasons they can reject orders of same-sex couples.[57] Whether a vendor believes it religiously compelling to exclude homosexuals from public services or a business thinks it religiously imperative to deny women the autonomy right to choose certain contraceptives, the message of *Hobby Lobby* seems to be that religious aversion can gainsay persons' pursuits of happiness and government's policy to affirm their inalienable right in social settings. Faced with two conflicting statutory rights—the RFRA's prohibition against "substantially burden[ing] a person's exercise of religion" absent a compelling reason in the least restrictive manner and the ACA's mandate to provide for women's contraceptive needs—the Court simply dismissed the latter policy concern by simply claiming that favoring the for-profit corporation had "precisely zero"[58] effect on women's compelling healthcare interests. A maxim-based approach to constitutional interpretation requires a significantly more robust analysis of dignitary concerns (of religious parties and those seeking services that they believe abridge their free liberty interests), rather than dismissive statements of legislative policy, and a comprehensive review of public policy and its social effects in advancing equality, tranquility, safety, health, access to legal institutions and the privileges of citizenship, and any other factors relevant to the dispute at hand and to the Preamble's stated goal of establishing justice.

F. Concluding Remarks

The overarching maxim of constitutional law provides a normative foundation for exercising authority for the individual and collective benefit of the people as members of various communities. The structure of government—in the allocation of responsibilities between the several branches and between federal and state governments—is predicated on a mandate to safeguard inalienable rights and pursue policies conducive to the general welfare. This broad ideal allows for like-minded and adversarial parties to deliberate on the basis of a common, normative groundwork for resolving constitutional disputes and advancing legislative initiatives. The maxim of constitutional governance is not meant to provide definitive formal resolution for the many sets of legal issues facing society. Rather, the unified constitutional maxim defines national commitment for all public conduct and democratic oversight. This is critical to setting the legitimate parameters of constitutional policy orientation and decision making. Without a core commitment, constitutional interpretation is blown by the winds of popular opinion and self-interested assertions of political powers.

The statements of government purpose found in the Declaration of Independence and the Preamble to the Constitution are short and easy to remember. The elegance of these documents and their attraction to ordinary people in the quest to live as equals not subject to arbitrary state abuses of power facilitates consensus building, the development of public morality, and the creation of civil rules for the resolution of conflicts. Where people feel that the system is fair, they are more likely to work within the established laws and institutions for modifying existing order rather than acting subversively. The people entrust public servants to enact institutionally consistent and predictable laws for the enjoyment of inalienable rights and the resolution of conflicting interests.

Standing alone, the general statements of the Declaration and Preamble cannot provide concrete answers about the specific responsibilities allocated to the three branches. General terms like safety, happiness, liberty, inalienable rights, general welfare, and the like have always required elaboration, refinement, and correction. The maxim of liberal equality for the common good stands at a high point of constitutional abstraction, and yet it provides judges, legislators, and ordinary citizens alike with the necessary reference point for the interpretation of other constitutional principles—such as due process, equal protection, free speech, search and seizure, and cruel and unusual punishments. Taken together, the history, tradition, aspirations, social structures, progressive thinking, and much more goes into the creation of concrete statutes and then to their application in appropriate scenarios. Abstractions are crucial for placing limits on state actions and establishing mutually recognized standards of public behavior on which even opposing sides to contentious debates can agree. Without a mutually agreed-upon foundation for government, too much is left to arbitrary rule by powerful interest groups and those holding the reins of power. The maxim of constitutional governance sets the requisite priorities for a pluralistic, representative society. The constitutional fulcrum serves as the guidepost of legitimate government, and provides the people with the standard of public accountability. And a judicial doctrine that requires proportionate considerations of all relevant liberty interests and legislative reasons to pursue a policy for the benefit of the general welfare is likely to benefit free and equal representative government "of the people, by the people, and for the people."

NOTES

Introduction

1. Arizona State Legislature v. Arizona Indep. Redistricting Comm'n, 2015 WL 2473452, at *19 (U.S. June 29, 2015).
2. JOHN HART ELY, DEMOCRACY AND DISTRUST: A THEORY OF JUDICIAL REVIEW 76 (1980).
3. ROBERT ALEXY, A THEORY OF CONSTITUTIONAL RIGHTS 6–10 (Julian Rivers trans. 2010).
4. Marbury v. Madison, 5 U.S. 137, 178 (1803); Cooper v. Aaron, 358 U.S. 1, 18 (1958).
5. See THE FEDERALIST No. 48 (James Madison), at 306 (Clinton Rossiter ed., 1961); THE FEDERALIST No. 69 (Alexander Hamilton).
6. NICOLAI HARTMANN, ETHICS 68–69, 71–72 (1932).
7. ALEXY, supra, at 12–13.
8. AHARON BARAK, PROPORTIONALITY: CONSTITUTIONAL RIGHTS AND THEIR LIMITATIONS 73 (2012).
9. See, e.g., HENRY M. HART, JR., Holmes' Positivism—An Addendum, 64 HARV. L. REV. 929 (1951); HERBERT WECHSLER, Toward Neutral Principles of Constitutional Law, 73 HARV. L. REV. 1 (1959); HENRY M. HART, JR. & ALBERT M. SACKS, THE LEGAL PROCESS: BASIC PROBLEMS IN THE MAKING AND APPLICATION OF LAW (William N. Eskridge, Jr. & Philip P. Frickey eds., 1994).
10. Laurence H. Tribe, The Puzzling Persistence of Process-Based Constitutional Theories, 89 YALE L.J. 1063, 1077–78 (1980); Frank I. Michelman, The Not So Puzzling Persistence of the Futile Search: Tribe on Proceduralism in Constitutional Theory, 42 TULSA L. REV. 891, 897–98 (2007).
11. See JOHN HART ELY, DEMOCRACY AND DISTRUST, supra, at 100, 181–83.
12. See JÜRGEN HABERMAS, BETWEEN FACTS AND NORMS: CONTRIBUTIONS TO A DISCOURSE THEORY OF LAW AND DEMOCRACY 110, 263, 278–79 (William Rehg trans., 1996); JÜRGEN HABERMAS, MORAL CONSCIOUSNESS AND COMMUNICATIVE ACTION 198 (Christian Lenhardt & Shierry Weber Nicholsen trans., 1990).
13. HABERMAS, BETWEEN FACTS AND NORMS, supra, at 453 (Habermas calls the following "the leading question of modern natural law": "what rights must citizens mutually grant one another if they decide to constitute themselves as a voluntary association of legal consociates and legitimately to regulate their living together by means of positive law?").
14. 60 U.S. 393 (1857).
15. 62 U.S. 506, 524, 526 (1858).
16. For a defense of the original position and the veil of ignorance see JOHN RAWLS, A THEORY OF JUSTICE (1971).
17. See Laurence H. Tribe, A Constitution We Are Amending: In Defense of a Restrained Judicial Role, 97 HARV. L. REV. 433, 442 (1983) ("The value of the Constitution as an evolving repository of the nation's core political ideals and as a record of the nation's deepest ideological battles depends significantly on the limitation of its substantive content to what all (or nearly

all) perceive to be fundamentals; a document cluttered with regulatory specifics could command no such respect").

18. Jack M. Balkin, Living Originalism 7 (2011).

19. Philip Bobbitt, Constitutional Interpretation 12–13 (1991).

20. Mark Tushnet, *Justification in Constitutional Adjudication: A Comment on Constitutional Interpretation*, 72 Tex. L. Rev. 1707, 1720 (1994).

21. Mark Tushnet, Taking the Constitution Away from the Courts 13 (1999). Jack Balkin has also argued that the substantive vision of the Constitution's political and substantive framework lies in the Preamble and Declaration of Independence. Jack M. Balkin, *Nine Perspectives on Living Originalism*, 2012 U. Ill. L. Rev. 815, 856–57.

22. Sanford Levinson, *On Positivism and Potted Plants: "Inferior" Judges and the Task of Constitutional Interpretation*, 25 Conn. L. Rev. 843, 850 (1993).

23. John Hart Ely, Democracy and Distrust, *supra*, at 49, 74, 87–88; Alexander Tsesis, *Self-Government and the Declaration of Independence*, 97 Cornell L. Rev. 693, 701–10 (2012) (describing the Declaration of Independence as "the substance of the law, and the Constitution as the framework for upholding it"); Alexander Tsesis, *Furthering American Freedom: Civil Rights & the Thirteenth Amendment*, 45 B.C. L. Rev. 307, 365 (2004) (discussing congressional enforcement power under the Thirteenth Amendment as upholding the promises of the Declaration of Independence and the Preamble).

24. H. Jefferson Powell, The Moral Tradition of American Constitutionalism: A Theological Interpretation 188–89 (1993).

25. Ronald Dworkin, Freedom's Law: The Moral Reading of the American Constitution 2, 17, 35, 73 (1996).

26. Daniel A. Farber & Suzanna Sherry, Desperately Seeking Certainty: The Misguided Quest for Constitutional Foundations 4, 139 (2002).

27. *See, e.g.*, Martin H. Redish & Matthew B. Arnould, *Judicial Review, Constitutional Interpretation, and the Democratic Dilemma: Proposing a "Controlled Activism" Alternative*, 64 Fla. L. Rev. 1485, 1488–89 (2012).

28. Robert H. Bork, *The Constitution, Original Intent, and Economic Rights*, 23 San Diego L. Rev. 823, 823 (1986).

29. William J. Brennan, Jr., *Constitutional Adjudication and the Death Penalty: A View from the Court*, 100 Harv. L. Rev. 313, 325 (1986).

30. Plessy v. Ferguson, 163 U.S. 537 (1896).

31. Dred Scott v. Sandford, 60 U.S. 393 (1856).

32. Lochner v. New York, 198 U.S. 45 (1905); Adkins v. Children's Hosp. of the District of Columbia, 261 U.S. 525 (1923).

33. *See* Alexander Tsesis, *Free Speech Constitutionalism*, 2015 U. of Ill. L. Rev. 1015; Tsesis, *Self-Government and the Declaration of Independence, supra*, at 693.

Chapter 1

1. The substance of a speech delivered by James Wilson, Esq. Explanatory of the general principles of the proposed Fæderal Constitution . . . on . . . the 24th of November, 1787, at 8 (1787).

2. James Wilson, Lectures on Law, *in* 2 Works of the Honourable James Wilson 436 (1804).

3. *Id.* at 303, 359, 422; James Wilson, Argument on the Power of Congress of the Old Confederacy to Incorporate the Bank of America, *in* The Works of James Wilson 549, 566 (1896); John Adams, A Defence of the Constitutions of Government of the United States of America 87 (1788).

4. James Wilson, Nov. 28, 1787, *in* 2 The Documentary History of the Ratification of the Constitution 383–84 (Merril Jensen ed., 1976).

5. 2 Debates in the Several State Conventions on the Adoption of the Federal Constitution 456–57 (Jonathan Elliot ed., 1836).

6. The substance of a speech delivered by James Wilson, at 7.

7. 1 LECTURES ON LAW, *in* 1 THE WORKS OF THE HONOURABLE JAMES WILSON 305 (Bird Wilson ed., 1804).
8. *See, e.g.,* Nestor, *Letter to the President of the United States,* GENERAL ADVERTISER (Philadelphia), Aug. 12, 1794, at 1.
9. *See Philadelphia, December 20,* CUMBERLAND GAZETTE (Portland, Maine), Jan. 24, 1788, at 4.
10. M'Culloch v. State, 17 U.S. 316, 377 (1819).
11. One means legislatures have chosen for dealing with them include hate crimes laws. All fifty states and the federal government enforce various versions of such laws against the commission of crimes motivated by negative attitudes targeting statutorily identified groups. This legislative approach is not only a constitutionally reasonable use of authority but a required public duty to safeguard equal civil liberties for equal citizens.
12. John E. Finn, *Transformation or Transmogrification?,* 10 CONST. POL. ECON. 355, 355 (1999).
13. Robert Post, *Fashioning the Legal Constitution: Culture, Courts, and Law,* 117 HARV. L. REV. 4, 8 (2003).
14. *See, e.g.,* Bd. of Trs. of the Univ. of Ala. v. Garrett, 531 U.S. 356 (2001); Kimel v. Fla. Bd. of Regents, 528 U.S. 62, 91 (2000).
15. Davis v. Bandemer, 478 U.S. 109, 123–24 (1986). On the history of the Fourteenth Amendment and its lack of protection of voter rights see ALEXANDER TSESIS, FOR LIBERTY AND EQUALITY 192–93 (2008).
16. Wesberry v. Sanders, 376 U.S. 1, 7–8 (1964).
17. Reynolds v. Sims, 377 U.S. 533 (1964).
18. *See, e.g.,* Griswold v. Connecticut, 381 U.S. 479, 482 (1965).
19. *Id.*
20. ARISTOTLE, POLITICS Book I, ch. 2, 1253a.

Chapter 2

1. J. HARVIE WILKINSON III, COSMIC CONSTITUTIONAL THEORY: WHY AMERICANS ARE LOSING THEIR INALIENABLE RIGHT TO SELF-GOVERNANCE (2012).
2. WILKINSON, *supra,* at 6.
3. WILKINSON, *supra,* at 7.
4. J. Harvie Wilkinson, III, *The Role of Reason in the Rule of Law,* 56 U. CHI. L. REV. 779, 803 (1989).
5. *Id.* at 792.
6. 410 U.S. 113 (1973).
7. 531 U.S. 98 (2000).
8. DANIEL A. FARBER & SUZANNA SHERRY, DESPERATELY SEEKING CERTAINTY: THE MISGUIDED QUEST FOR CONSTITUTIONAL FOUNDATIONS (2002).
9. ALEXANDER TSESIS, FOR LIBERTY AND EQUALITY: THE LIFE AND TIMES OF THE DECLARATION OF INDEPENDENCE (2012).
10. The Confederate Constitution prohibited the enactment of any law "denying or impairing the right of property in Negro Slaves." The Oregon Constitution of 1857 prohibited blacks from entering the state. CONFEDERATE CONST. art. I, § 9, cl. 4; 1857 Constitution of Oregon, § 35, *available at* (http://bluebook.state.or.us/state/constitution/orig/unnumbered.htm).
11. *State Convention,* Friday, November 30, INDEP. GAZETTEER (Phila.), Jan. 3, 1788, at 2.
12. *From the Republican Ledger,* THE EXAMINER, No. VII, CONST. TELEGRAPHE (Bos.), Feb. 1, 1800, at 1 (asserting this statement of human rights in defense of the French Revolution).
13. *New-York, October 2,* YOUTH'S NEWS PAPER (N.Y.C.), Oct. 7, 1797, at 16.
14. Jack Rakove, *Fitly Spoken, New Republic,* Aug. 9, 2012, *available at* http://www.tnr.com/book/review/liberty-equality-alexander-tsesis?page=0,1; DAVID ARMITAGE, THE DECLARATION OF INDEPENDENCE: A GLOBAL HISTORY 21 (2007).
15. 1 DEBATES OF THE CONVENTION, OF THE STATE OF PENNSYLVANIA, ON THE CONSTITUTION, PROPOSED FOR THE GOVERNMENT OF THE UNITED STATES 59, 63 (1788).
16. Hancock's Message to the Massachusetts Legislature, Jan. 31, 1792, *in* ACTS AND RESOLVES PASSED BY THE GENERAL COURT (Mass. Gen. Ct.) 691, 692 (Boston: Thomas Adams 1792).

17. Samuel Adams, *Mass. Lieutenant Governor, Speech to the Massachusetts House of Representatives and Senate* (Jan. 17, 1794), MASS. MAG., Jan. 1794, at 59, 63.

18. Speech of Samuel Adams, *in Domestic Occurrences*, MASS. MAG., Jan. 1794, at 59, 62–64.

19. *Id.*

20. *See, e.g.*, A LAW GRAMMAR 10 (1791); A Bostonian, *A View of Federal Government, in* 1 THE AMERICAN MUSEUM 269, 271–72 (No. 1, 1790).

21. STEPHEN JOHNSON, INTEGRITY AND PIETY THE BEST PRINCIPLES OF A GOOD ADMINISTRATION OF GOVERNMENT 5–6 (New London, Green 1770).

22. THE AMERICAN IN ALGIERS, OR THE PATRIOT OF SEVENTY-SIX IN CAPTIVITY 23–26 (New York, Buel 1797).

23. ANTHONY BENEZET, SHORT OBSERVATIONS ON SLAVERY 2 (Phila., Joseph Crukshank 1781). For a similar reliance on the Declaration as a statement of national principle, see THE CONSTITUTION OF THE PENNSYLVANIA SOCIETY, FOR PROMOTING THE ABOLITION OF SLAVERY, AND THE RELIEF OF FREE NEGROES, UNLAWFULLY HELD IN BONDAGE 21 (Phila., Francis Bailey 1788); JAMES DANA, THE AFRICAN SLAVE TRADE. A DISCOURSE DELIVERED IN THE CITY OF NEW-HAVEN, SEPTEMBER 9, 1790, BEFORE THE CONNECTICUT SOCIETY FOR THE PROMOTION OF FREEDOM 28 (New Haven, Thomas & Samuel Green 1791); WARNER MIFFLIN, A SERIOUS EXPOSTULATION WITH THE MEMBERS OF THE HOUSE OF REPRESENTATIVES OF THE UNITED STATES 9 (Phila., Poughkeepsie, Dutchess Cnty. 1794).

24. ANTHONY BENEZET, SERIOUS CONSIDERATIONS ON SEVERAL IMPORTANT SUBJECTS 28 (Phila., Joseph Crukshank 1778).

25. JACOB GREEN, A SERMON DELIVERED AT HANOVER (IN NEW-JERSEY) APRIL 22D, 1778, at 12–13 (Chatham, N.J., Shepard Kollock 1779).

26. DAVID COOPER, A SERIOUS ADDRESS TO THE RULERS OF AMERICA, ON THE INCONSISTENCY OF THEIR CONDUCT RESPECTING SLAVERY 12 (Trenton, N.J., Isaac Collins 1783).

27. *Id.* at 6–13.

28. GEORGE BUCHANAN, AN ORATION UPON THE MORAL AND POLITICAL EVIL OF SLAVERY 13–14 (Balt., Philip Edwards 1793).

29. *American Intelligence*, FREEMAN'S J.; OR, N.-AM. INTELLIGENCER (Phila.), Aug. 24, 1791, at 3.

30. Letter from Thomas Jefferson to Henry Lee (May 8, 1825), *in* 10 THE WRITINGS OF THOMAS JEFFERSON 342, 343 (Paul Leicester Ford ed., 1899).

31. Paul W. Kahn & Kiel Brennan-Marquez, *Statutes and Democratic Self-Authorship*, 56 WM. & MARY L. REV. 140 (2014).

32. A Ploughman, *To the People*, INDEP. GAZETTEER (Phila.), Oct. 5, 1782, at 1.

33. Mark D. Walters, *Mohegan Indians v. Connecticut (1705–1773) and the Legal Status of Aboriginal Customary Laws and Government in British North America*, 33 OSGOODE HALL L.J. 785 (1996); DAVID W. MILLER, INDIAN LANDS IN THE SOUTHEAST (2011); C. A. WESLAGER, DELAWARE'S FORGOTTEN FOLK: THE STORY OF THE MOORS AND NANTICOKES 54 (1943); JOSEPH D. DOUGLAS, DEAL, RACE AND CLASS IN COLONIAL VIRGINIA 116 (1993).

34. *Miscellanies*, NEW-HAVEN GAZETTE & CONN. MAG., Mar. 1, 1787, at 9.

35. SAMUEL ADAMS, THE RIGHTS OF THE COLONISTS, A LIST OF VIOLATIONS OF RIGHTS AND A LETTER OF CORRESPONDENCE (Nov. 20, 1772), *available at* http:// www.constitution.org/ bcp/right_col.htm.

36. 4 JOHN ADAMS, THOUGHTS ON GOVERNMENT, in THE WORKS OF JOHN ADAMS 193, 193 (Charles Francis Adams ed., Bos., Charles C. Little & James Brown 1865).

37. 1 JOHN DICKINSON, AN ADDRESS TO THE COMMITTEE OF CORRESPONDENCE IN BARBADOS, in THE WRITINGS OF JOHN DICKINSON 251, 262 (Paul Leicester Ford ed., Phila., Historical Soc'y of Pa. 1895).

38. Letter from Samuel Adams to John Adams, (Nov. 25, 1790), *in* 4 SAMUEL ADAMS, THE WRITINGS OF SAMUEL ADAMS 344, 344 (Harry Alonzo Cushing ed., 1908).

39. JAMES OTIS, THE RIGHTS OF THE BRITISH COLONIES ASSERTED AND PROVED 10 (Bos., Edes & Gill 1764).

40. *See* THE DECLARATION OF INDEPENDENCE para. 11 (U.S. 1776) (asserting several condemnations against the King of England: "He has made Judges dependent on his Will alone, for the Tenure of their Offices, and the Amount and Payment of their Salaries"); *see id.* para. 7

("He has dissolved Representative Houses repeatedly, for opposing with manly Firmness his Invasions on the Rights of the People."). The reverse is also true. Congress cannot use its authority to infringe on presidential, Article II powers. *See* Bowsher v. Synar, 478 U.S. 714, 726 (1986) ("Congress cannot reserve for itself the power of removal of an officer charged with the execution of the laws except by impeachment.").

41. *A Citizen, A Word of Advice*, PA. PACKET (Phila.), Nov. 5, 1785, at 2.

42. THE FEDERALIST No. 47 (James Madison), at 323, 323 (Jacob E. Cooke ed., 1961). In Federalist 48, James Madison pointed out that the concentration of power in the hands of the executive or legislative branches can lead to tyranny. THE FEDERALIST No. 48 (James Madison), *supra*, at 332, 333, 338. Alexander Hamilton, writing in Federalist 73, pointed out that the judiciary too can become a tool for tyranny if it becomes overly entangled in executive politics. THE FEDERALIST No. 73 (Alexander Hamilton), *supra*, 492, 499. Hamilton argued against anti-Federalists who were concerned that the exclusive concentration of power in the Supreme Court to interpret the Constitution would result in an entity that could mold the meaning of the document to its own opinion with no possibility of revision by the legislature. THE FEDERALIST No. 81, *supra*, 541, 542.

43. JACK M. BALKIN, CONSTITUTIONAL REDEMPTION: POLITICAL FAITH IN AN UNJUST WORLD 18 (2011).

44. E-mail from Ernest A. Young, Professor of Law, Duke University School of Law, to Alexander Tsesis (Mar. 16, 2015 2:28 PM) (on file with author).

45. TSESIS, FOR LIBERTY AND EQUALITY, *supra*, at 168–73.

Chapter 3

1. Martin Luther King, Jr., *I Have a Dream* (Aug. 28, 1963), *available at* http://www.usconstitution.net/dream.html.

2. Martin Luther King, Jr., *The American Dream* (delivered at Ebenezer Baptist Church, Atlanta, Ga., July 4, 1965), *available at* https://kinginstitute.stanford.edu/king-papers/documents/american-dream-sermon-delivered-ebenezer-baptist-church..

3. Martin Luther King, Jr., *A Christmas Sermon on Peace* (delivered on Ebenezer Baptist Church, Atlanta, Ga., Dec. 24, 1967), *available at* http://www.ecoflourish.com/Primers/education/Christmas_Sermon.html).

4. ROGERS M. SMITH, CIVIC IDEALS 35–39 (1997); Rogers M. Smith, *Beyond Tocqueville, Myrdal, and Hartz: The Multiple Traditions in America*, 87 AM. POL. SCI. REV. 549, 549 (1993).

5. CHARLES L. BLACK, JR., NEW BIRTH OF FREEDOM: HUMAN RIGHTS, NAMED & UNNAMED 35, 38 (1997).

6. Daniel Webster, *Adams and Jefferson: Discourse in Commemoration of the Lives and Services of John Adams and Thomas Jefferson, Delivered in Faneuil Hall* (Aug. 2, 1826), *in* THE SPEECHES OF DANIEL WEBSTER 183, 199 (B. F. Tefft ed., 1880).

7. King, Jr., *I Have a Dream, supra*.

8. EDWARD GRAY, AN ORATION, DELIVERED JULY 5, 1790, at 8–9 (1790).

9. *See* Letter from Thomas Jefferson to Henry Lee (May 8, 1825), *in* THE WRITINGS OF THOMAS JEFFERSON 342, 343 (Paul Leicester Ford ed., 1899).

10. David P. Currie, *The Civil War Congress*, 73 U. CHI. L. REV. 1131, 1213 (2006) ("[B]y its plain terms the Guarantee Clause applies only to states").

11. Frank I. Michelman, *Traces of Self-Government*, 100 HARV. L. REV. 4 (1986).

12. M. E. BRADFORD, A BETTER GUIDE THAN REASON: FEDERALISTS AND ANTI-FEDERALIST 41 ("Declaration is not implicit in the Constitution except as it made possible free ratification by the independent states. In truth, many rights are secured under the Constitution that are not present in the Declaration, however it be construed").

13. Stern v. Marshall, 131 S. Ct. 2594, 2609 (2011); O'Donoghue v. United States, 289 U.S. 516, 531 (1933).

14. Jones v. United States, 526 U.S. 227, 246 (1999); Adams v. United States *ex rel.* McCann, 317 U.S. 269, 276 (1942).

15. Arizona State Legislature v. Arizona Indep. Redistricting Comm'n, 2015 WL 2473452, at *19 (2015).

16. Ferrell v. Dallas Indep. Sch. Dist., 393 U.S. 856, 856 (1968) (Douglas, J., dissenting to writ petition).

17. Abraham Lincoln, *Fragment on the Constitution and the Union, in* 4 THE COLLECTED WORKS OF ABRAHAM LINCOLN 169 (Roy Basler ed., 1953); *also available at* http://teachingameri-canhistory.org/library/document/fragment-on-the-constitution-and-union/.

18. *Id.*

19. Carlton F.W. Larson, *The Declaration of Independence: A 225th Anniversary Re-Interpretation,* 76 WASH. L. REV. 701, 763 (2001).

20. Saikrishna B. Prakash, *America's Aristocracy,* 109 YALE L.J. 541, 553–54 (1999).

21. Troxel v. Granville, 530 U.S. 57, 91 (2000) (Scalia, J., dissenting).

22. Akhil Reed Amar, *The Central Meaning of Republican Government: Popular Sovereignty, Majority Rule, and the Denominator Problem,* 65 U. COLO. L. REV. 749, 749 (1994).

23. Reynolds v. Sims, 377 U.S. 533 (1964); Wesberry v. Sanders, 376 U.S. 1, 18 (1964).

24. Gray v. Sanders, 372 U.S. 368, 381(1963).

25. *Compare* White v. Weiser, 412 U.S. 783 (1969) *to* Mahan v. Howell, 410 U.S. 315 (1973).

26. RONALD DWORKIN, LAW'S EMPIRE 238 *et seq.* (1986).

27. *See* Sanford Levinson, *Taking Law Seriously: Reflections on "Thinking Like a Lawyer,"* 30 Stan. L. Rev. 1071, 1108 n.155 (1978); Robert Justin Lipkin, *Beyond Skepticism, Foundationalism and the New Fuzziness: The Role of Wide Reflective Equilibrium in Legal Theory,* 75 CORNELL L. REV. 811, 842 (1990) ("In Dworkin's view, despite disagreement, there is one and only one correct answer to legal questions. Disagreement as to the correct answer in Dworkin's view, even disagreement after careful and sophisticated deliberation, does not preclude there being one right answer. After all, truth does not entail proof. A legal proposition might be true despite our failure."); David Wolitz, *Indeterminacy, Value Pluralism, and Tragic Cases,* 62 BUFF. L. REV. 529, 578 (2014) ("Those who deny legal indeterminacy, such as Dworkin, usually argue that because the law rationally determines one right answer, the judge's duty is to reason to that uniquely correct answer.").

28. Aharon Barak, *A Judge on Judging: The Role of A Supreme Court in A Democracy,* 116 HARV. L. REV. 16, 22 (2002) ("Is Hercules the proper model by which we should judge? Whatever the philosophical answer may be, the reality is that the large majority of judges on supreme courts think, as I do, that in some cases they do have a choice. In such cases, it is not that their decisions legitimate their rulings, but rather that their decisions are based on a legitimacy that precedes the rulings. Their judicial discretion is an expression of this legitimacy.").

29. *Instructions to the Representatives of the Town of Boston,* NEW ENG. CHRON. (Bos.), May 30, 1776, at 2.

30. *See, e.g.,* for a mid-Atlantic view: *A Citizen, A Word of Advice: or, The Pennsylvania Assemblyman's Vade Maeum,* PA. PACKET (Phila.), Nov. 5, 1785, at 2.

31. THE FEDERALIST No. 47, at 297 (James Madison), (Clinton Rossiter ed., 1961).

32. *A Dialogue Between a Ruler and a Subject,* ESSEX GAZETTE (Salem), Mar. 24, 1772, at 138 ("[I]t is an old maxim, that the body of the people never can be deceived; that the wisdom of the state lies with them, and they always judge right with regard to the conduct of their rulers."); *By the Great and General Court of the Colony of Massachusetts-Bay,* PA. EVENING POST (Phila.), Feb. 27, 1776, at 99. The author noted: "It is a maxim that in every government, there must exist somewhere, a supreme, sovereign, absolute, and uncontroulable [sic] power: But this power resides always in the body of the people; and it never was, or can be delegated to one man, or a few; the great Creator having never given to men a right to vest others with authority over them, unlimited either in duration or degree." *Id.*

33. McDonald v. City of Chicago, 130 S. Ct. 3020, 3059 (2010) (Thomas, J., concurring).

34. Charles L. Black, Jr., *Further Reflections on the Constitutional Justice of Livelihood,* 86 COLUM. L. REV. 1103, 1103 (1986).

35. CONG. GLOBE, 38th Cong., 2d Sess. 142 (1864) (Orth).

36. CONG. GLOBE, 39th Cong., 1st Sess. 1152 (1866).

37. CONG. GLOBE, 39th Cong., 1st Sess. 5 (1865).

38. ALEXANDER TSESIS, THE THIRTEENTH AMENDMENT AND AMERICAN FREEDOM: A LEGAL HISTORY 37–48 (2004).

39. Jones v. Alfred H. Mayer, 392 U.S. 409, 440 (1968).

40. Cong. Globe, 39th Cong., 1st Sess. 2961 (1866).

41. Charles Fairman, *Does the Fourteenth Amendment Incorporate the Bill of Rights?: The Original Understanding*, 2 STAN. L. REV. 5, 73 (1949), *quoting from* CIN. COM., Aug. 9, 1866, at 2.

42. Cong. Globe, 39th Cong., 1st Sess. 2539 (1866).

43. *The Soldiers in Council!*, ADAMS SENTINEL (Gettysburg, Pa.), June 19, 1866, at 4.

44. CONG. GLOBE, 40th Cong., 3d Sess. 100 app. (1869).

45. *Id.* at 903 (Sumner); *id.* at 200 app (Loughridge).

46. CONG. GLOBE, 39th Cong., 1st Sess. 833 (1866).

47. *Id.*

48. *See* Charles Sumner's statement on this point at CONG. GLOBE, 39th Cong., 1st Sess., at 2033 (Apr. 19, 1866).

49. *Id.* at 1078.

50. *See, e.g.*, CONG. GLOBE, 39th Cong., 1st Sess., at 1319 (statement of Rep. Sidney Holmes of New York).

51. CONG. GLOBE, 39th Cong., 2d Sess., at 81 (Dec. 12, 1866).

52. AN ACT TO ENABLE THE PEOPLE OF NEBRASKA TO FORM A CONSTITUTION AND STATE GOVERNMENT, AND FOR THE ADMISSION OF SUCH STATE INTO THE UNION . . . § 4, *in* THE STATUTES OF NEBRASKA lvii, lviii (Chicago: Culver, Page & Hoyne, printers, 1867?).

53. CONG. GLOBE, 39th Cong., 2d Sess., at 329–30 (Jan. 8, 1867).

54. NEBRASKA BLUE BOOK AND HISTORICAL REGISTER, 1918, at 71 (1918).

55. *See, e.g.*, COLORADO, ENABLING ACT (MARCH 3, 1875), *available at* http://class-wp.digitaltrike. com/wp-content/uploads/2012/09/Enabling_Act1.pdf; AN ACT TO PROVIDE FOR THE DIVISION OF DAKOTA INTO TWO STATES AND TO ENABLE THE PEOPLE OF NORTH DAKOTA, SOUTH DAKOTA, MONTANA, AND WASHINGTON TO FORM CONSTITUTIONS AND STATE GOVERNMENTS AND TO BE ADMITTED INTO THE UNION ON AN EQUAL FOOTING WITH THE ORIGINAL STATES, AND TO MAKE DONATIONS OF PUBLIC LANDS TO SUCH STATES (Feb. 22, 1889), *available at* http://www.leg.wa.gov/History/State/Pages/enabling. aspx; AN ACT TO ENABLE THE PEOPLE OF UTAH TO FORM A CONSTITUTION AND STATE GOVERNMENT, AND TO BE ADMITTED INTO THE UNION ON AN EQUAL FOOTING WITH THE ORIGINAL STATES, *available at* http://archives.utah.gov/research/exhibits/Statehood/ 1894text.htm; Franz v. Autry, 91 P. 193, 203 (Okla. 1907) (construing the enabling act of Oklahoma to include the following propositions: "The [state constitutional] convention has and can exercise plenary powers subject to the limitations: (1) That the Constitution shall be republican in form; (2) that it shall not be repugnant to the Constitution of the United States and the principles of the Declaration of Independence; (3) that no distinction shall be made on account of race or color; and (4) that the convention shall accept by ordinance irrevocable all the terms and conditions of the enabling act."); ENABLING ACT FOR NEW MEXICO, Act of June 20, 1910, 36 Stat. 557 § 2, *available at* https://www.nmmi.edu/academics/documents/ enabling_act1.pdf; § 20; ENABLING ACT [ARIZONA], Act of June 20, 1910, 36 Stat. 557 § 20, *available at* http://www.azleg.state.az.us/const/enabling.pdf; AN ACT TO PROVIDE FOR THE ADMISSION OF THE STATE OF HAWAI'I INTO THE UNION § 3 (Mar. 18, 1959), *available at* http://www.hawaii-nation.org/admission.html#%C2%A7%203.

56. CONG. GLOBE, 39th Cong., 1st Sess. 129 (1866).

57. Civil Rights Act, ch. 31, 14 Stat. 27 (1866).

58. 42 U.S.C. §§1981 & 1982.

59. CONG. GLOBE, 39th Cong., 1st Sess. 1159 (1866).

60. CONG. GLOBE, 39th Cong., 1st Sess. 474–75 (1866).

61. CONG. GLOBE, 39th Cong., 1st Sess. 1757 (1866).

62. *Id.* at 1151.

63. CONG. GLOBE, 41st Cong., 2d Sess. 3434 (May 13, 1870).

64.. CONG. GLOBE, 42nd Cong., 2nd Sess. at 244 (Dec. 20, 1871).

65. Civil Rights Act of 1875, 3d CONG. REC., at 996, 1011 (Feb. 4, 1875).

66. Michael W. McConnell, *Originalism and the Desegregation Decisions*, 81 VA. L. REV. 947 (1995); CONG. GLOBE, 41st Cong., 2d Sess., at 3434 (May 13, 1870); *id.* at 3267 (May 9, 1872).

67. CONG. GLOBE, 42d Cong., 2d Sess. , at 728–29 (Jan. 31, 1872).

68. *See id.* at 730 (Senator Lot Morrill); *see also id.* at 760–61, 826 (Feb. 1, 1872) (Senator Matthew H. Carpenter).
69. *Id.* at 828 (Feb. 5, 1872).
70. *Id.*
71. CONG. GLOBE, 42nd Cong., 2d Session, Appendix, at 29 (Feb. 6, 1872).
72. CONG. GLOBE, 42nd Cong., 2d Session, at 762 (Feb. 1, 1872).
73. *Id.* at 847 (Feb. 6, 1872).
74. Alexander Tsesis, *Principled Governance: The American Creed and Congressional Authority*, 41 CONN. L. REV. 679, 701–05 (2009).
75. Civil Rights Cases, 109 U.S. 3 (1883).

Chapter 4

1. United States v. Virginia, 518 U.S. 515, 531 (1996).
2. Regents of Univ. of Cal. v. Bakke, 438 U.S. 265, 389 (1978) (Marshall, J., separate opinion).
3. 17 U.S. 316 (1819).
4. 32 U.S. 243, 247 (1833).
5. *M'Culloch*, 17 U.S. at 404.
6. James Wilson, Speech to the Pennsylvania Convention (Dec. 11, 1787), *in* PENNSYLVANIA AND THE FEDERAL CONSTITUTION, 1787–1788, at 391 (John Bach McMaster & Frederick D. Stone eds., Phila., Historical Soc'y of Pa. 1888).
7. 1 JOSEPH STORY, COMMENTARIES ON THE CONSTITUTION OF THE UNITED STATES § 459 (Bos., Billiard, Gray & Co. 1833); G.W.F. Mellen, AN ARGUMENT ON THE UNCONSTITUTIONALITY OF SLAVERY 344, 363–64 (Bos., Saxton & Peirce 1841).
8. 1 STORY, *supra*, at §460.
9. Charles L. Black, Jr., *On Reading and Using the Ninth Amendment, in* POWER AND POLICY IN QUEST OF LAW 187, 192 (Myers S. McDougal & W. Michael Reisman eds., 1985).
10. TUSHNET, TAKING THE CONSTITUTION AWAY FROM THE COURTS 13 (1999).
11. CHARLES L. BLACK, JR., STRUCTURE AND RELATIONSHIP IN CONSTITUTIONAL LAW 42–43 (1969).
12. On Norther abolition *see* ALEXANDER TSESIS, WE SHALL OVERCOME: A HISTORY OF CIVIL RIGHTS AND THE LAW 31–33 (2008); ALRTHUR ZILVERSMIT, THE FIRST EMANCIPATION: THE ABOLITION OF SLAVERY IN THE NORTH (1967).
13. JOHN PARRISH, REMARKS ON THE SLAVERY OF THE BLACK PEOPLE 8 (Phila., Kimber, Conrad & Co. 1806).
14. *Philadelphia, December 8*, CUMBERLAND GAZETTE (Portland, Me.), Jan. 3, 1788, at 1.
15. ARTICLES OF CONFEDERATION OF 1781, art. II ("Each State retains its sovereignty, freedom and independence, and every power, jurisdiction and right, which is not by this confederation expressly delegated to the United States, in Congress assembled.").
16. *Speech of John Williams, in* THE DEBATES AND PROCEEDINGS OF THE CONVENTION OF THE STATE OF NEW-YORK, ASSEMBLED AT POUGHKEEPSIE, ON THE 17TH JUNE, 1788, at 91 (N.Y.C., Francis Childs 1788), *available at* http://www.constitution.org/rc/rat_ny.htm.
17. THE FEDERALIST No. 84 (Alexander Hamilton), at 512 (Clinton Rossiter ed., 1961).
18. A NATIVE OF VIRGINIA, OBSERVATIONS UPON THE PROPOSED PLAN OF FEDERAL GOVERNMENT 10 (1788).
19. 1 STORY, *supra*, at §445.
20. Roe v. Wade, 410 U.S. 179, 210 (1973) (Douglas, J., concurring).
21. Holder v. Humanitarian Law Project, 130 S. Ct. 2705, 2731 (2010); *see* Alexander Tsesis, *Inflammatory Speech: Offense versus Incitement*, 97 MINN. L. REV. 1145, 1146–49, 1188–95 (2013).
22. 197 U.S. 11, 22 (1905).
23. 5 U.S. 137, 174 (1803).
24. Buck v. Bell, 274 U.S. 200, 208 (1927).
25. Goldberg v. Kelly, 397 U.S. 254, 265 (1970) (quoting U.S. Const. pmbl.).
26. Downes v. Bidwell, 182 U.S. 244, 377–78 (1901) (Harlan, J., dissenting).

27. JAMES SULLIVAN, OBSERVATIONS UPON THE GOVERNMENT OF THE UNITED STATES OF AMERICA 26 (1791).

28. James Madison, 1 THE CONGRESSIONAL REGISTER; OR, HISTORY OF THE PROCEEDINGS AND DEBATES OF THE FIRST HOUSE OF REPRESENTATIVES 427 (June 8, 1789).

29. RESULT OF THE CONVENTION OF DELEGATES HOLDEN AT IPSWICH IN THE COUNTY OF ESSEX 11 (1778).

30. DAVID RAMSAY, AN ENQUIRY INTO THE CONSTITUTIONAL AUTHORITY OF THE SUPREME FEDERAL COURT, OVER THE SEVERAL STATES, IN THEIR POLITICAL CAPACITY 11–12 (Charleston, W.P. Young 1792).

31. District of Columbia v. Heller, 554 U.S. 570, 579 (2008).

32. Martin v. Hunter's Lessee, 14 U.S. 304, 351 (1816) ("The constitution of the United States was ordained and established, not by the states in their sovereign capacities, but emphatically, as the preamble of the constitution declares, by 'the people of the United States.'").

33. 42 U.S.C. §§1396a(a)(10)(A)(i)–(ii) and 1396d(a).

34. Gray v. Sanders, 372 U.S. 368, 379–80 (1963).

35. JOHN L. MOTLEY, CAUSES OF THE CIVIL WAR IN AMERICA 10 (1861).

36. JAMES IREDELL, CONVENTION OF NORTH CAROLINA (July 22, 1788), in 4 THE DEBATES IN THE SEVERAL STATE CONVENTIONS ON THE ADOPTION OF THE FEDERAL CONSTITUTION 228, 230 (Jonathan Elliot ed., 1891).

37. White v. Hart, 80 U.S. 646, 650 (1872).

38. Letter from Thomas Jefferson to James Madison, Sept. 6, 1789, *available at* http://press-pubs. uchicago.edu/founders/documents/v1ch2s23.html ("Every constitution then, and every law, naturally expires at the end of 19 years.").

39. Goldberg, *supra*, at 265 (1970).

40. San Antonio Indep. Sch. Dist. v. Rodriguez, 411 U.S. 1, 58–59 (1973).

41. *Cf. Goldberg, supra*, at 265 (discussing welfare as a fulfillment of the Preamble's "General Welfare" and "Blessings of Liberty" clauses.).

42. *San Antonio Indep. School Dist., supra*, at 35.

Chapter 5

1. Ernest A. Young, *Making Federalism Doctrine: Fidelity, Institutional Competence, and Compensating Adjustments*, 46 WM. & MARY L. REV. 1733, 1741 (2005).

2. 531 U.S. 98 (2000).

3. Civil Rights Cases, 109 U.S. 3, 11 (1883).

4. Eric Foner, *The Supreme Court and the History of Reconstruction—and Vice-Versa*, 112 COLUM. L. REV. 1585, 1604 (2012).

5. DAVID BLIGHT, RACE AND REUNION: THE CIVIL WAR IN AMERICAN MEMORY (2001).

6. JÜRGEN HABERMAS, BETWEEN FACTS AND NORMS 107 (MIT Press, William Rehg trans., 1996) (1992).

7. ALEXANDER TSESIS, DESTRUCTIVE MESSAGES: HOW HATE SPEECH PAVES THE WAY FOR HARMFUL SOCIAL MOVEMENTS 188 (N.Y.U. Press 2002).

8. *See* R. M. HARE, THE LANGUAGE OF MORALS 24, 32, 46, 91 (1952); Mark T. Nelson, 32 RELIGIOUS STUDIES 15, 20 (1996) (providing a formal description of Hare's theory); N. Fotion, *Commending and Evaluating*, 12 PHILOS. Q. 73, 73–75 (1962).

9. H.L.A. Hart, *Positivism and the Separation of Law and Morals, in* THE PHILOSOPHY OF LAW 17, 32–34 (R. M. Dworkin ed., 1977); H.L.A. HART, THE CONCEPT OF LAW 88–117 (2d ed. 1994); JOSEPH RAZ, THE AUTHORITY OF LAW: ESSAYS ON LAW AND MORALITY 158 (1979).

10. Lon L. Fuller, *Positivism and Fidelity to Law—A Reply to Professor Hart*, 71 HARV. L. REV. 630 (1957); LON L. FULLER, THE MORALITY OF LAW 42, 44 (rev. ed. 1964).

11. H.L.A. Hart, *Positivism and the Separation of Law and Morals*, 71 HARV. L. REV. 593, 624–29 (1958); HART, CONCEPT OF LAW ch. 5 (1961).

12. HART, CONCEPT OF LAW, *supra*, at 266.

13. Gary Peller, *Neutral Principles in the 1950s*, 21 U. MICH. J.L. REFORM 561, 567 (1988).

14. Maurice Finkelstein, *Judical Self-Limitation*, 37 HARV. L. REV. 338, 362 (1924).
15. Walter Wheeler Cook, *The Logical and Legal Bases of the Conflict of Laws*, 33 YALE L.J. 457, 486–87 (1924).
16. Jerome Frank, *A Plea for Lawyer-Schools*, 56 YALE L.J. 1303, 1323–24 (1947).
17. See ALEXANDER TSESIS: WE SHALL OVERCOME: A HISTORY OF CIVIL RIGHTS AND THE LAW 61–63 (2008).
18. *See contra* Carl Llewellyn, *Some Realism about Realism*, 44 HARV. L. REV. 1222, 1223 (1931) (asserting that Realists "want to check ideas, and rules, and formulas by facts to keep them close to facts.").
19. Brown v. Allen, 344 U.S. 443, 540 (1953) (Jackson, J., concurring).
20. William J. Brennan, Jr., *The Constitution of the United States: Contemporary Ratification*, 27 S. TEX. L. REV. 433, 434 (1986).
21. Jack M. Balkin, *Original Meaning and Constitutional Redemption*, 24 CONST. COMMENT. 427, 462–63 (2007); J. M. Balkin, *The Declaration and the Promise of a Democratic Culture*, 4 WIDENER L. SYMP. J. 167, 179 (1999).
22. Mark V. Tushnet, *The Hardest Question in Constitutional Law*, 81 MINN. L. REV. 1, 28 (1996).
23. J. M. BALKIN, CONSTITUTIONAL REDEMPTION: POLITICAL FAITH IN AN UNJUST WORLD 4, 19 (2011); E-mail from Mark Tushnet to Alexander Tsesis (Apr. 28, 2013) (on file with author).
24. James E. Fleming, *Fidelity to Natural Law and Natural Rights in Constitutional Law*, 69 FORDHAM L. REV. 2285, 2291 (2001).
25. James E. Fleming, *Securing Deliberative Autonomy*, 48 STAN. L. REV. 1, 16 (1995).
26. James E. Fleming, *The Natural Rights-Based Justification for Judicial Review*, 69 FORDHAM L. REV. 2119, 2120 (2001).
27. My extrapolation of Fleming's position is partly predicated on the normative statement of his often coauthor, Sotirios Barber of "the family of justice-seeking constitutionalists" as the group of theorists "who can accept (1) a description of the Constitution as an instrument of justice, conceived as a substantive state of affairs, (2) some conception of the Constitution's affirmative ends, and (3) the view that the Constitution obligates elected officials to pursue such ends." Sotirios A. Barber, "Justice-Seeking Constitutionalism and Its Critics," Presented at the New York University School of Law (Apr. 20, 1995), *quoted in* Anthony J. Sebok, *The Insatiable Constitution*, 70 S. CAL. L. REV. 417, 420–21 (1997).
28. Philip Bobbitt, *Reflections Inspired by My Critics*, 72 Tex. L. Rev. 1869, 1954–55 (1994).
29. Ian Bartrum, *Constitutional Value Judgments and Interpretive Theory Choice*, 40 FLA. ST. U. L. REV. 259, 287 (2013).

Chapter 6

1. *James Madison, President's Message*, N.Y. COM. ADVERTISER, Dec. 6, 1816, at 2.
2. ARCHIBALD H. GRIMKE, WILLIAM LLOYD GARRISON: THE ABOLITIONIST 354 (1891).
3. I've catalogued a more extensive list of slave-protecting portions of the Constitution in ALEXANDER TSESIS, WE SHALL OVERCOME: A HISTORY OF CIVIL RIGHTS AND THE LAW 33–36 (2008).
4. *Address of the National Convention of Abolitionists Held in Albany, July 31, 1839*, LIBERATOR, Aug. 23, 1839, at 1.
5. Frederick Douglass, *Oath To Support the Constitution*, NORTH STAR, Apr. 5, 1850, at 2.
6. *See* Aziz Z. Huq, *Enforcing (but Not Defending) 'Unconstitutional' Laws*, 98 VA. L. REV. 1001, 1052–58 (2012).
7. *See, e.g.*, Wesberry v. Sanders, 376 U.S. 1, 18 (1964); Gomillion v. Lightfoot, 364 U.S. 339, 347–48 (1960).
8. Cooper v. Aaron, 358 U.S. 1, 18 (1958).
9. City of Boerne v. Flores, 521 U.S. 507, 519–20, 536 (1997).
10. Youngstown Sheet & Tube Co. v. Sawyer, 343 U.S. 579 (1952).
11. For a distinction between constitutional interpretation and construction see Lawrence B. Solum, *Originalism and Constitutional Construction*, 82 FORDHAM L. REV. 453, 456–57, 459, 472 (2013).

Chapter 7

1. Kyllo v. United States, 533 U.S. 27 (2001).
2. *See, e.g.,* Lawrence B. Solum, *Originalism & Constitutional Construction,* 82 FORDHAM L. REV. 453 (2013); Lawrence B. Solum, *Communicative Content and Legal Content,* 89 NOTRE DAME L. REV. 479 (2013).
3. Lawrence B. Solum, *The Interpretation-Construction Distinction,* 27 CONST. COMMENT. 95, 104 (2010).
4. Solum, 82 FORDHAM L. REV. at 457.
5. KEITH E. WHITTINGTON, CONSTITUTIONAL INTERPRETATION 6, 11 (1999).
6. Jack M. Balkin, *Framework Originalism and the Living Constitution,* 103 Nw. U. L. REV. 549, 559–60 (2009).
7. In re Winship, 397 U.S. 358, 364 (1970).
8. Plessy v. Ferguson, 163 U.S. 537 (1896).
9. Brown v. Board of Ed., 347 U.S. 483 (1954).
10. 42 U.S.C. §300gg-4(a) (2012).
11. National Federation of Indep. Bus. v. Sebelius, 132 S. Ct. 2566 (2012) .
12. *Id.* at 2611–12 (Ginsburg, J., concurring).
13. 42 U.S.C. §2000a(b).
14. 42 U.S.C. §2000d.
15. Thomas Hobbes wrote that people "transfer" some of their "natural rights" to another to better achieve the "peace of mankind." THOMAS HOBBES, LEVIATHAN Part I, ch. 15, at 71, 77 (1651).
16. DONALD H. REGAN, UTILITARIANISM AND CO-OPERATION 124 (1980).
17. Aziz Z. Huq, *Enforcing (but Not Defending) 'Unconstitutional' Laws,* 98 VA. L. REV. 1001, 1057–58 (2012).
18. H.L.A. HART, THE CONCEPT OF LAW 100–10 (1961); H.L.A. Hart, *Positivism and the Separation of Law and Morals,* 71 HARV. L. REV. 593, 626 (1958) ("[T]here are laws which may have any degree of iniquity or stupidity and still be laws. And conversely there are rules that have every moral qualification to be laws but yet are not laws.").
19. Some of the greatest administrative programs in US history have been run by the Freedman's Bureau, the Social Security Administration, the Federal Trade Administration, the Federal Communications Commission, the National Labor Relations Board, and the Public Broadcasting Service.
20. Amartya Sen, *Liberty, Unanimity and Rights,* 43 ECONOMICA 217, 217 (1976).
21. 42 U.S.C §1981.
22. Saxbe v. Washington Post Co., 417 U.S. 843, 863 (1974) (Powell, J., dissenting).
23. *See* Michael H. v. Gerald D., 491 U.S. 110 (1989).
24. Schenck v. United States, 249 U.S. 47, 52 (1919) .
25. *Id.* ("The most stringent protection of free speech would not protect a man in falsely shouting fire in a theater and causing a panic").
26. Chaplinsky v. New Hampshire, 315 U.S. 568, 572 (1942).
27. Griswold v. Connecticut, 381 U.S. 479, 484 (1965); Zablocki v. Redhail, 434 U.S. 374 (1978).
28. *Zablocki,* 434 U.S. at 384.
29. Obergefell v. Hodges, 135 S. Ct. 2584 (2015); United States v. Windsor, 133 S. Ct. 2675, 2692 (2013).
30. Meyer v. Nebraska, 262 U.S. 390, 399 (1923).
31. Griswold v. Connecticut, 381 U.S. 479 (1965).
32. Palmore v. Sidoti, 466 U.S. 429 (1984); *Windsor,* 133 S. Ct. at 2696.
33. 18 U.S.C. §249.

Chapter 8

1. Robert H. Bork, *Neutral Principles and Some First Amendment Problems,* 47 IND. L.J. 1, 8 (1971).
2. Robert H. Bork, *The Constitution, Original Intent, and Economic Rights,* 23 SAN DIEGO L. REV. 823, 823 (1986).

3. Raoul Berger, Government by Judiciary: The Transformation of the Fourteenth Amendment 108 & n.71, 402 (2d ed. 1997).

4. The Hon. Edwin Meese III, Att'y Gen. of the U.S., *Address before the D.C. Chapter of the Federalist Society Lawyers Division at the Golden Palace* 8, 10, 12–13 (Nov. 15, 1985), *available at* http://www.justice.gov/ag/aghistory/meese/1985/11-15-1985.pdf.

5. Keith E. Whittington, Constitutional Interpretation: Textual Meaning, Original Intent, and Judicial Review 124–25, 155–56 (1999); Michael W. McConnell, *The Role of Democratic Politics in Transforming Moral Convictions into Law*, 98 Yale L.J. 1501, 1529 (1989).

6. Randy J. Kozel, *Settled Versus Right: Constitutional Method and the Path of Precedent*, 91 Texas L. Rev. 1843, 1870–71 (2013).

7. Richard S. Kay, *Original Intention and Public Meaning in Constitutional Interpretation*, 103 Nw. U. L. Rev. 703, 721 (2009).

8. Thomas B. Colby & Peter J. Smith, *Living Originalism*, 59 Duke L.J. 239, 251–52, 254–55 (2009).

9. Larry B. Solum, *What Is Originalism?: The Evolution of Contemporary Originalist Theory, in* The Challenge of Originalism: Essays in Constitutional Theory 12, 36 (Grant Huscroft & Bradley W. Miller eds., 2011).

10. Andrew Koppelman, *Originalism, Abortion, and the Thirteenth Amendment*, 112 Colum. L. Rev. 1917, 1918 (2012).

11. *Heller*, 554 U.S. 570, 636 (2008); Greene, *How Constitutional Theory Matters*, 72 Ohio St. L.J. 1183, 1193 (2011); Reva B. Siegel, *Heller & Originalism's Dead Hand—In Theory and Practice*, 56 UCLA L. Rev. 1399, 1415–16 (2009).

12. United States v. Jones, 132 S. Ct. 945, 949 (2012) (holding that "the Government's installation of a GPS device on a target's vehicle, and its use of that device to monitor the vehicle's movements, constitutes a 'search'").

13. Kyllo v. United States, 533 U.S. 27, 40 (2001) (holding that the use of a thermal heat device to ascertain behavior occurring inside a home was a "search" for Fourth Amendment purposes).

14. Katz v. United States, 389 U.S. 347, 353 (1967) (deciding that people have a reasonable expectation of privacy in phone booths, where they are protected against unreasonable searches).

15. 514 U.S. 779 (1995).

16. *U.S. Term Limits*, 514 U.S. 779, 783 (1995).

17. Jack M. Balkin, Living Originalism 12–13 (2011).

18. Balkin, *Framework Originalism and the Living Constitution*, 103 Nw. U. L. Rev. 549, 551.

19. Balkin, Living Originalism, *supra*, at 4, 12–13; Jack M. Balkin, *Nine Perspectives on Living Originalism*, 2012 U. Ill. L. Rev. 815, 817; Jack M. Balkin, *Framework, supra*, at 551–53.

20. 410 U.S. 113 (1973).

21. Balkin, Living Originalism, *supra*, at 215–18.

22. Balkin, *Nine Perspectives, supra*, at 846.

23. *Lawrence*, 539 U.S. 558 (2003); *Griswold*, 381 U.S. 479 (1965).

24. David A. Strauss, *Can Originalism Be Saved?*, 92 B.U. L. Rev. 1161, 1166 (2012).

25. David A. Strauss, The Living Constitution 1, 3 (2010).

26. Balkin, Living Originalism, *supra*, at 123–24.

27. William J. Brennan, Jr., *The Constitution of the United States: Contemporary Ratification*, 27 S. Tex. L. Rev. 433, 434 (1986).

28. Bruce Ackerman, *2006 Oliver Wendell Holmes Lectures: The Living Constitution*, 120 Harv. L. Rev. 1737, 1801 (2007).

29. Strauss, Living Constitution, *supra*, at 3.

30. 60 U.S. (19 How.) 393 (1857).

31. 198 U.S. 45 (1905).

32. The Civil Rights Cases, 109 U.S. 3, 17 (1883).

33. Bradwell v. Illinois, 83 U.S. (16 Wall.) 130, 137–39, 142 (1873).

34. *Brown*, 347 U.S. 483, 493–94 (1954).

35. *McLaurin*, 339 U.S. 637, 641–42 (1950); *Sweatt*, 339 U.S. 629, 633–34 (1950), *Plessy*, 163 U.S. 537 (1896).

36. Herbert Wechsler, *Toward Neutral Principles of Constitutional Law*, 73 HARV. L. REV. 1, 32–34 (1959).
37. JOHN RAWLS, A THEORY OF JUSTICE 101 (1971).
38. Sch. Dist. of Abington v. Schempp, 374 U.S. 203, 230 (1963) (Brennan, J., concurring).
39. 300 U.S. 379, 392–93 (1937).
40. 312 U.S. 100, 114 (1941).
41. 404 U.S. 71, 74 (1971).
42. *Bradwell*, 83 U.S. (16 Wall.) 130, 139 (1873); *Minor*, 88 U.S. (21 Wall.) 162, 174–75 (1874).
43. 538 U.S. 721, 725, 729–35 (2003).
44. PHILIP BOBBITT, CONSTITUTIONAL INTERPRETATION xii–xvii, 12–13 (1991); Philip Bobbitt, *Reflections Inspired by My Critics*, 72 TEXAS L. REV. 1869, 1913–14 (1994).
45. Dred Scott v. Sandford, 60 U.S. (19 How.) 393, 404–05 (1856).
46. BOBBITT, CONSTITUTIONAL INTERPRETATION, *supra*, at 14.
47. W.C.N., *Meeting of Colored Citizens*, LIBERATOR (Bos.), July 9, 1858, at 112.
48. *National Resolves*, N.H. STATESMAN (Concord), Aug. 13, 1859, at 4.
49. BOBBITT, CONSTITUTIONAL INTERPRETATION, *supra*, at 4–5.
50. BOBBITT, CONSTITUTIONAL INTERPRETATION, *supra*, at 21.
51. PHILIP BOBBITT, CONSTITUTIONAL FATE: THEORY OF THE CONSTITUTION 94 (1982).
52. BOBBITT, CONSTITUTIONAL INTERPRETATION, *supra*, at 22.
53. Herbert Wechsler, *Toward Neutral Principles of Constitutional Law*, 73 HARV. L. REV. 1, 16, 19, 32–34 (1959).
54. RONALD DWORKIN, A MATTER OF PRINCIPLE 69 (1985).
55. *Id.*
56. Alexander Tsesis, *Self-Government and the Declaration of Independence*, 97 CORNELL L. REV. 693, 735–41 (2012).
57. United States v. Carolene Prods. Co., 304 U.S. 144, 153 n.4 (1938) (stating that heightened scrutiny may be appropriate in cases involving interference with the political process and discrimination against "discrete and insular minorities").
58. LOUIS MICHAEL SEIDMAN, ON CONSTITUTIONAL DISOBEDIENCE 69–74 (2012); Louis Michael Seidman, *The Secret History of American Constitutional Skepticism: A Recovery and Preliminary Evaluation*, 17 U. PA. J. CONST. L. 1 (2014).
59. The Supreme Court has recognized rights to privacy in a variety of cases: Lawrence v. Texas, 539 U.S. 558, 578 (2003); Roe v. Wade, 410 U.S. 113, 164 (1973); Eisenstadt v. Baird, 405 U.S. 438, 443 (1972); Griswold v. Connecticut, 381 U.S. 479, 485 (1965). The Court has found support for protecting the right to travel in a variety of constitutional provisions, including the Privileges and Immunities Clause, the Due Process Clause, the Equal Protection Clause, and the Commerce Clause. Saenz v. Roe, 526 U.S. 489, 501 (1999); United States v. Guest, 383 U.S. 745, 758–59 (1966); Zemel v. Rusk, 381 U.S. 1, 14 (1965); Twining v. New Jersey, 211 U.S. 78, 96–97 (1908); Paul v. Virginia, 75 U.S. (8 Wall.) 168, 180 (1869). The Court found that parental autonomy is constitutionally protected in Meyer v. Nebraska, 262 U.S. 390 (1923).
60. SEIDMAN, ON CONSTITUTIONAL DISOBEDIENCE at 115.
61. *Id.* at 136.
62. Louis Michael Seidman, *Political and Constitutional Obligation*, 93 B.U. L. REV. 1257, 1257 (2013).
63. ALAN GEWIRTH, REASON AND MORALITY 135 (1978).
64. MARK TUSHNET, TAKING THE CONSTITUTION AWAY FROM THE COURTS 13 (1999).
65. *Id.* at 11–13, 181–82.
66. EDWARD GRAY, AN ORATION, DELIVERED JULY 5, 1790, at 9 (1790).
67. Marin Scordato, *Distinction Without a Difference: A Reappraisal of the Doctrine of Prior Restraint*, 68 N.C. L. REV. 1, 4 (1989).

Chapter 9

1. Citizens United v. Fed. Election Comm'n, 558 U.S. 310 (2010).
2. Austin v. Mich. Chamber of Commerce, 494 U.S. 652, 659 (1990), *overruled by Citizens United v. FEC, supra.*

3. 132 S. Ct. 2490 (2012).

4. Transcript of Oral Argument at 33, *Citizens United,* Transcript 08-205, at 33, *available at* http://www.supremecourt.gov/oral_arguments/argument_transcript/2008.

5. Arizona Free Enter. Club's Freedom Club PAC v. Bennett, 131 S. Ct. 2806, 2821 (2011).

6. Roosevelt, *Excerpt from his 1944 State of the Union* (Jan. 11, 1944), *available at* http://www.fdrlibrary.marist.edu/archives/address_text.html.

7. JOHN LOCKE, SECOND TREATISE OF GOVERNMENT § 6 (Peter Laslett ed., Mentor Press 3d Repr.) (1690).

8. *See, e.g., Political Maxims,* NEW-YORK DAILY GAZETTE, Oct. 29, 1789, at 2; An American, *For the Gazette* (Letter to the Editor, July 16, 1795), GAZETTE OF THE UNITED STATES (Phila., Pa.), July 17, 1795, at 3; *To Thomas M'Kean Esq., Governor Elect of the Commonwealth of Pennsylvania,* PHILADELPHIA GAZETTE, Nov. 8, 1799, at 3.

9. U.S. Const. art. I, § 8, cl.1; Social Security Act Amendments of 1965, Title XIX, 79 Stat. 286, 343–52 (1965).

10. 42 U.S.C. §§300gg, 300gg-1(a), 300gg-5, 300gg-11, 300gg-12 (Supp. V 2012).

11. 42 U.S.C. §1396d(y)(1).

12. *NFIB,* 132 S. Ct. at 2601.

13. Florida *ex rel.* Atty. Gen. v. U.S. Dep't of Health & Human Servs., 648 F.3d 1235, 1267 (11th Cir. 2011).

14. West Coast Hotel Co. v. Parrish, 300 U.S. 379 (1937); United States v. Darby, 312 U.S. 100 (1941).

15. *Wickard v. Filburn,* 317 U.S. 111 (1942).

16. Articles of Confederation, art. II.

17. *Coll. Sav. Bank,* 527 U.S. 666 (1999).

18. *Kimel,* 528 U.S. 62 (2000).

19. *Garrett,* 531 U.S. 356 (2001).

20. 109 U.S. 3 (1883).

21. *Marsh v. Alabama,* 326 U.S. 501 (1946).

22. Burton v. Wilmington Parking Auth., 365 U.S. 715 (1961).

23. Eric Foner, *The Supreme Court and the History of Reconstruction—and Vice-Versa,* 112 COLUM. L. REV. 1585, 1604 (2012).

24. MICHAEL J. KLARMAN, FROM JIM CROW TO CIVIL RIGHTS: THE SUPREME COURT AND THE STRUGGLE FOR RACIAL EQUALITY 152 (2004).

25. Robert J. Glennon Jr. & John E. Nowak, *A Functional Analysis of the Fourteenth Amendment "State Action" Requirement,* 1976 SUP. CT. REV. 221, 225–26 (noting that the traditional "all-or-nothing theory" of state action became increasingly difficult to accept); Charles L. Black, Jr., *The Supreme Court, 1966 Term—Foreword: "State Action," Equal Protection, and California's Proposition 14,* 81 HARV. L. REV. 69, 95 (1967) (contemplating the consequences of a shift away from strict state action doctrine); William W. Van Alstyne & Kenneth L. Karst, *State Action,* 14 STAN. L. REV. 3, 5–8 (1961) (addressing the ad hoc state action doctrines emerging from Fourteenth and Fifteenth Amendment cases); Harold W. Horowitz, *The Misleading Search for "State Action" Under the Fourteenth Amendment,* 30 S. CAL. L. REV. 208, 218 (1957) (stating that a private corporation may be an unconstitutional state actor even though it is not a state agent).

26. Their suggestions tie back to the Court's holding that court enforcement of racial covenants is a form of state action. Shelley v. Kraemer, 334 U.S. 1, 19 (1948).

27. *See* Shelley v. Kraemer, 334 U.S. 1 (1948).

28. United States v. Morrison, 529 U.S. 598 (2000).

29. *Id.* at 632–33 (Souter, J., dissenting).

30. Joseph R. Biden, Jr., *The Civil Rights Remedy of the Violence Against Women Act: A Defense,* 37 HARV. J. ON LEGIS. 1, 9 (2000).

31. S. Rep. No. 102–197, at 45–48 (1991).

32. *See* Bell v. Maryland, 378 U.S. 226 (1964); Christopher W. Schmidt, *The Sit-Ins and the State Action Doctrine,* 18 WM. & MARY BILL RTS. J. 767, 795–98 (2010).

33. Personnel Adm'r v. Feeney, 442 U.S. 256, 286 (1979).

34. J.E.B. v. Alabama *ex rel.* T.B., 511 U.S. 127, 139 n.11 (1994).

35. City of Boerne v. Flores, 521 U.S. 507, 518 (1997).

36. *Morrison*, 529 U.S. at 628–31 (Souter, J., dissenting).

37. 400 U.S. 112 (1970); Reva Siegel and Robert Post, *Equal Protection by Law: Federal Antidiscrimination Legislation After* Morrison *and* Kimel, 110 YALE L.J. 441, 478 (2000).

38. *Morrison*, 529 U.S. at 666 (Breyer, J., dissenting).

39. *McClung*, 379 U.S. 294 (1964); *Heart of Atlanta Motel, Inc.*, 379 U.S. 241 (1964).

40. Even before *Morrison*, in another 5–4 case, *United States v. Lopez*, the Court struck down a federal statute against the possession of firearms near a school. 514 U.S. 549 (1995). The Court's rulings both diminished Congress's power to act on rational findings that something substantially affects interstate commerce and they increased judicial oversight authority. *Lopez* concerned the Gun-Free School Zones Act of 1990, which provided criminal penalties for persons who knowingly possessed firearms in a defined school zone. Chief Justice William Rehnquist, writing for the majority, found the Act unconstitutional. The ruling in *Lopez* was the first time in 60 years that the Court found a federal statute exceeded Congress's power to regulate interstate commerce. Rehnquist's opinion weakened Congress's Commerce Clause power by forgoing the rational basis test inquiry and, instead, examining whether the law had a "substantial effect" on interstate commerce. The Court found the congressional record lacked adequate evidence that guns carried in a school zone had a substantial effect on interstate commerce. Writing for the dissent in *Lopez*, Justice Stephen Breyer argued that the case should be decided through the rational basis lens of interpretation. He further pointed out that precedents allowed the national regulation of activity that had a significant, not necessarily substantial, effect on interstate commerce. The majority's demand from Congress for a greater proof of economic effect enabled the majority to set aside a federal law spurred by the legislative intent to preserve safe education for the happiness of individuals and the community.

41. CONG. GLOBE, 38th Cong., 1st Sess. 1443 (1864).

42. CONG. GLOBE, 38th Cong., 1st Sess. 1319 (1864).

43. *Id.* at 2989.

44. *Id.* at 1200.

45. *Jones*, 392 U.S. 409 (1968).

46. 1 LAURENCE H. TRIBE, AMERICAN CONSTITUTIONAL LAW 927 (3d ed. 2000).

47. Pub. L. No. 111–84, §§4701–4713, 123 Stat. 2835, 2835–44 (2009).

48. United States v. Cannon, 750 F.3d 492 (5th Cir. 2014); United States v. Hatch, 722 F.3d 1193 (10th Cir. 2013).

49. Melissa Seifer Briggs, *Exempt or Not Exempt: Mandated Prescription Contraception Coverage and the Religious Employer*, 84 OR. L. REV. 1227, 1229 (2005).

50. Burwell v. Hobby Lobby Stores, Inc., 134 S. Ct. 2751 (2014).

51. Hobby Lobby Stores, Inc. v. Sebelius, 723 F.3d 1114, 1144 (10th Cir. 2013).

52. Hands on Originals, Inc. v. Lexington-Fayette Urban County Human Rights Commission, C.A. No. 14-CI-04474 (Fayette Cir. Ct. Apr. 27, 2015), *available at* https://perma.cc/75FY-Z77D.

53. *Cf.* Heart of Atlanta Motel, Inc. v. United States, 379 U.S. 241, 250 (1964) ("The Senate Commerce Committee made it quite clear that the fundamental object of Title II was to vindicate 'the deprivation of personal dignity that surely accompanies denials of equal access to public establishments.'").

54. Tony & Susan Alamo Found. v. Sec'y of Labor, 471 U.S. 290 (1985).

55. *Hobby Lobby*, 134 S. Ct. at 2788 (Ginsburg, J., dissenting).

56. *Id.* at 2780–81 (majority opinion).

57. *See, e.g.*, Verified Petition, Odgaard v. Iowa Civil Rights Comm'n, No. CVCV046451 (Polk Cty., Iowa, Dist. Ct. Oct. 7, 2013); Ruling on Defendants' Motion to Dismiss, Odgaard v. Iowa Civil Rights Comm'n, No. CVCV046451 (Apr. 3, 2014) (granting motion to dismiss); Ingersoll v. Arlene's Flowers, Am. Civil Liberties Union (Oct. 11, 2013), *available at* http://perma.cc/KZ4Y-RRTB; Elane Photography, LLC v. Willock, 309 P.3d 53 (2013).

58. *Hobby Lobby*, 134 S. Ct. at 2760.

INDEX